INJUSTICE™2

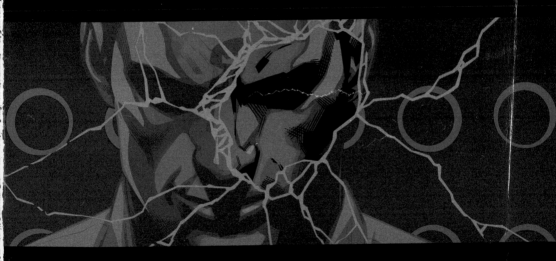

VOLUME 1

INJUS

TOM TAYLOR
Writer

**BRUNO REDONDO   DANIEL SAMPERE   MIKE S. MILLER
JUAN ALBARRAN   VICENTE CIFUENTES**
Artists

REX LOKUS   J. NANJAN
Colorists

WES ABBOTT
Letterer

INJUSTICE 2

VOLUME 1

SUPERMAN created by JERRY SIEGEL and JOE SHUSTER
By special arrangement with the Jerry Siegel Family

SUPERGIRL based on the characters created by JERRY SIEGEL & JOE SHUSTER

BASED ON THE VIDEO GAME *INJUSTICE 2*

JIM CHADWICK Editor – Original Series
SUSIE ESPARZA
ROB LEVIN Assistant Editors – Original Series
JEB WOODARD Group Editor – Collected Editions
PAUL SANTOS Editor – Collected Edition
STEVE COOK Design Director – Books
LOUIS PRANDI Publication Design

BOB HARRAS Senior VP – Editor-in-Chief, DC Comics
PAT McCALLUM Executive Editor, DC Comics

DIANE NELSON President
DAN DiDIO Publisher
JIM LEE Publisher
GEOFF JOHNS President & Chief Creative Officer
AMIT DESAI Executive VP – Business & Marketing Strategy,
     Direct to Consumer & Global Franchise Management
SAM ADES Senior VP & General Manager, Digital Services
BOBBIE CHASE VP & Executive Editor, Young Reader & Talent Development
MARK CHIARELLO Senior VP – Art, Design & Collected Editions
JOHN CUNNINGHAM Senior VP – Sales & Trade Marketing
ANNE DePIES Senior VP – Business Strategy, Finance & Administration
DON FALLETTI VP – Manufacturing Operations
LAWRENCE GANEM VP – Editorial Administration & Talent Relations
ALISON GILL Senior VP – Manufacturing & Operations
HANK KANALZ Senior VP – Editorial Strategy & Administration
JAY KOGAN VP – Legal Affairs
JACK MAHAN VP – Business Affairs
NICK J. NAPOLITANO VP – Manufacturing Administration
EDDIE SCANNELL VP – Consumer Marketing
COURTNEY SIMMONS Senior VP – Publicity & Communications
JIM (SKI) SOKOLOWSKI VP – Comic Book Specialty Sales & Trade Marketing
NANCY SPEARS VP – Mass, Book, Digital Sales & Trade Marketing
MICHELE R. WELLS VP – Content Strategy

INJUSTICE 2 VOLUME 1

Published by DC Comics. Compilation and all new material
Copyright © 2017 DC Comics. All Rights Reserved. Originally
published in single magazine form in INJUSTICE 2 1-6.
Copyright © 2017 DC Comics. All Rights Reserved. All
characters, their distinctive likenesses and related elements
featured in this publication are trademarks of DC Comics. The
stories, characters and incidents featured in this publication
are entirely fictional. DC Comics does not read or accept
unsolicited submissions of ideas, stories or artwork.

DC Comics, 2900 West Alameda Ave., Burbank, CA 91505
Printed by LSC Communications, Kendallville, IN, USA.
9/22/17. First Printing.
ISBN: 978-1-4012-7441-2

Library of Congress Cataloging-in-Publication Data is available.

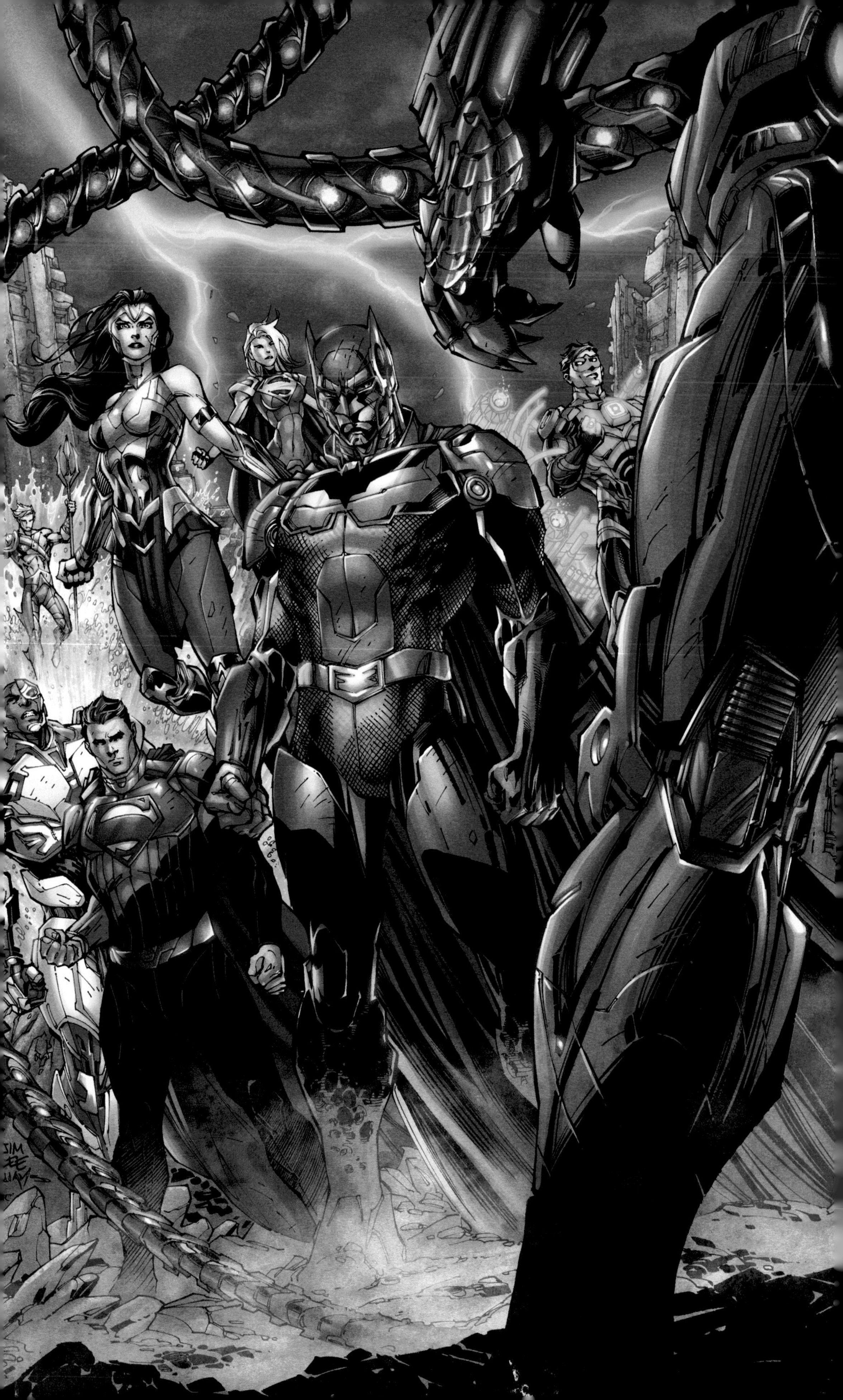

“Two Speeding Bullets”

Bruno Redondo Penciller **Juan Albarran** Inker

Rex Lokus Colorist Cover art by **Jim Lee, Scott Williams** and **Alex Sinclair**

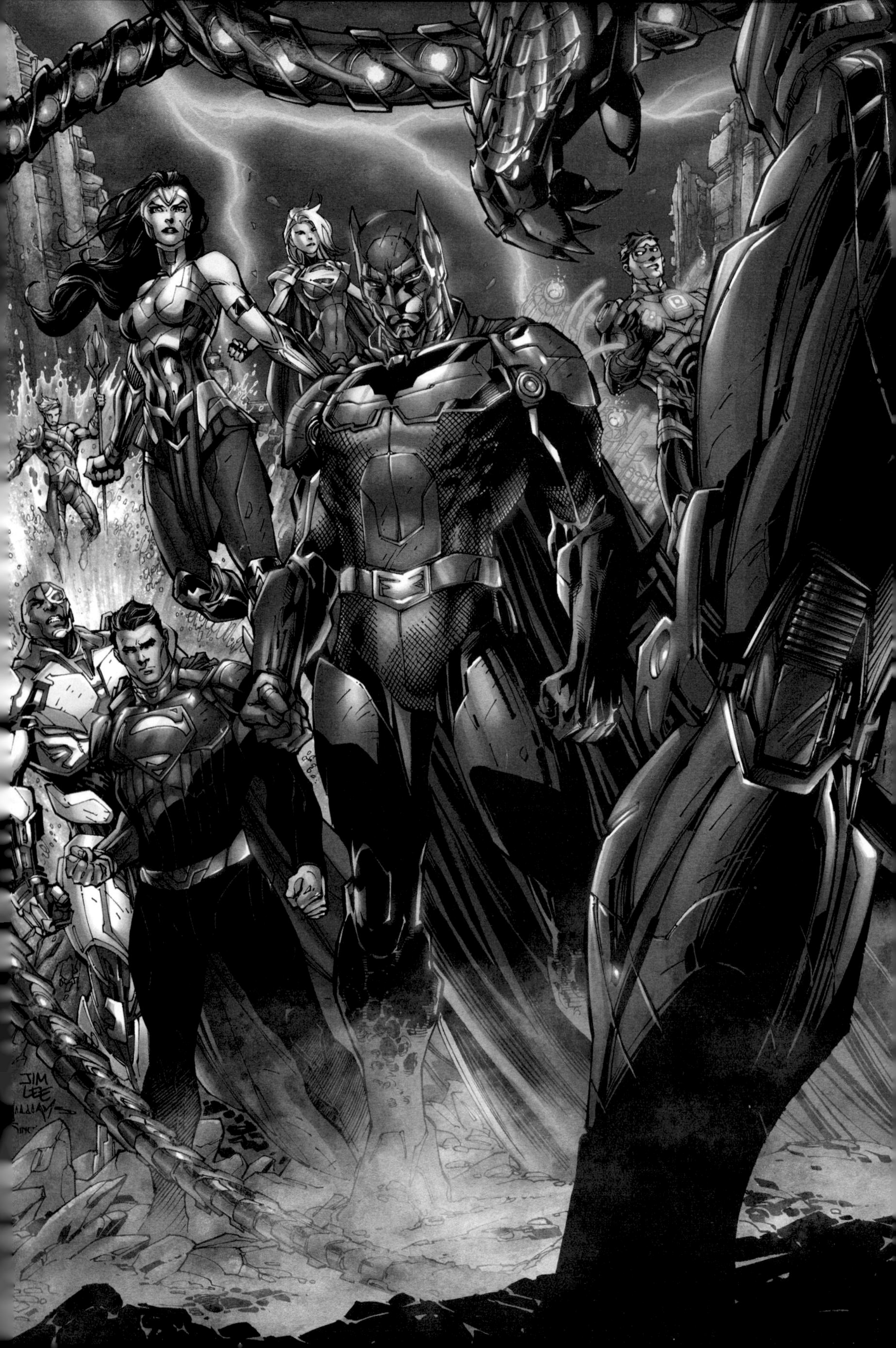

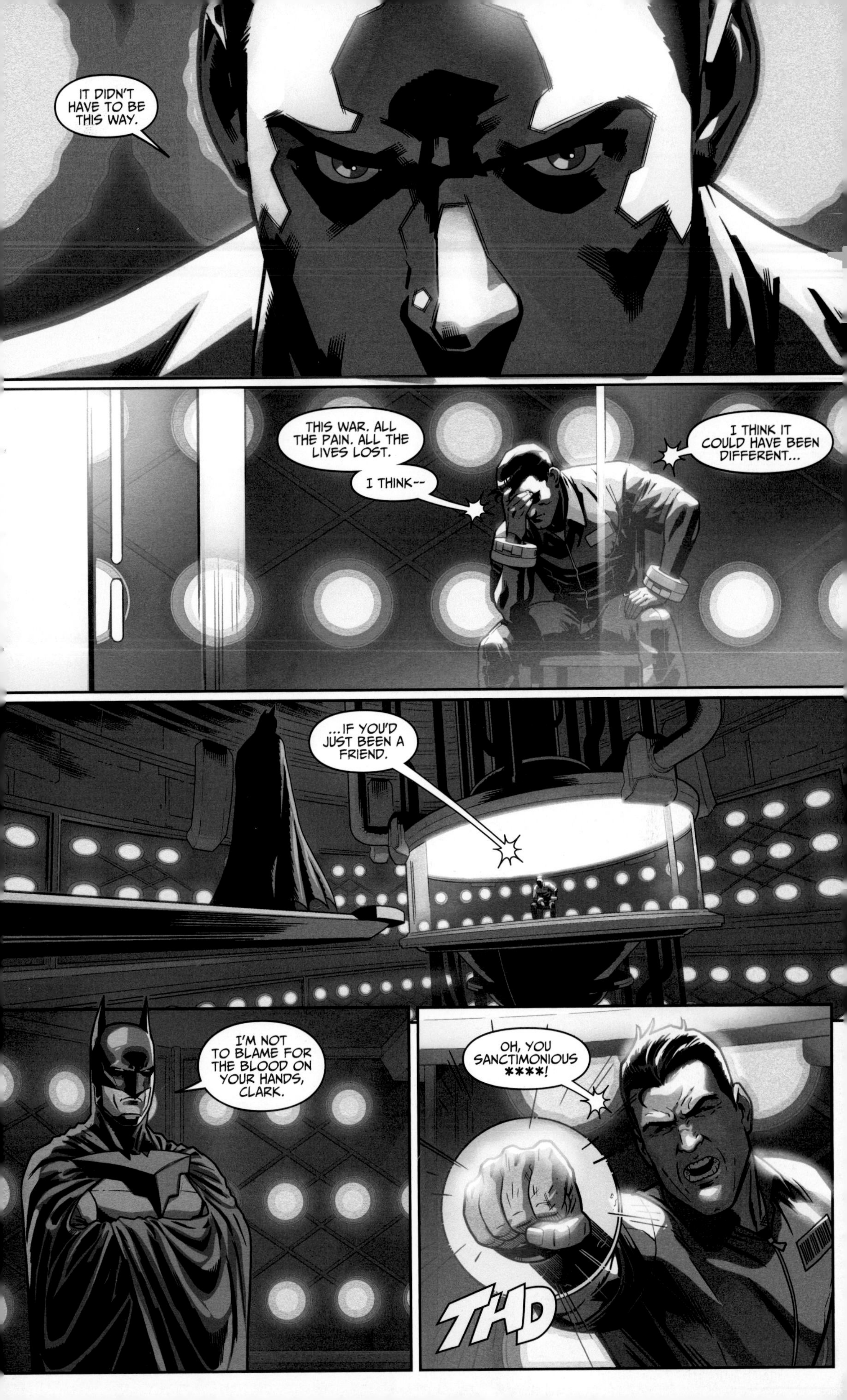

IT DIDN'T HAVE TO BE THIS WAY.
THIS WAR. ALL THE PAIN. ALL THE LIVES LOST.
I THINK--
I THINK IT COULD HAVE BEEN DIFFERENT...
...IF YOU'D JUST BEEN A FRIEND.
I'M NOT TO BLAME FOR THE BLOOD ON YOUR HANDS, CLARK.
OH, YOU SANCTIMONIOUS ****!
THD

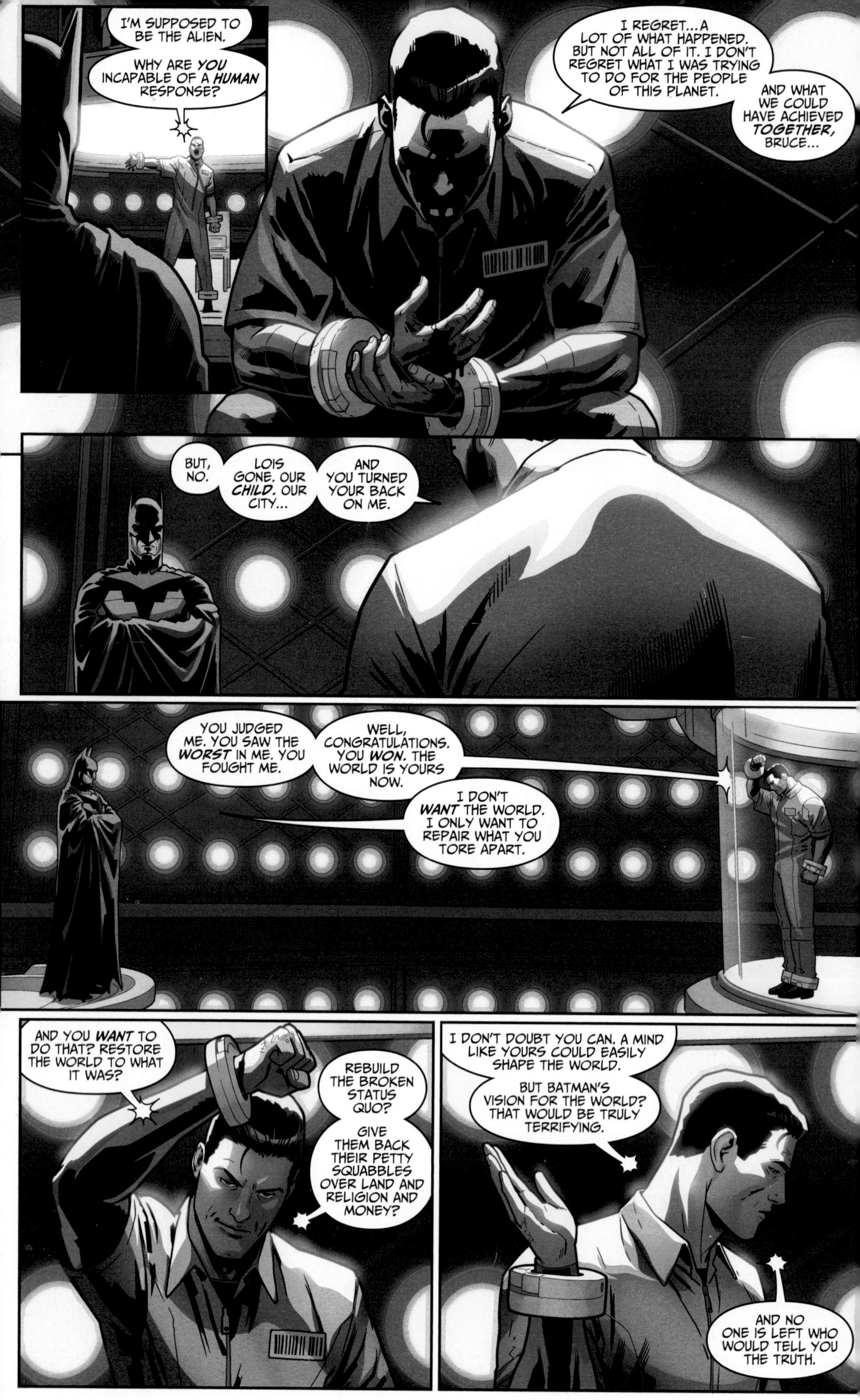
I'M SUPPOSED TO BE THE ALIEN.
WHY ARE *YOU* INCAPABLE OF A *HUMAN* RESPONSE?
I REGRET...A LOT OF WHAT HAPPENED. BUT NOT ALL OF IT. I DON'T REGRET WHAT I WAS TRYING TO DO FOR THE PEOPLE OF THIS PLANET.
AND WHAT WE COULD HAVE ACHIEVED *TOGETHER,* BRUCE...
BUT, NO.
LOIS GONE. OUR *CHILD.* OUR CITY...
AND YOU TURNED YOUR BACK ON ME.
YOU JUDGED ME. YOU SAW THE *WORST* IN ME. YOU FOUGHT ME.
WELL, CONGRATULATIONS. YOU *WON.* THE WORLD IS YOURS NOW.
I DON'T *WANT* THE WORLD. I ONLY WANT TO REPAIR WHAT YOU TORE APART.
AND YOU *WANT* TO DO THAT? RESTORE THE WORLD TO WHAT IT WAS?
REBUILD THE BROKEN STATUS QUO?
GIVE THEM BACK THEIR PETTY SQUABBLES OVER LAND AND RELIGION AND MONEY?
I DON'T DOUBT YOU CAN. A MIND LIKE YOURS COULD EASILY SHAPE THE WORLD.
BUT BATMAN'S VISION FOR THE WORLD? THAT WOULD BE TRULY TERRIFYING.
AND NO ONE IS LEFT WHO WOULD TELL YOU THE TRUTH.

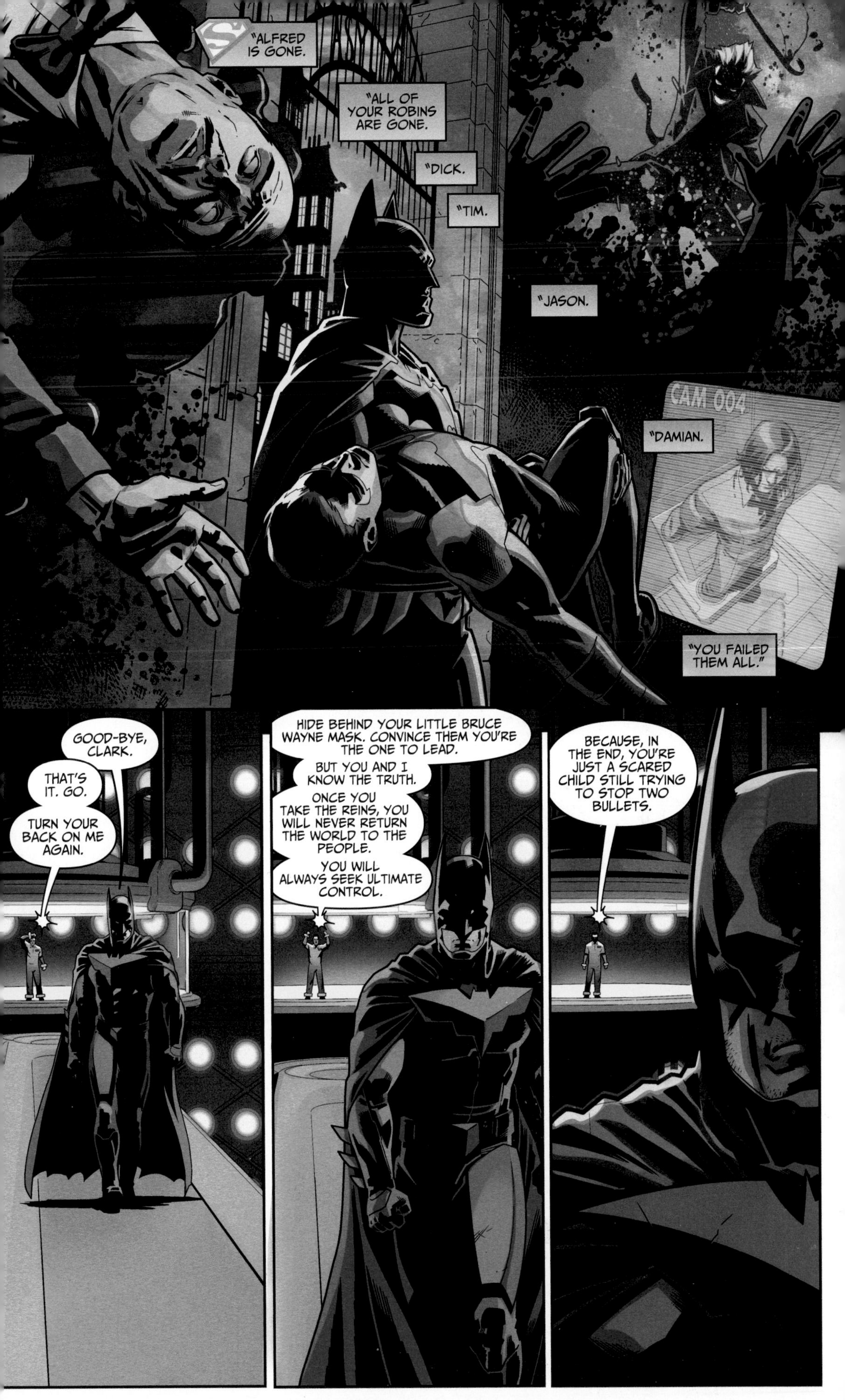
"ALFRED IS GONE.
"ALL OF YOUR ROBINS ARE GONE.
"DICK.
"TIM.
"JASON.
CAM 004
"DAMIAN.
"YOU FAILED THEM ALL."
GOOD-BYE, CLARK.
THAT'S IT. GO.
TURN YOUR BACK ON ME AGAIN.
HIDE BEHIND YOUR LITTLE BRUCE WAYNE MASK. CONVINCE THEM YOU'RE THE ONE TO LEAD.
BUT YOU AND I KNOW THE TRUTH.
ONCE YOU TAKE THE REINS, YOU WILL NEVER RETURN THE WORLD TO THE PEOPLE.
YOU WILL ALWAYS SEEK ULTIMATE CONTROL.
BECAUSE, IN THE END, YOU'RE JUST A SCARED CHILD STILL TRYING TO STOP TWO BULLETS.

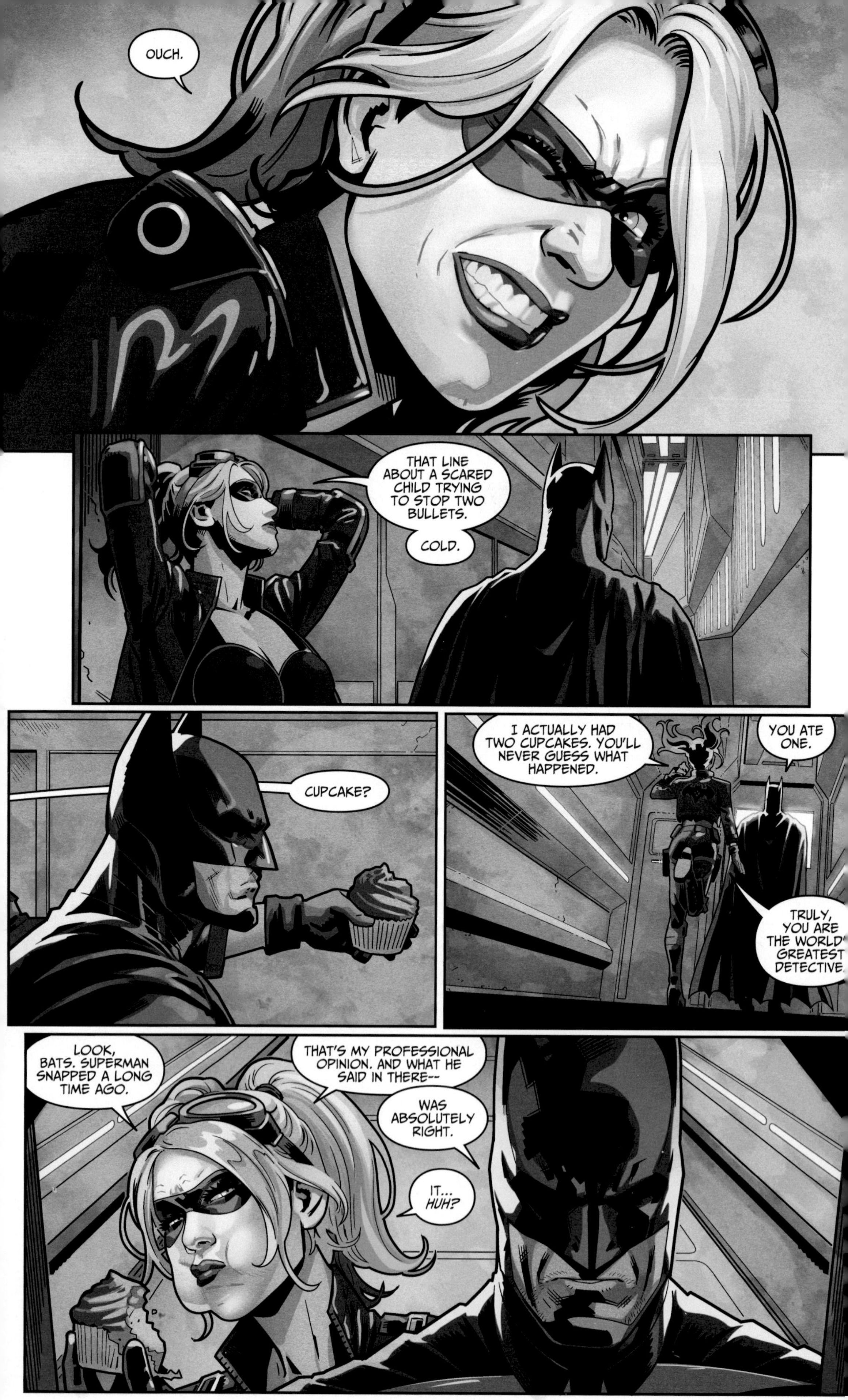
OUCH.
THAT LINE ABOUT A SCARED CHILD TRYING TO STOP TWO BULLETS.
COLD.
CUPCAKE?
I ACTUALLY HAD TWO CUPCAKES. YOU'LL NEVER GUESS WHAT HAPPENED.
YOU ATE ONE.
TRULY, YOU ARE THE WORLD' GREATEST DETECTIVE
LOOK, BATS. SUPERMAN SNAPPED A LONG TIME AGO.
THAT'S MY PROFESSIONAL OPINION. AND WHAT HE SAID IN THERE--
WAS ABSOLUTELY RIGHT.
IT... *HUH?*

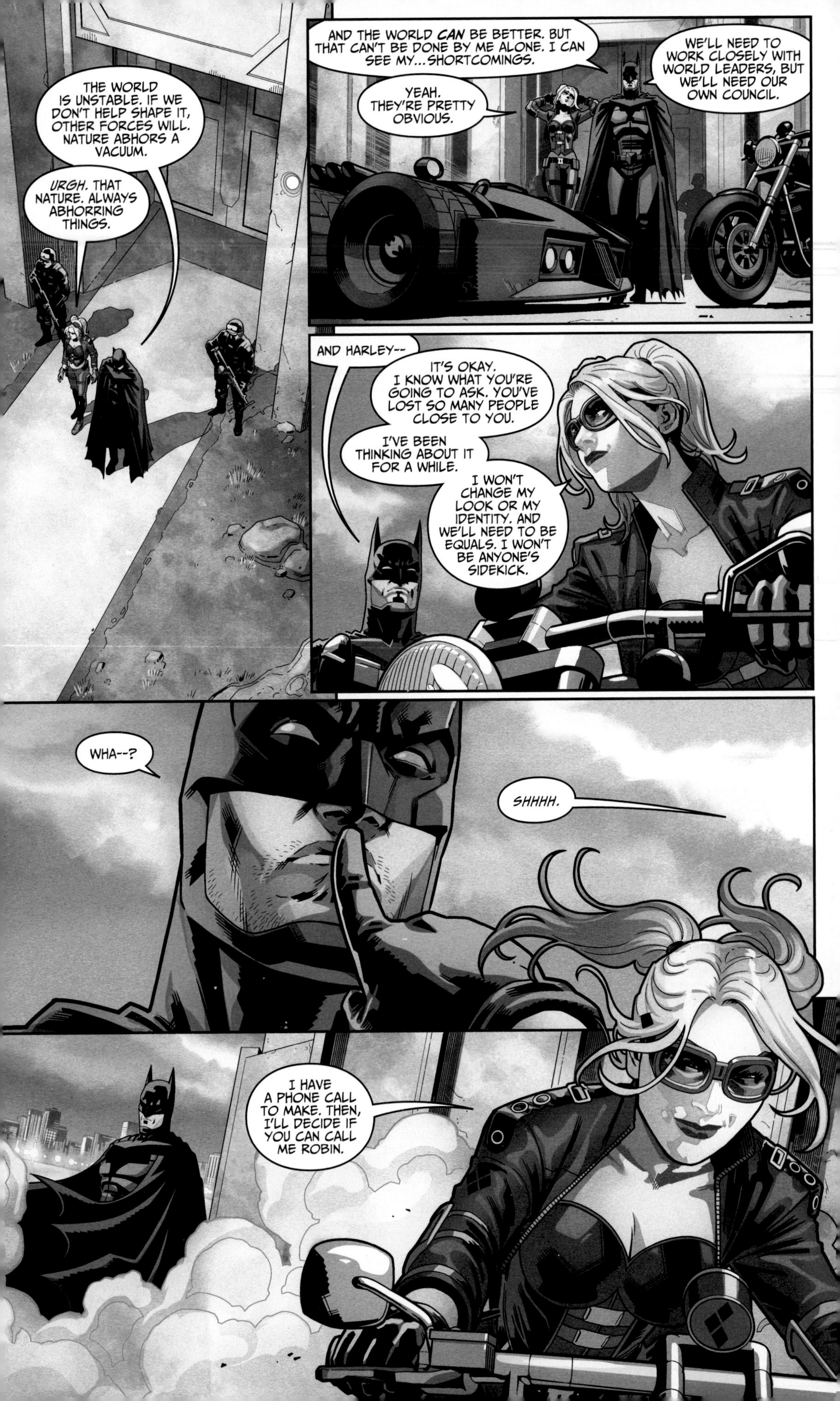
THE WORLD IS UNSTABLE. IF WE DON'T HELP SHAPE IT, OTHER FORCES WILL. NATURE ABHORS A VACUUM.
URGH. THAT NATURE. ALWAYS ABHORRING THINGS.
AND THE WORLD CAN BE BETTER. BUT THAT CAN'T BE DONE BY ME ALONE. I CAN SEE MY...SHORTCOMINGS.
YEAH. THEY'RE PRETTY OBVIOUS.
WE'LL NEED TO WORK CLOSELY WITH WORLD LEADERS, BUT WE'LL NEED OUR OWN COUNCIL.
AND HARLEY--
IT'S OKAY. I KNOW WHAT YOU'RE GOING TO ASK. YOU'VE LOST SO MANY PEOPLE CLOSE TO YOU.
I'VE BEEN THINKING ABOUT IT FOR A WHILE.
I WON'T CHANGE MY LOOK OR MY IDENTITY. AND WE'LL NEED TO BE EQUALS. I WON'T BE ANYONE'S SIDEKICK.
WHA--?
SHHHH.
I HAVE A PHONE CALL TO MAKE. THEN, I'LL DECIDE IF YOU CAN CALL ME ROBIN.

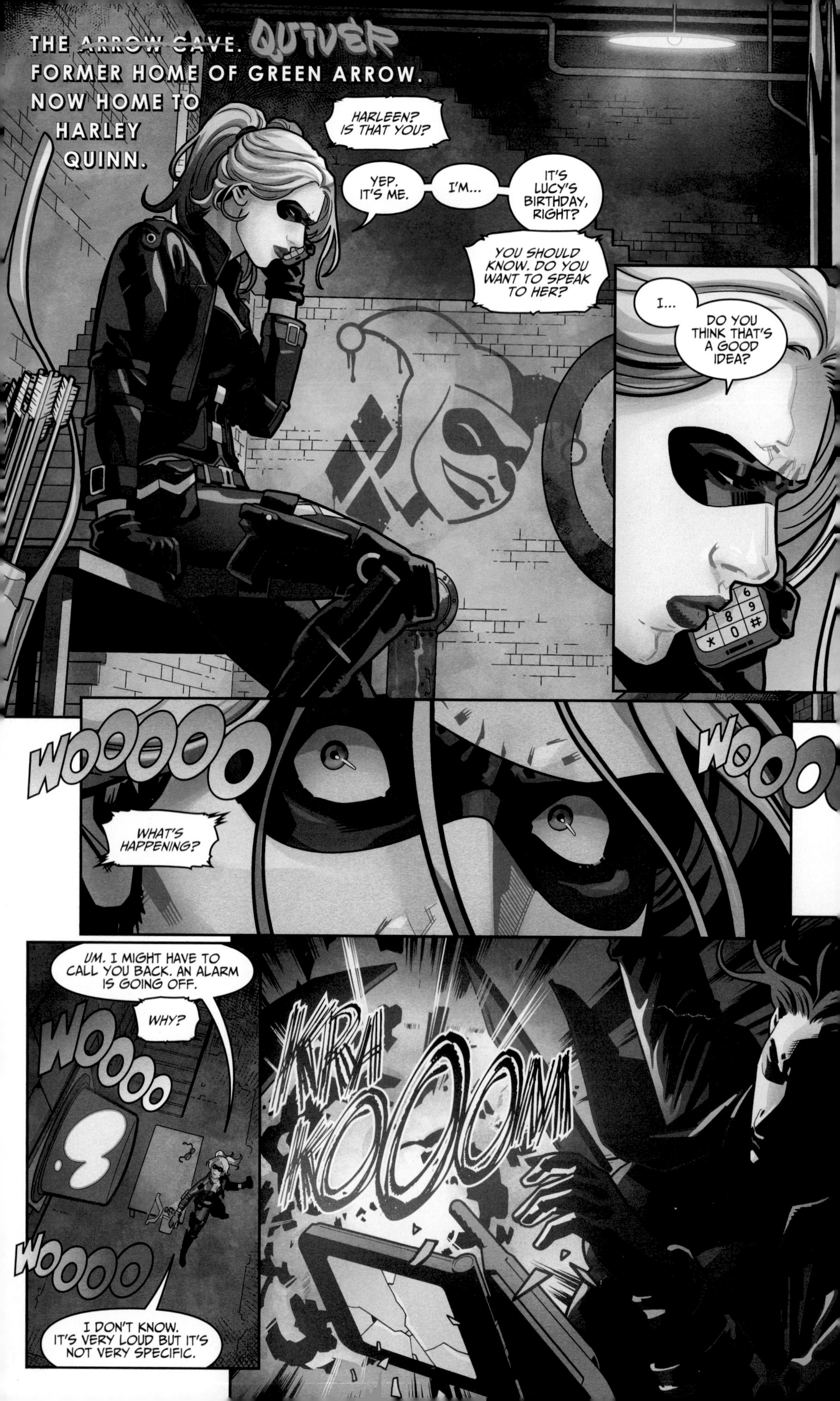

THE ARROW CAVE. QUIVER
FORMER HOME OF GREEN ARROW. NOW HOME TO HARLEY QUINN.
HARLEEN? IS THAT YOU?
YEP. IT'S ME.
I'M...
IT'S LUCY'S BIRTHDAY, RIGHT?
YOU SHOULD KNOW. DO YOU WANT TO SPEAK TO HER?
I...
DO YOU THINK THAT'S A GOOD IDEA?
WOOOOO
WOOO
WHAT'S HAPPENING?
UM. I MIGHT HAVE TO CALL YOU BACK. AN ALARM IS GOING OFF.
WHY?
WOOOO
WOOOO
I DON'T KNOW. IT'S VERY LOUD BUT IT'S NOT VERY SPECIFIC.
KRAKOOOOM

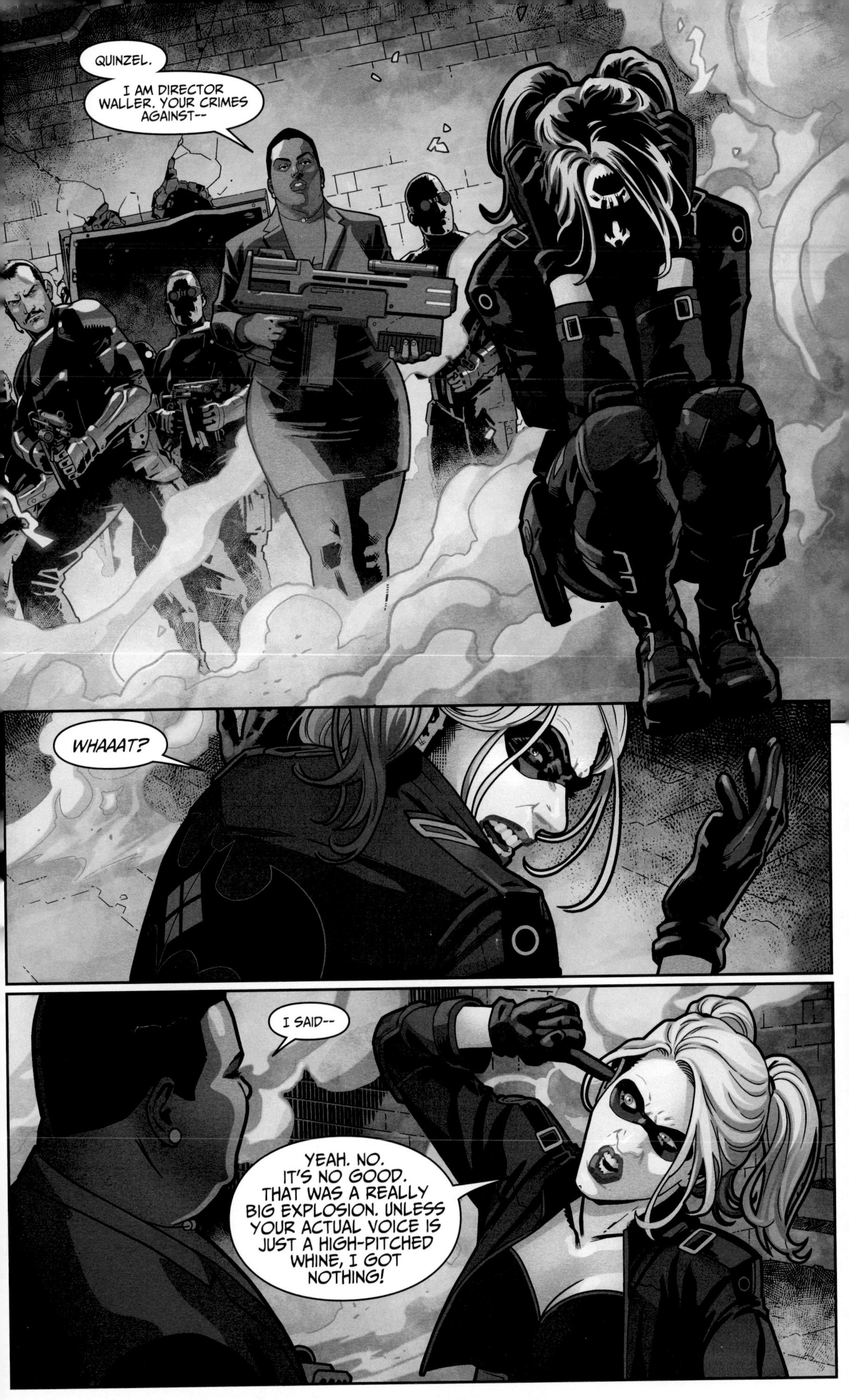
QUINZEL.
I AM DIRECTOR WALLER. YOUR CRIMES AGAINST--
WHAAAT?
I SAID--
YEAH. NO. IT'S NO GOOD. THAT WAS A REALLY BIG EXPLOSION. UNLESS YOUR ACTUAL VOICE IS JUST A HIGH-PITCHED WHINE, I GOT NOTHING!

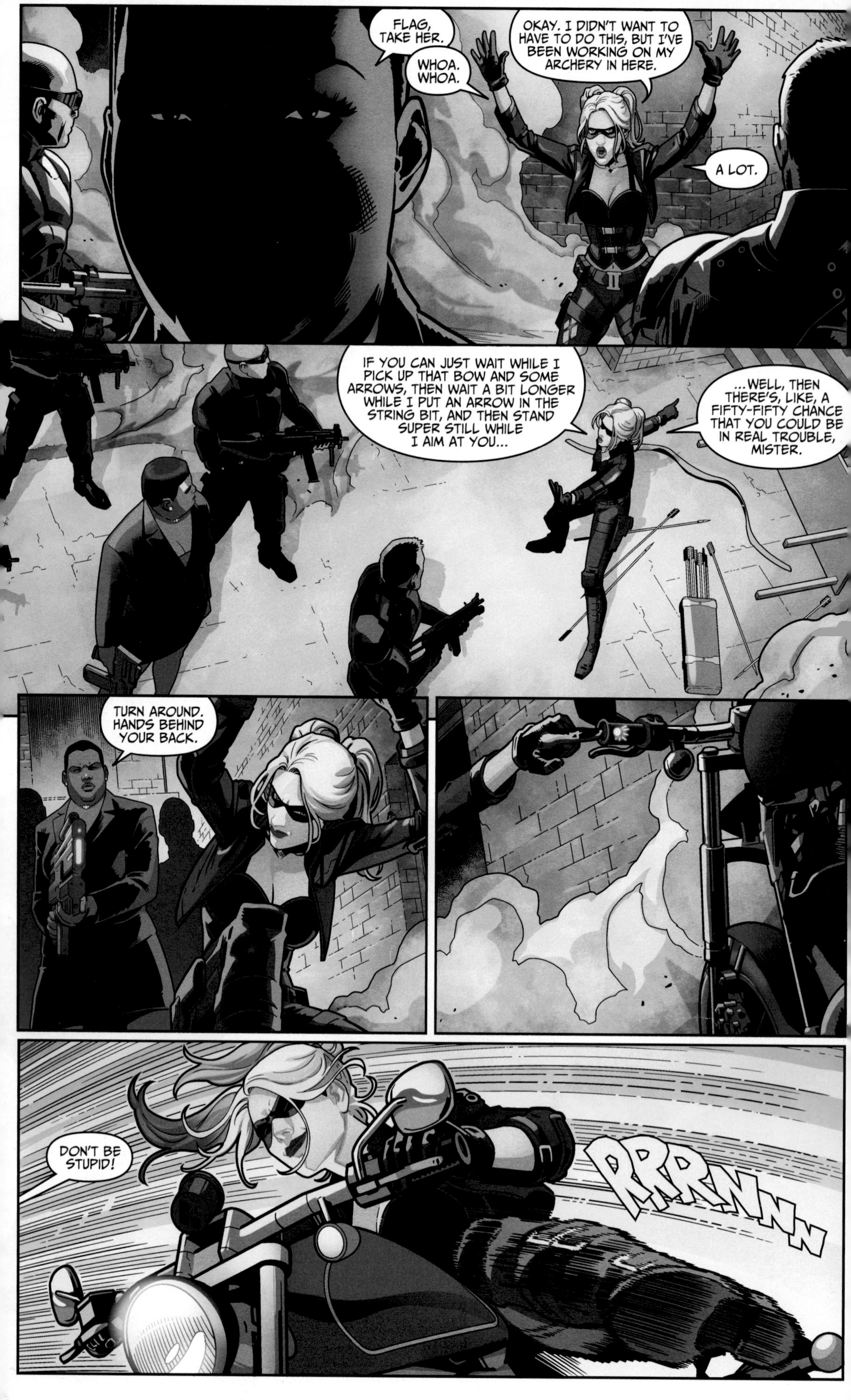
FLAG, TAKE HER.
WHOA. WHOA.
OKAY. I DIDN'T WANT TO HAVE TO DO THIS, BUT I'VE BEEN WORKING ON MY ARCHERY IN HERE.
A LOT.
IF YOU CAN JUST WAIT WHILE I PICK UP THAT BOW AND SOME ARROWS, THEN WAIT A BIT LONGER WHILE I PUT AN ARROW IN THE STRING BIT, AND THEN STAND SUPER STILL WHILE I AIM AT YOU...
...WELL, THEN THERE'S, LIKE, A FIFTY-FIFTY CHANCE THAT YOU COULD BE IN REAL TROUBLE, MISTER.
TURN AROUND. HANDS BEHIND YOUR BACK.
DON'T BE STUPID!
RRRRNNNN

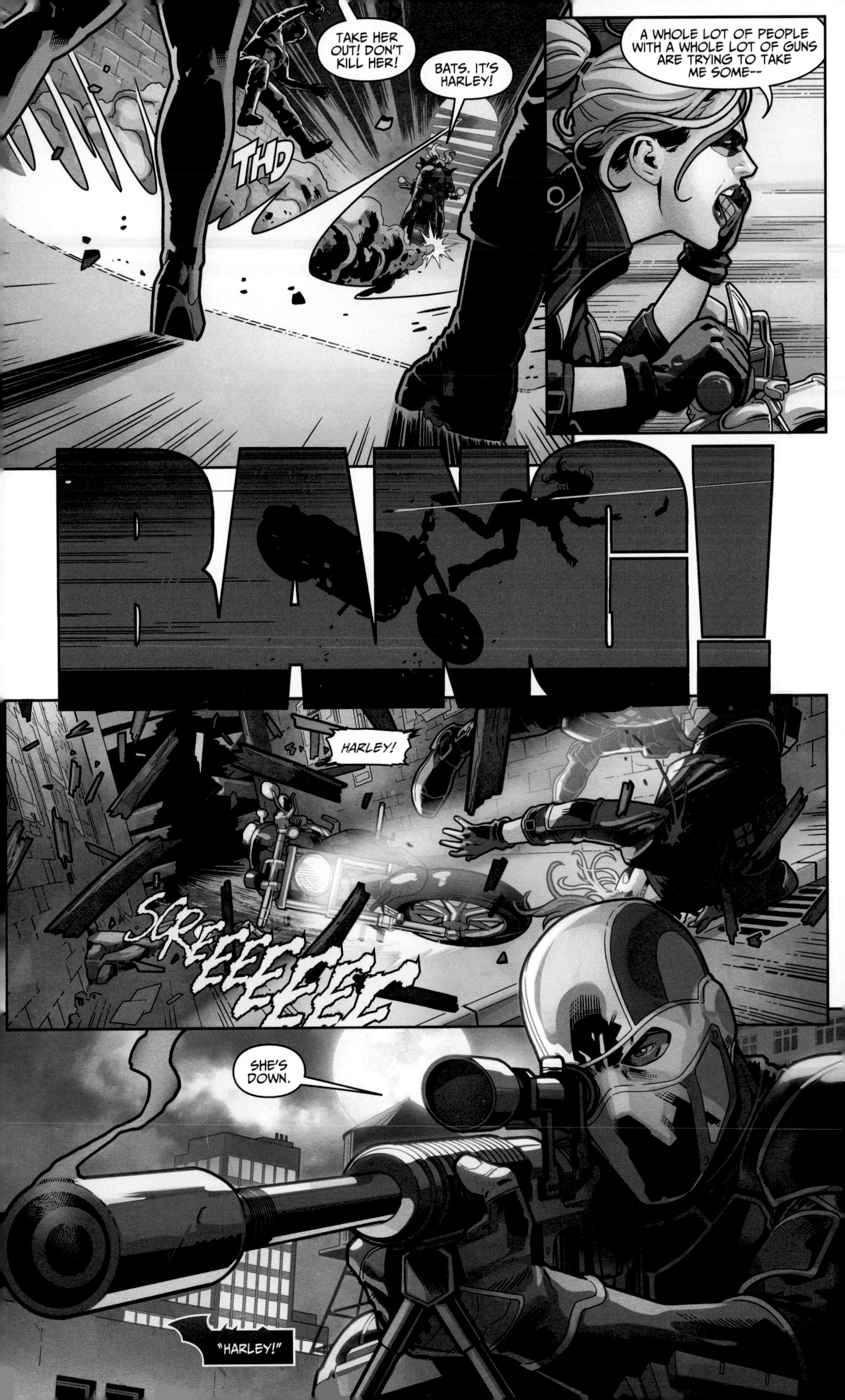
TAKE HER OUT! DON'T KILL HER!
BATS. IT'S HARLEY!
THD
A WHOLE LOT OF PEOPLE WITH A WHOLE LOT OF GUNS ARE TRYING TO TAKE ME SOME--
BANG!
HARLEY!
SCREEEEEEEE
SHE'S DOWN.
"HARLEY!"

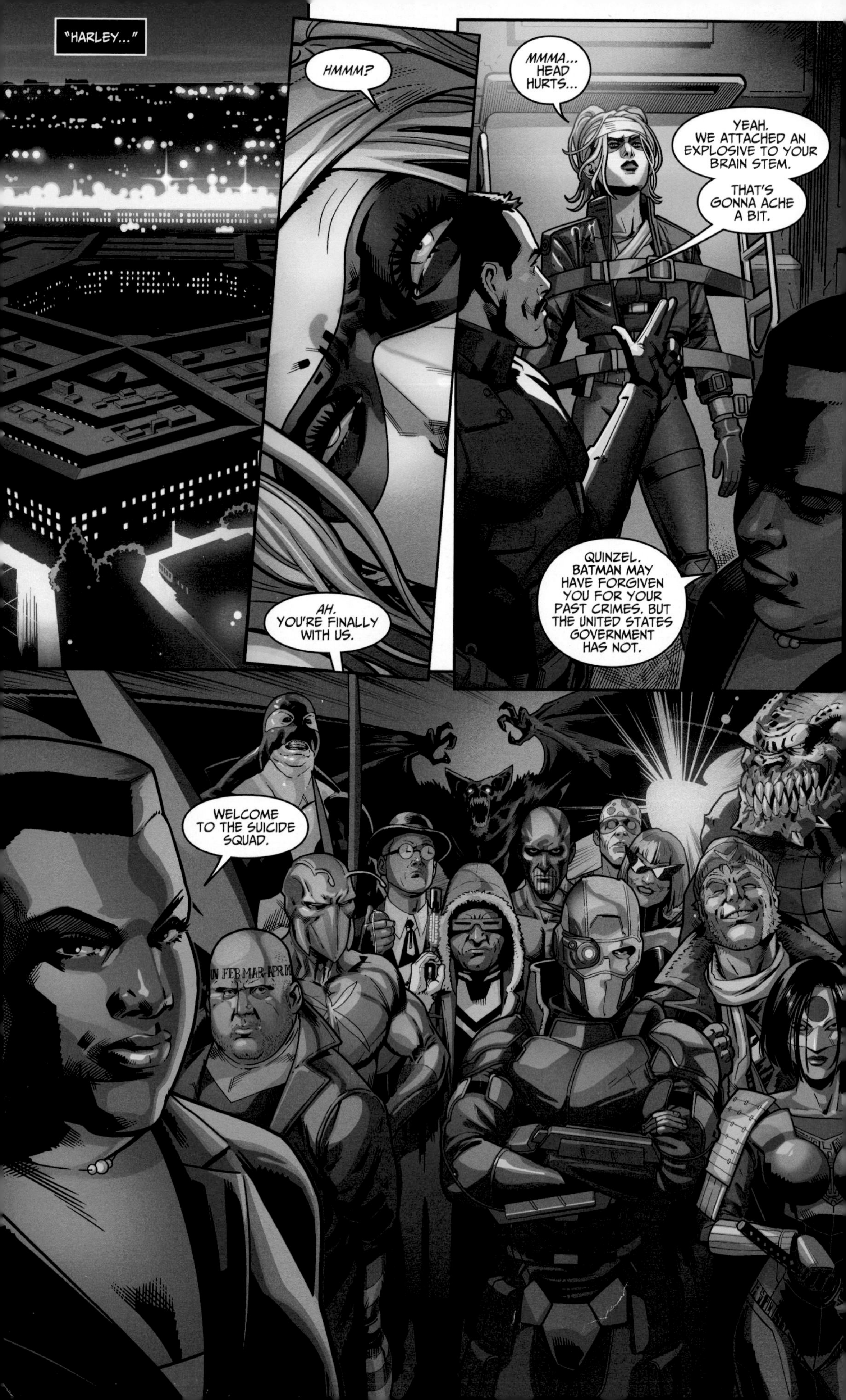
"HARLEY..."
HMMM?
AH. YOU'RE FINALLY WITH US.
MMMA... HEAD HURTS...
YEAH. WE ATTACHED AN EXPLOSIVE TO YOUR BRAIN STEM.
THAT'S GONNA ACHE A BIT.
QUINZEL. BATMAN MAY HAVE FORGIVEN YOU FOR YOUR PAST CRIMES. BUT THE UNITED STATES GOVERNMENT HAS NOT.
WELCOME TO THE SUICIDE SQUAD.

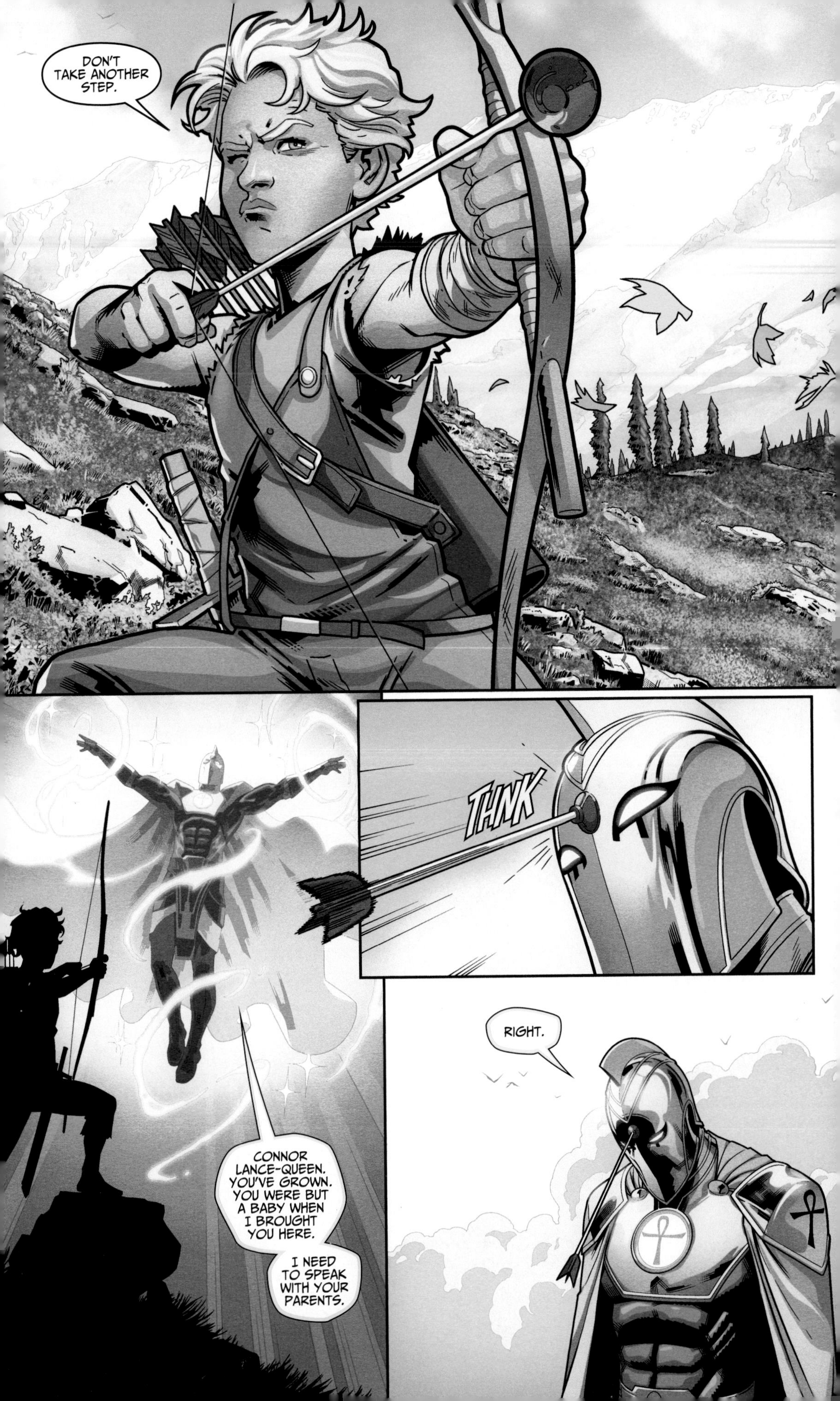
DON'T TAKE ANOTHER STEP.
CONNOR LANCE-QUEEN. YOU'VE GROWN. YOU WERE BUT A BABY WHEN I BROUGHT YOU HERE.
I NEED TO SPEAK WITH YOUR PARENTS.
THNK
RIGHT.

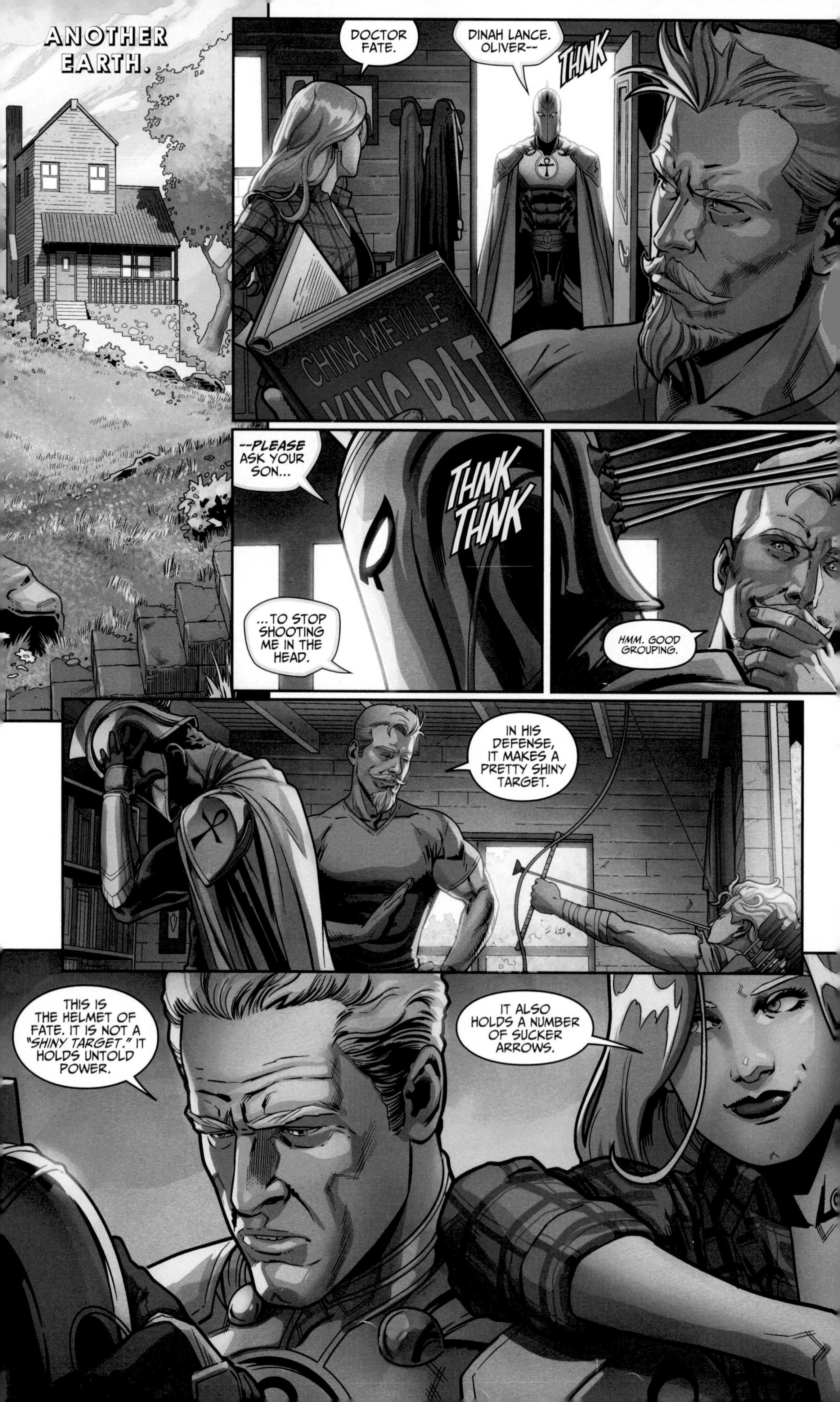
ANOTHER EARTH.
DOCTOR FATE.
DINAH LANCE. OLIVER--
THNK
CHINA MIÉVILLE
KING RAT
--PLEASE ASK YOUR SON...
THNK THNK
...TO STOP SHOOTING ME IN THE HEAD.
HMM. GOOD GROUPING.
IN HIS DEFENSE, IT MAKES A PRETTY SHINY TARGET.
THIS IS THE HELMET OF FATE. IT IS NOT A "SHINY TARGET." IT HOLDS UNTOLD POWER.
IT ALSO HOLDS A NUMBER OF SUCKER ARROWS.

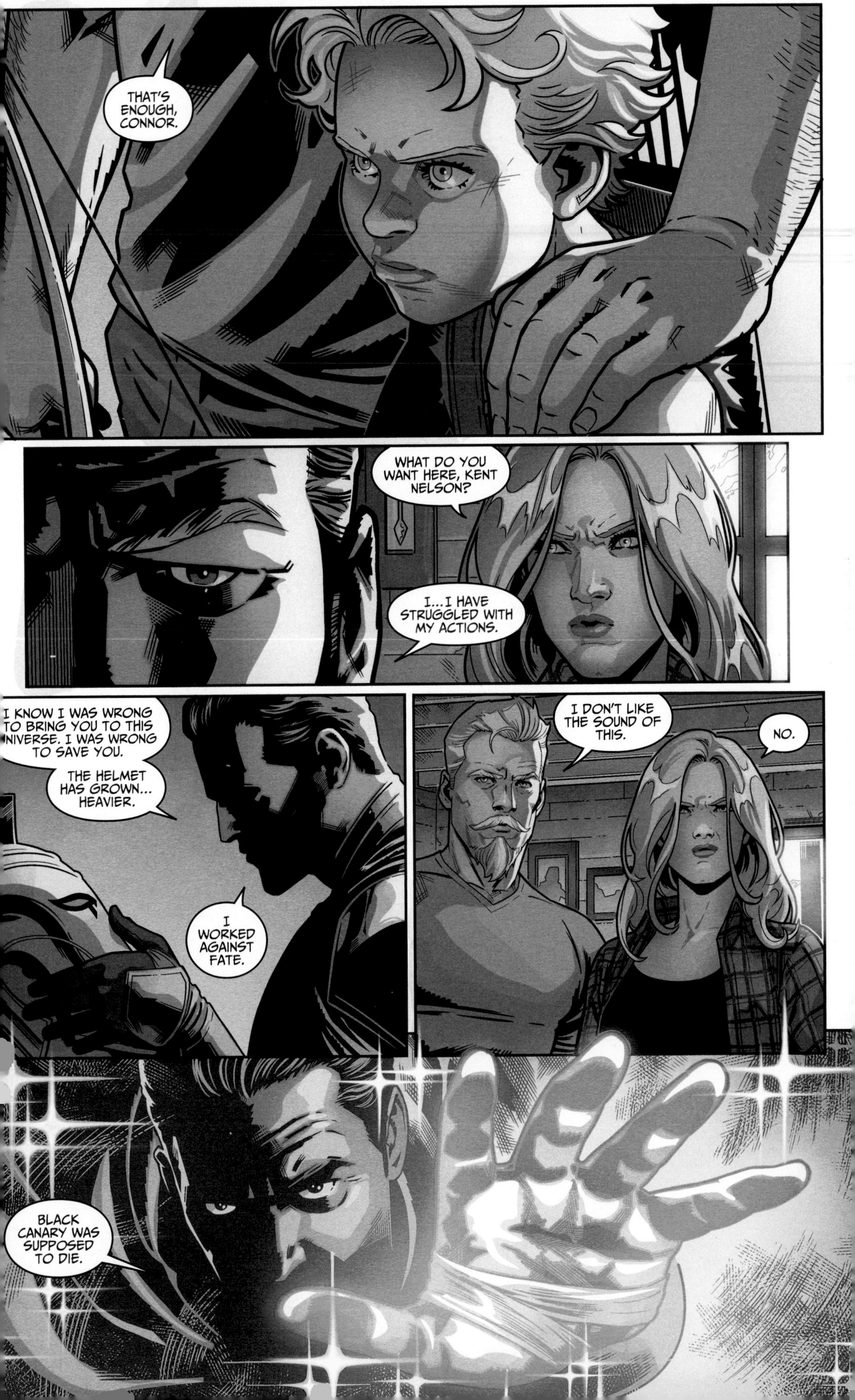
THAT'S ENOUGH, CONNOR.
WHAT DO YOU WANT HERE, KENT NELSON?
I...I HAVE STRUGGLED WITH MY ACTIONS.
I KNOW I WAS WRONG TO BRING YOU TO THIS NIVERSE. I WAS WRONG TO SAVE YOU.
THE HELMET HAS GROWN... HEAVIER.
I WORKED AGAINST FATE.
I DON'T LIKE THE SOUND OF THIS.
NO.
BLACK CANARY WAS SUPPOSED TO DIE.

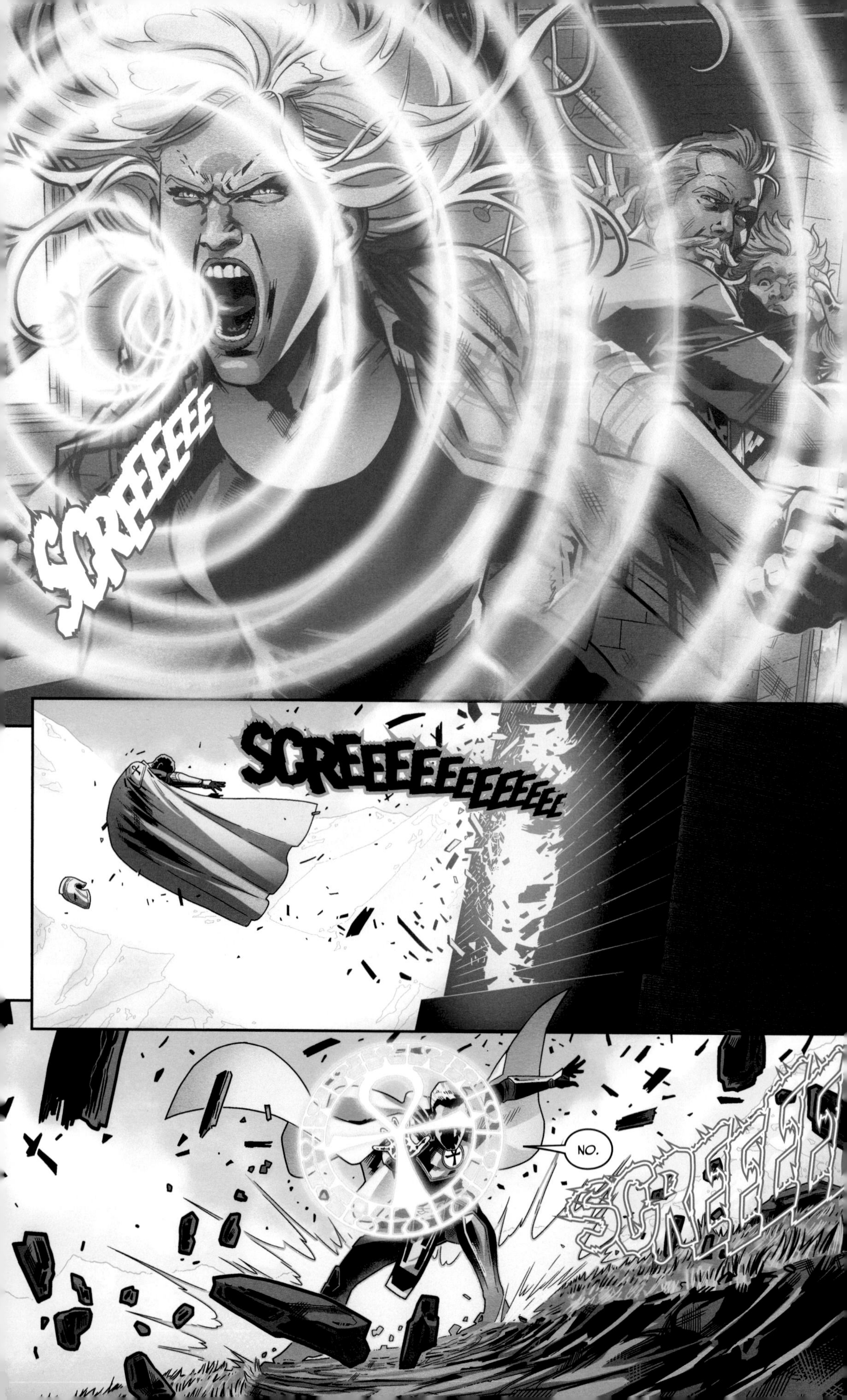
SCREEEEEE
SCREEEEEEEEEEEEEE
NO.
SCREEEEE

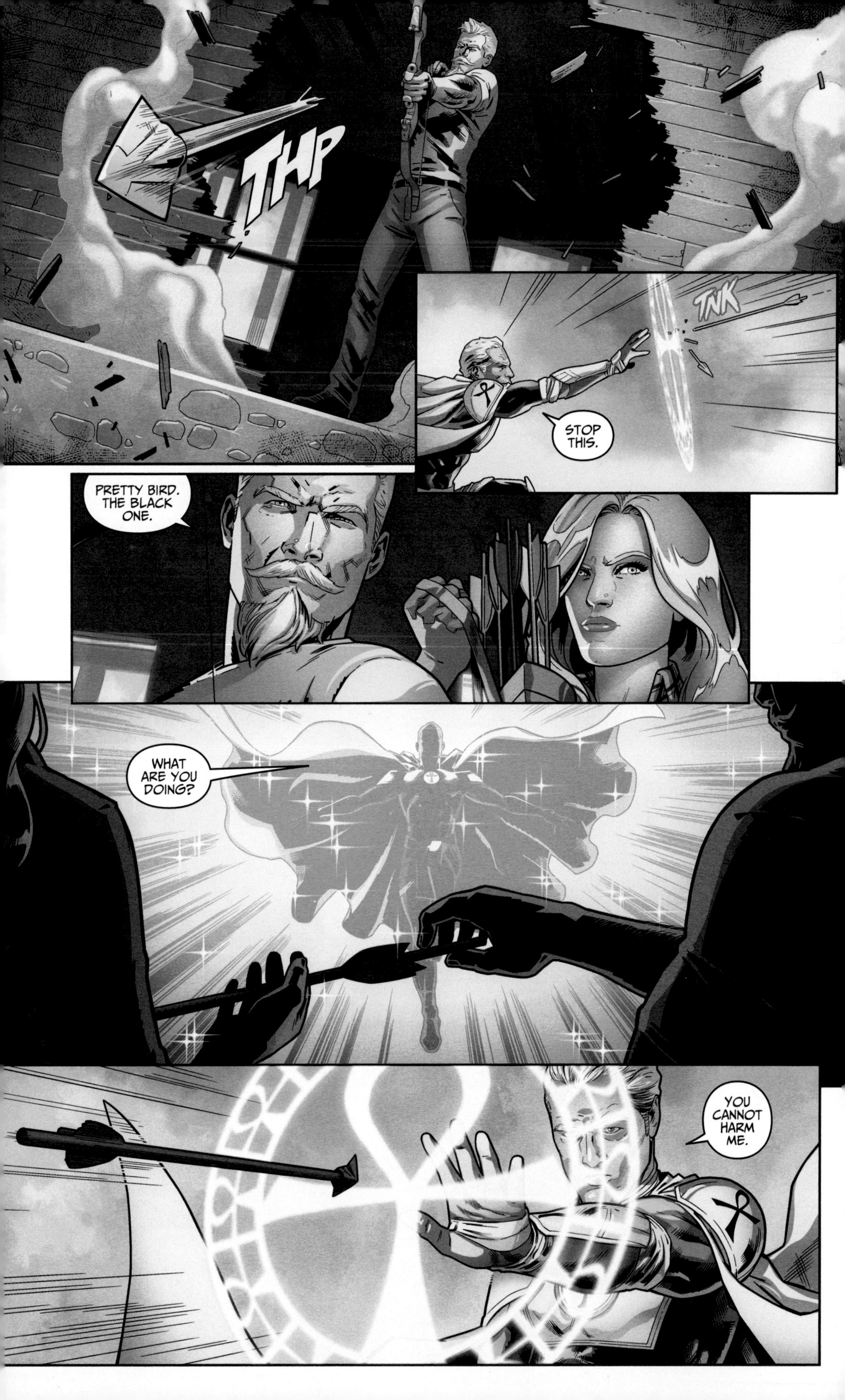
THP
TNK
STOP THIS.
PRETTY BIRD. THE BLACK ONE.
WHAT ARE YOU DOING?
YOU CANNOT HARM ME.

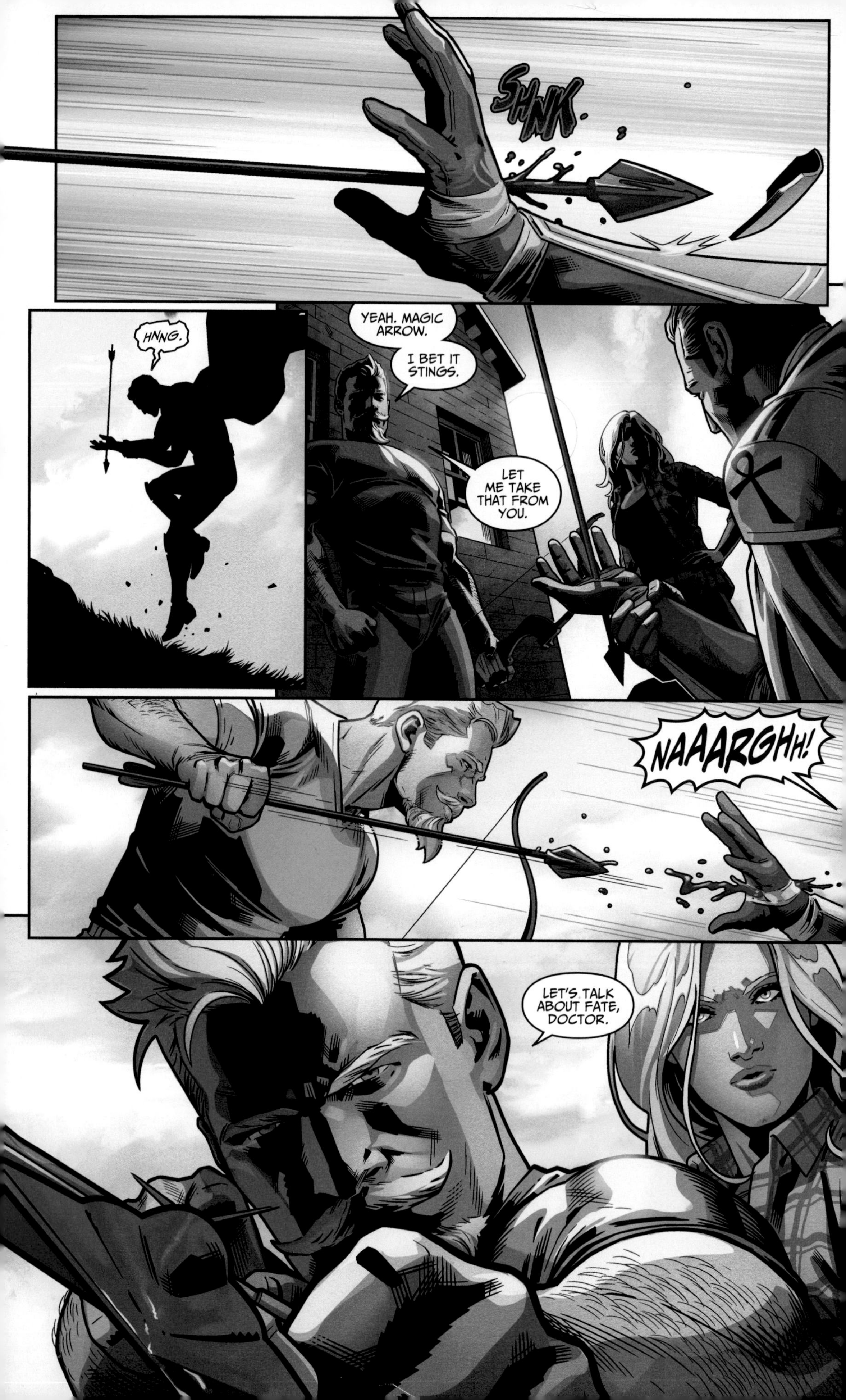
SHNK
HNNG.
YEAH. MAGIC ARROW.
I BET IT STINGS.
LET ME TAKE THAT FROM YOU.
NAAARGHH!
LET'S TALK ABOUT FATE, DOCTOR.

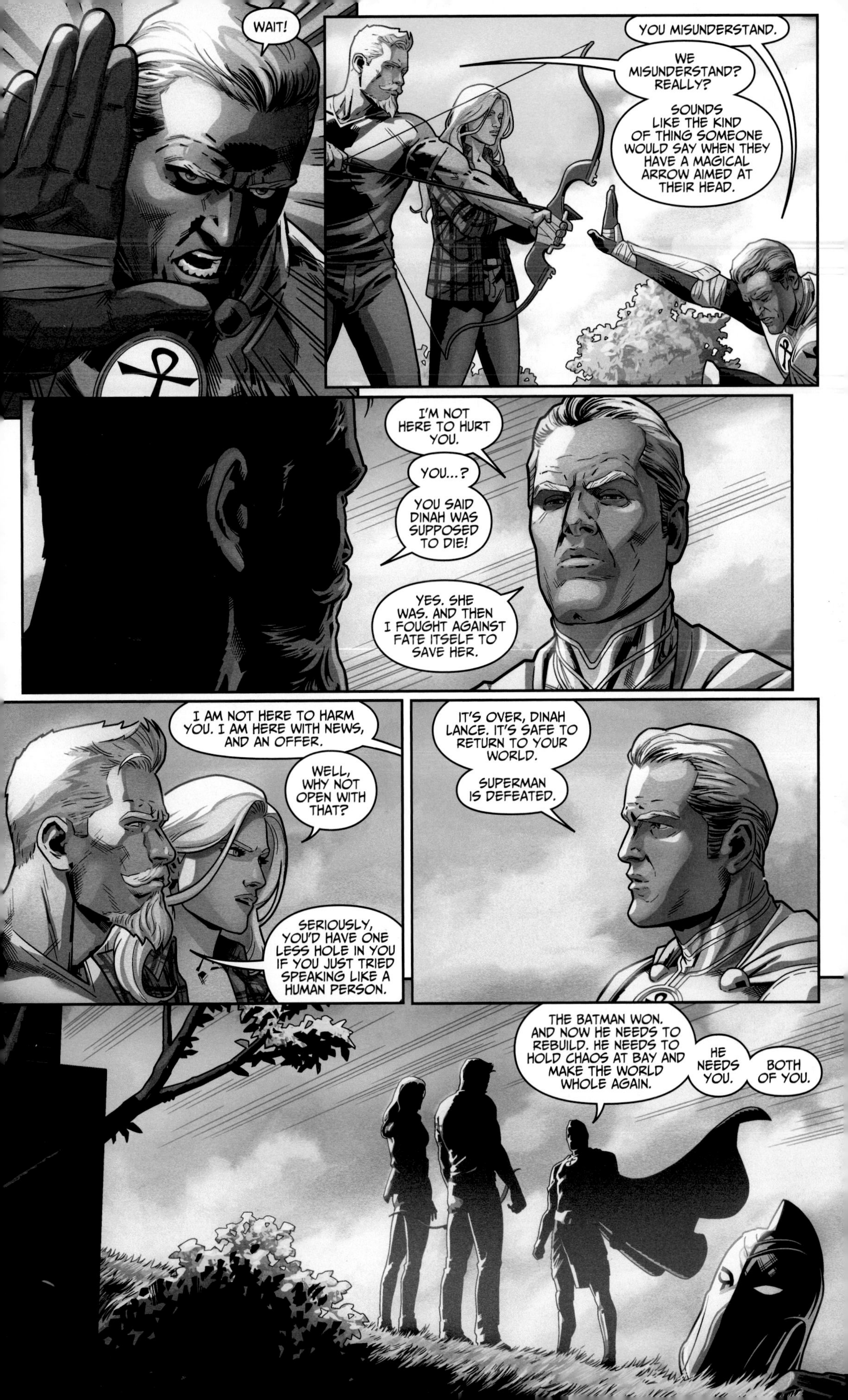
WAIT!
YOU MISUNDERSTAND.
WE MISUNDERSTAND? REALLY?
SOUNDS LIKE THE KIND OF THING SOMEONE WOULD SAY WHEN THEY HAVE A MAGICAL ARROW AIMED AT THEIR HEAD.
I'M NOT HERE TO HURT YOU.
YOU...?
YOU SAID DINAH WAS SUPPOSED TO DIE!
YES. SHE WAS. AND THEN I FOUGHT AGAINST FATE ITSELF TO SAVE HER.
I AM NOT HERE TO HARM YOU. I AM HERE WITH NEWS, AND AN OFFER.
WELL, WHY NOT OPEN WITH THAT?
SERIOUSLY, YOU'D HAVE ONE LESS HOLE IN YOU IF YOU JUST TRIED SPEAKING LIKE A HUMAN PERSON.
IT'S OVER, DINAH LANCE. IT'S SAFE TO RETURN TO YOUR WORLD.
SUPERMAN IS DEFEATED.
THE BATMAN WON. AND NOW HE NEEDS TO REBUILD. HE NEEDS TO HOLD CHAOS AT BAY AND MAKE THE WORLD WHOLE AGAIN.
HE NEEDS YOU.
BOTH OF YOU.

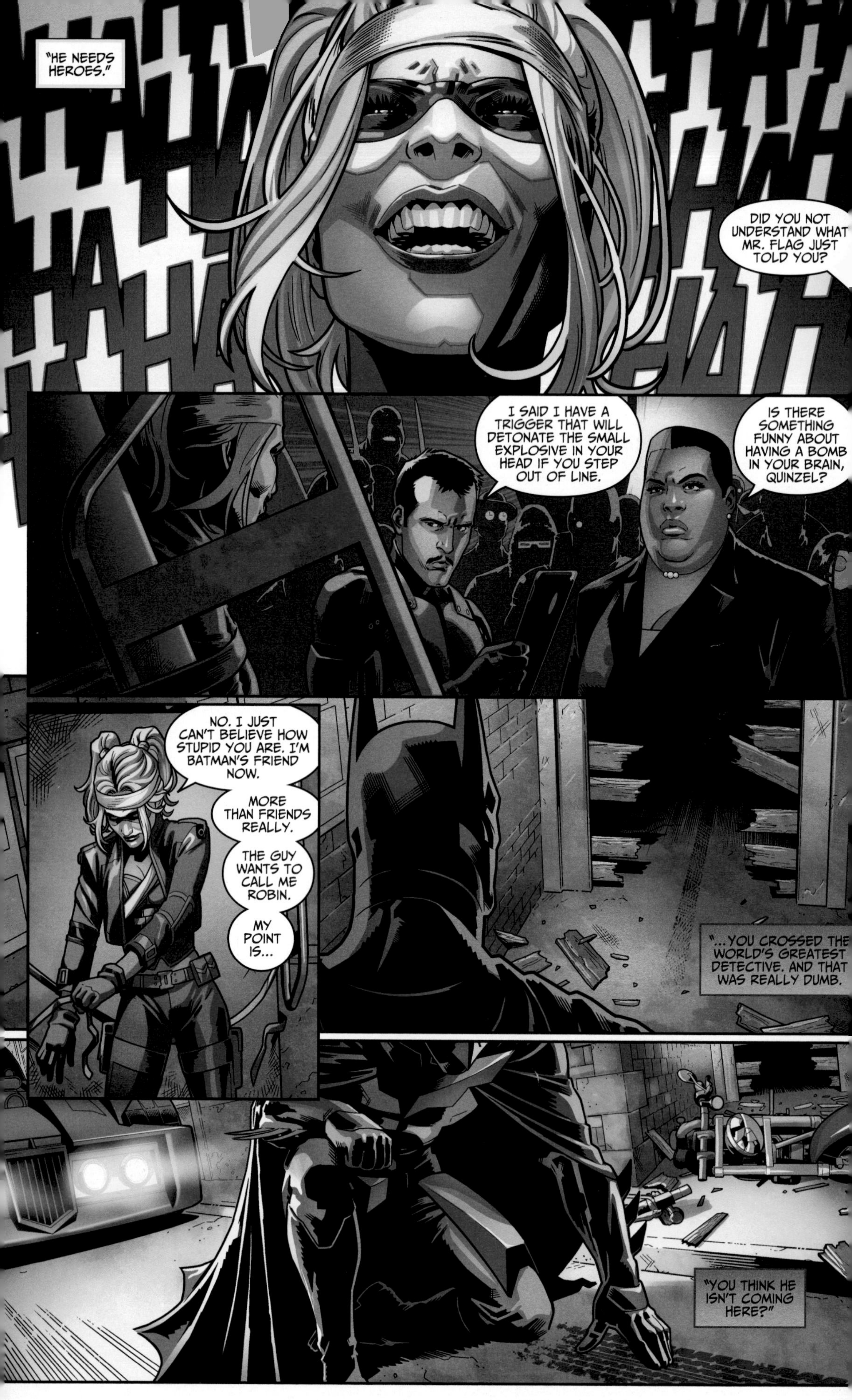
"HE NEEDS HEROES."
DID YOU NOT UNDERSTAND WHAT MR. FLAG JUST TOLD YOU?
I SAID I HAVE A TRIGGER THAT WILL DETONATE THE SMALL EXPLOSIVE IN YOUR HEAD IF YOU STEP OUT OF LINE.
IS THERE SOMETHING FUNNY ABOUT HAVING A BOMB IN YOUR BRAIN, QUINZEL?
NO. I JUST CAN'T BELIEVE HOW STUPID YOU ARE. I'M BATMAN'S FRIEND NOW.
MORE THAN FRIENDS REALLY.
THE GUY WANTS TO CALL ME ROBIN.
MY POINT IS...
"...YOU CROSSED THE WORLD'S GREATEST DETECTIVE. AND THAT WAS REALLY DUMB.
"YOU THINK HE ISN'T COMING HERE?"

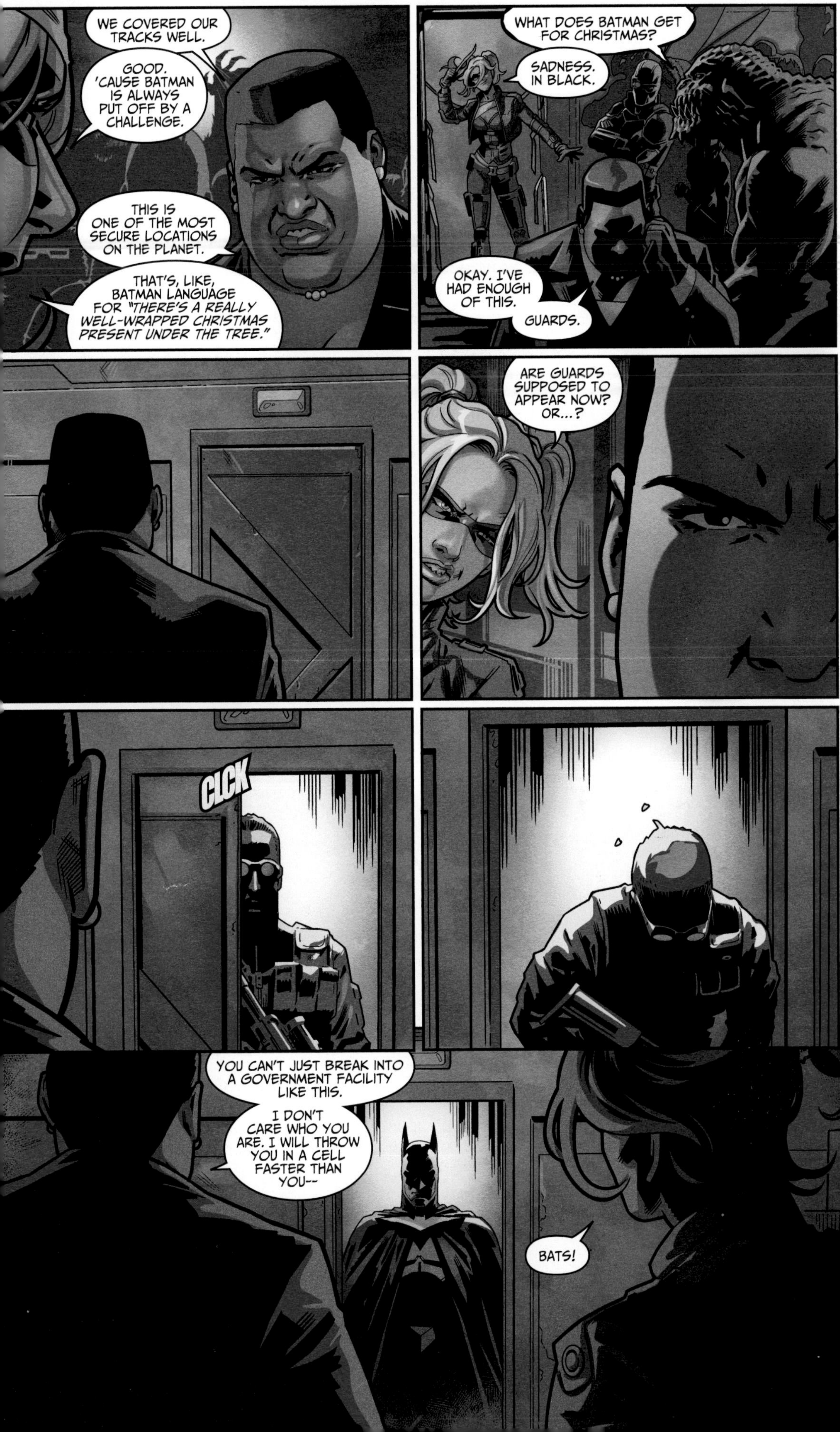
WE COVERED OUR TRACKS WELL.
GOOD. 'CAUSE BATMAN IS ALWAYS PUT OFF BY A CHALLENGE.
THIS IS ONE OF THE MOST SECURE LOCATIONS ON THE PLANET.
THAT'S, LIKE, BATMAN LANGUAGE FOR "THERE'S A REALLY WELL-WRAPPED CHRISTMAS PRESENT UNDER THE TREE."
WHAT DOES BATMAN GET FOR CHRISTMAS?
SADNESS. IN BLACK.
OKAY. I'VE HAD ENOUGH OF THIS.
GUARDS.
ARE GUARDS SUPPOSED TO APPEAR NOW? OR...?
CLCK
YOU CAN'T JUST BREAK INTO A GOVERNMENT FACILITY LIKE THIS.
I DON'T CARE WHO YOU ARE. I WILL THROW YOU IN A CELL FASTER THAN YOU--
BATS!

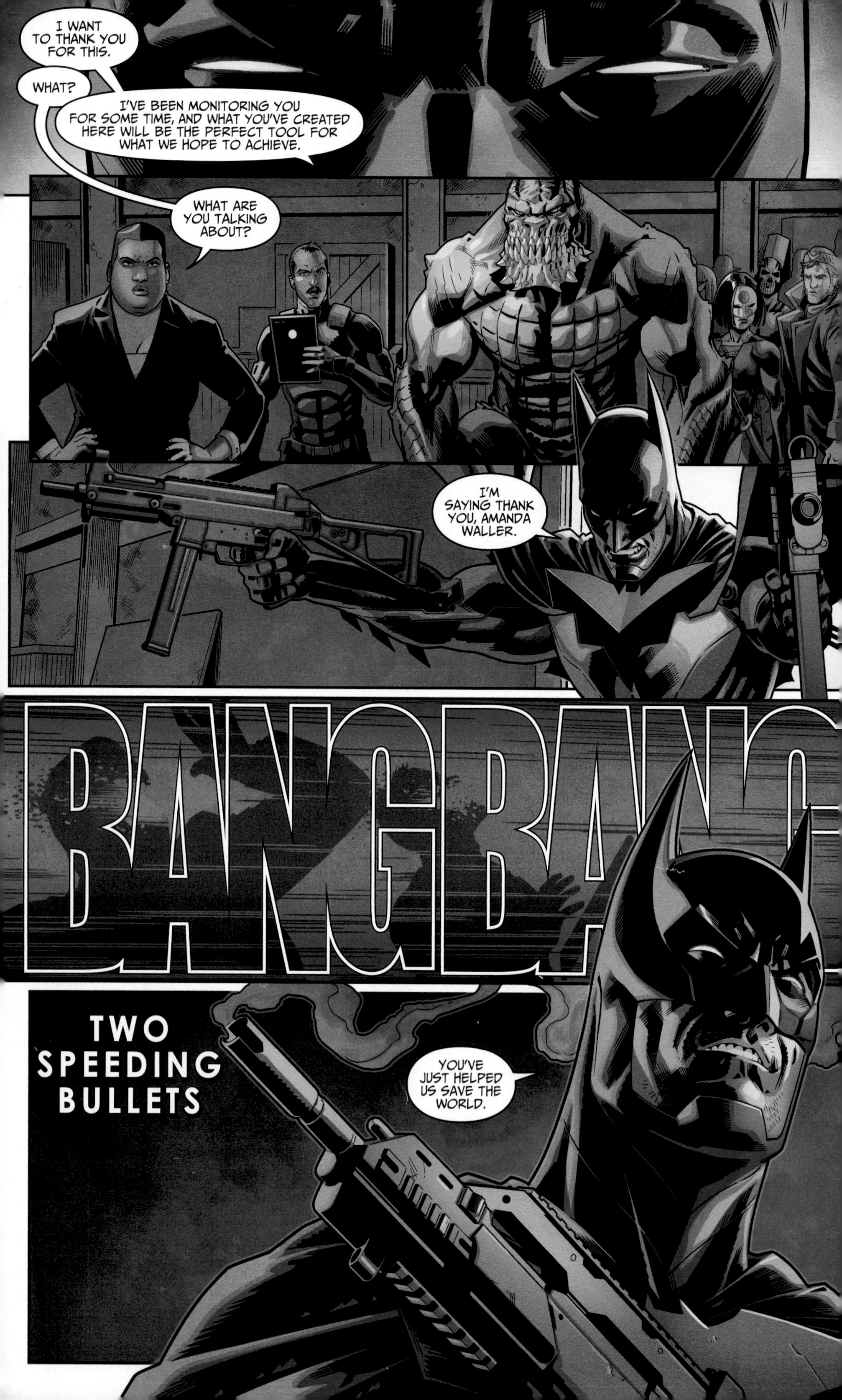
I WANT TO THANK YOU FOR THIS.
WHAT?
I'VE BEEN MONITORING YOU FOR SOME TIME, AND WHAT YOU'VE CREATED HERE WILL BE THE PERFECT TOOL FOR WHAT WE HOPE TO ACHIEVE.
WHAT ARE YOU TALKING ABOUT?
I'M SAYING THANK YOU, AMANDA WALLER.
BANGBANG
TWO SPEEDING BULLETS
YOU'VE JUST HELPED US SAVE THE WORLD.

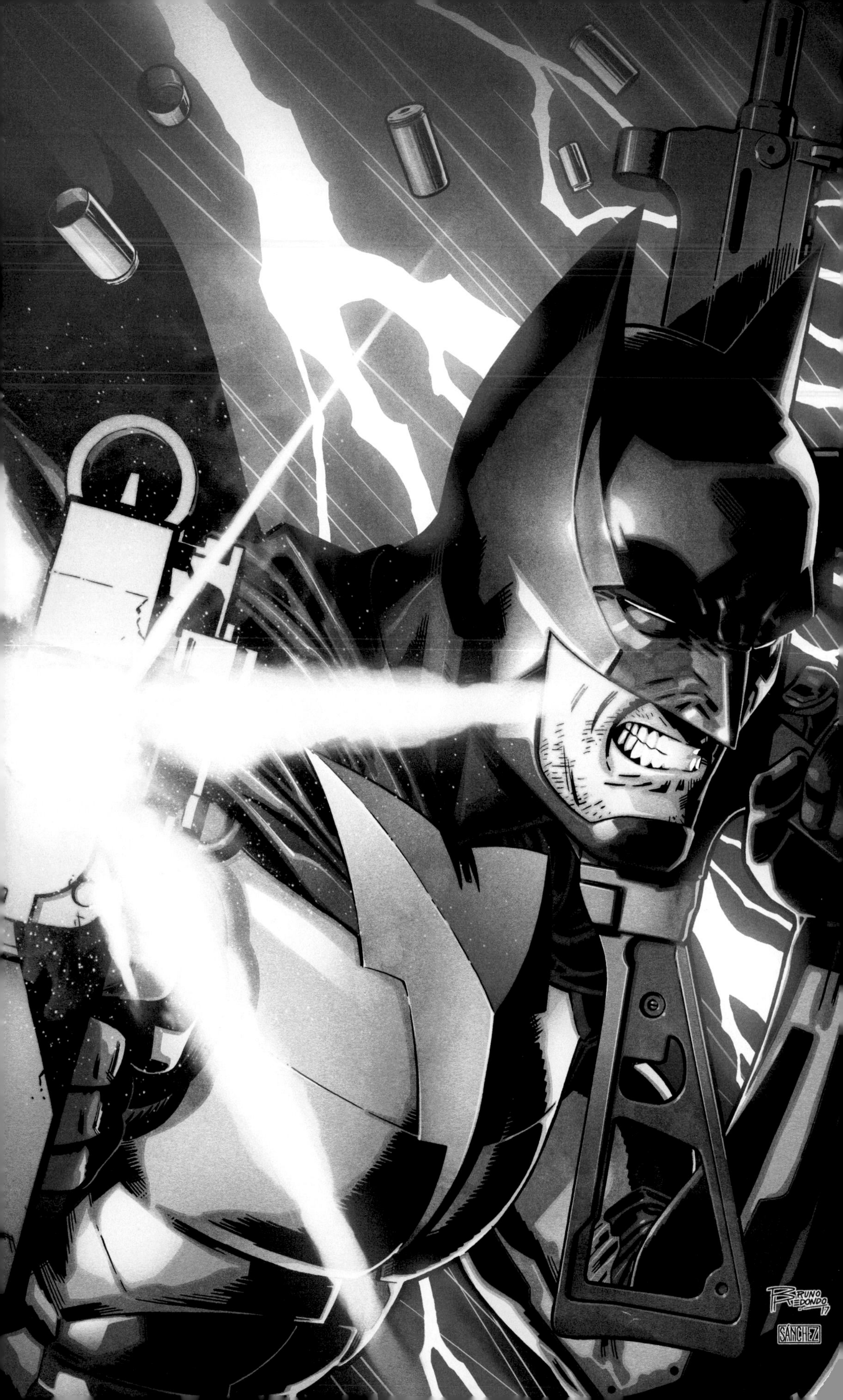
BRUNO REDONDO '17
SÁNCHEZ

"Things Go Boom"

Bruno Redondo Penciller **Juan Albarran** Inker

Rex Lokus Colorist Cover art by **Bruno Redondo** and **Alejandro Sanchez**

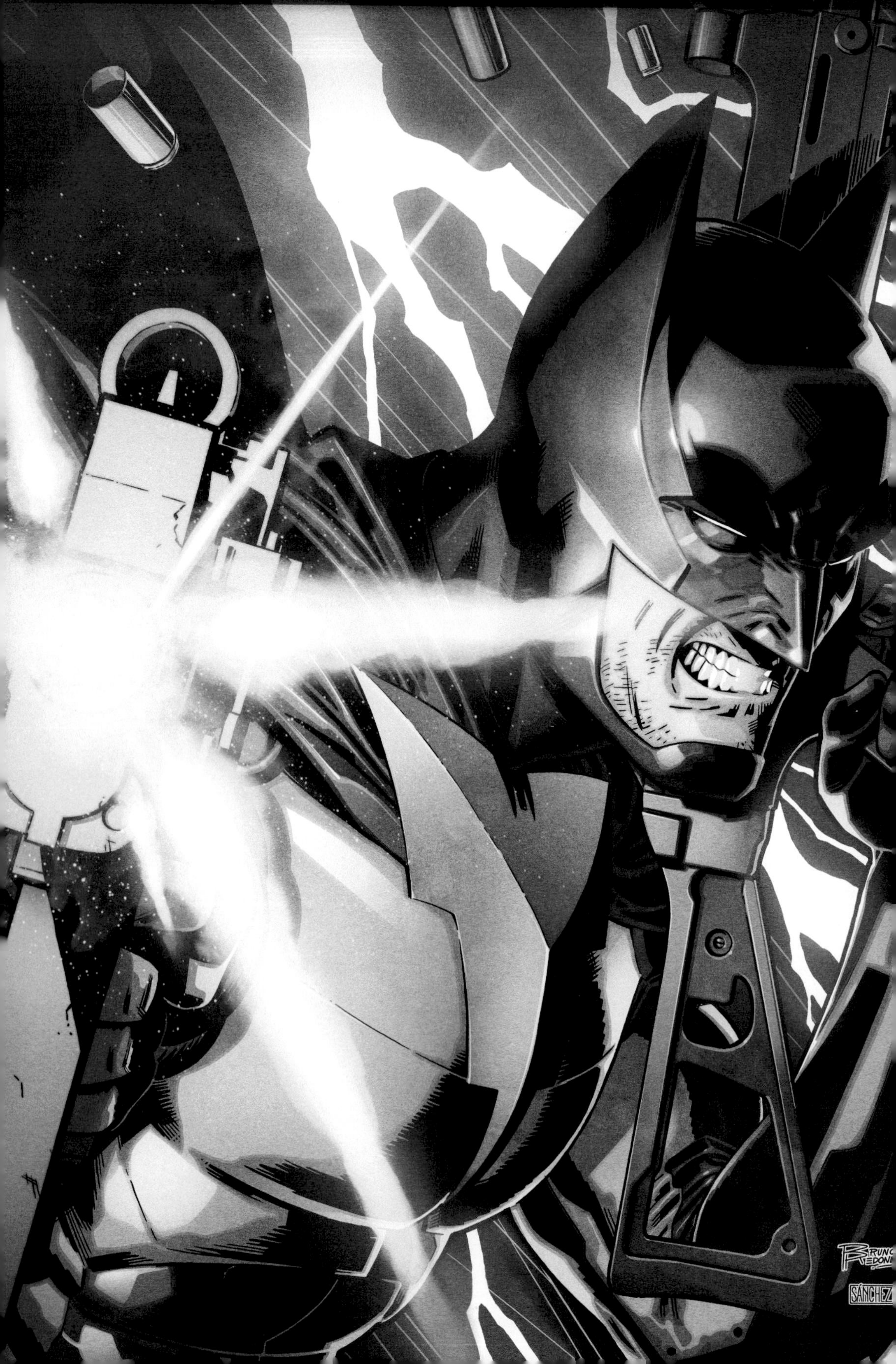

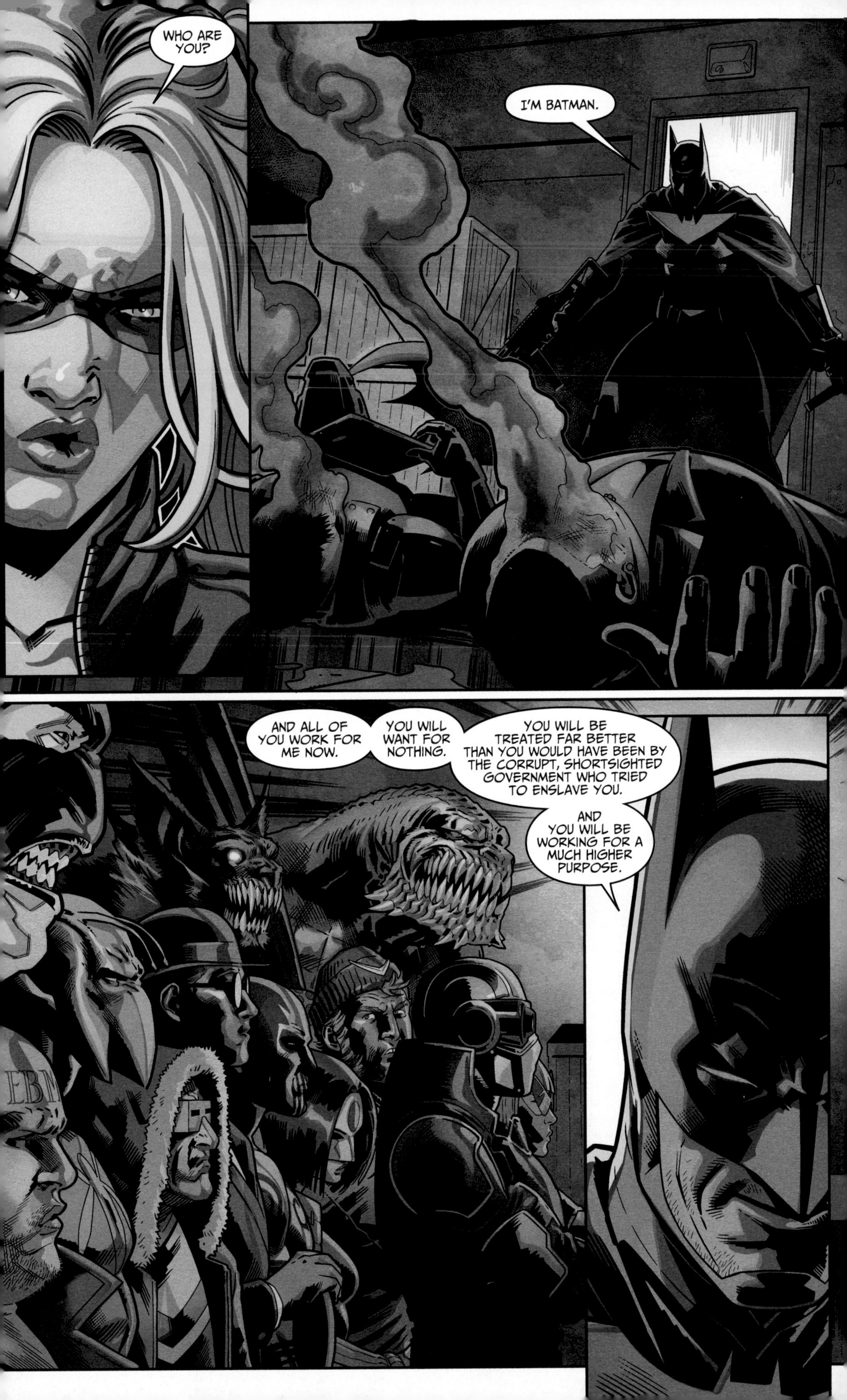
WHO ARE YOU?
I'M BATMAN.
AND ALL OF YOU WORK FOR ME NOW.
YOU WILL WANT FOR NOTHING.
YOU WILL BE TREATED FAR BETTER THAN YOU WOULD HAVE BEEN BY THE CORRUPT, SHORTSIGHTED GOVERNMENT WHO TRIED TO ENSLAVE YOU.
AND YOU WILL BE WORKING FOR A MUCH HIGHER PURPOSE.

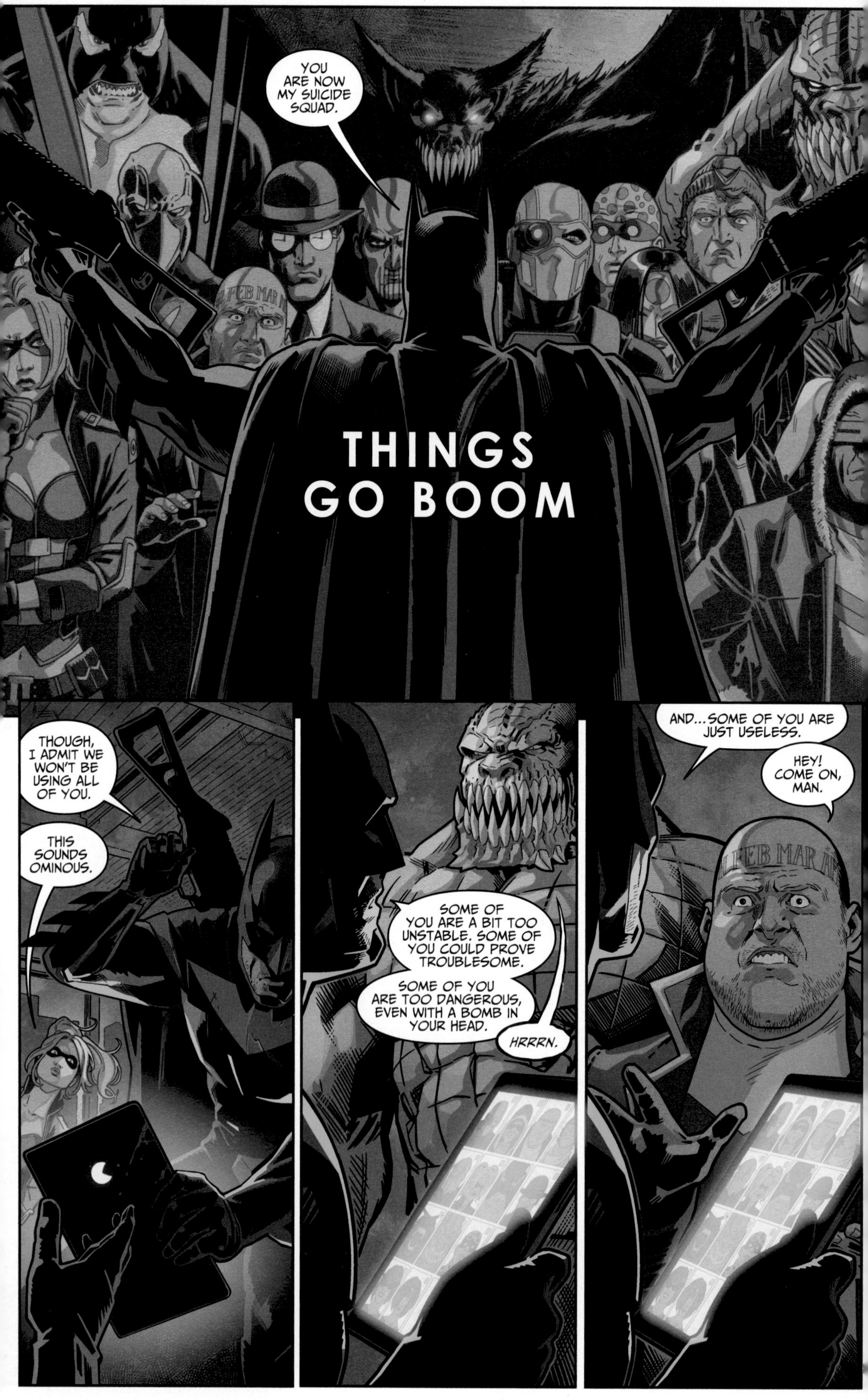
YOU ARE NOW MY SUICIDE SQUAD.
THINGS GO BOOM
THOUGH, I ADMIT WE WON'T BE USING ALL OF YOU.
THIS SOUNDS OMINOUS.
SOME OF YOU ARE A BIT TOO UNSTABLE. SOME OF YOU COULD PROVE TROUBLESOME.
SOME OF YOU ARE TOO DANGEROUS, EVEN WITH A BOMB IN YOUR HEAD.
HRRRN.
AND...SOME OF YOU ARE JUST USELESS.
HEY! COME ON, MAN.

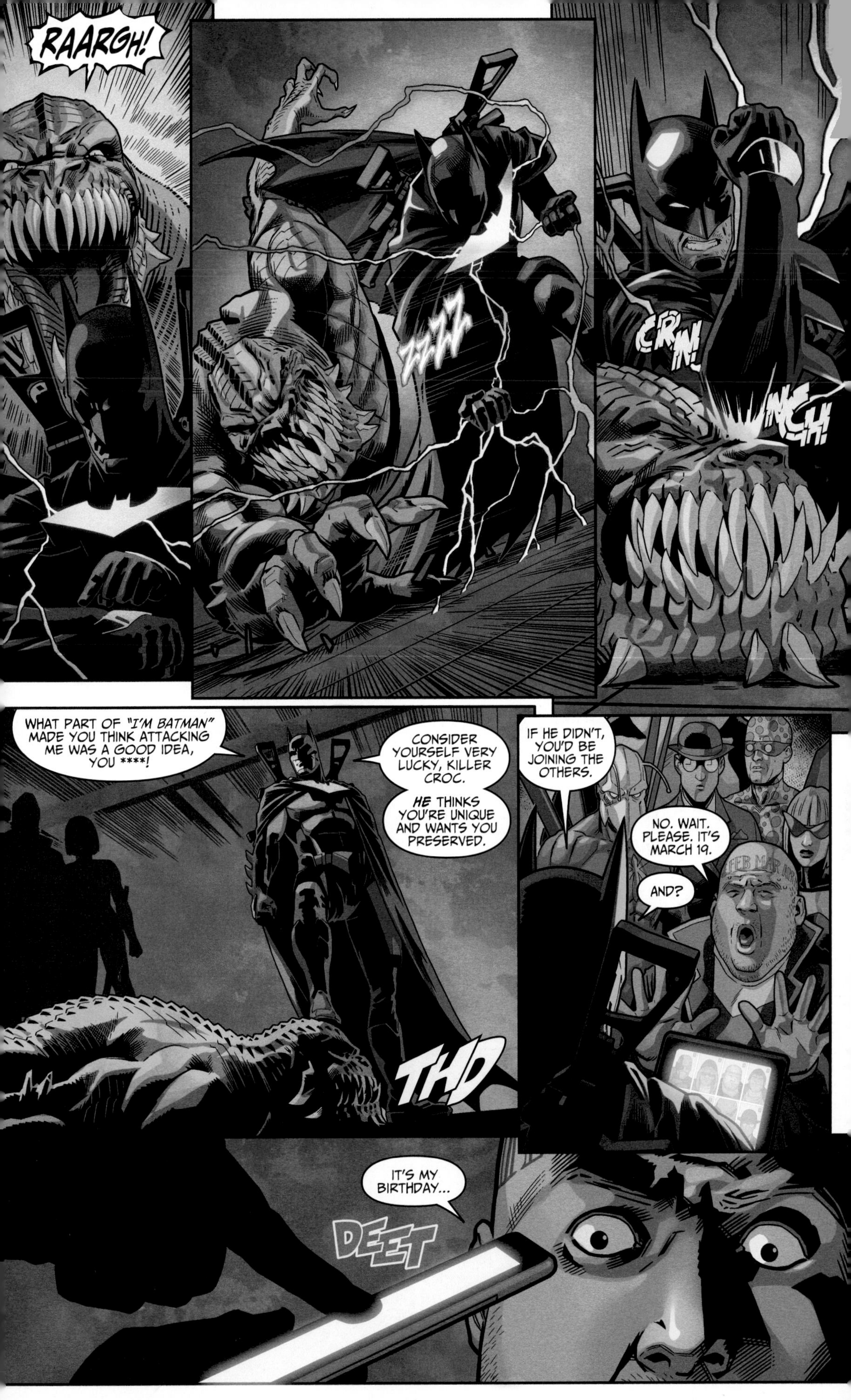
RAARGH!
ZZZZ
CRNCH!
WHAT PART OF "I'M BATMAN" MADE YOU THINK ATTACKING ME WAS A GOOD IDEA, YOU ****!
CONSIDER YOURSELF VERY LUCKY, KILLER CROC.
HE THINKS YOU'RE UNIQUE AND WANTS YOU PRESERVED.
THD
IF HE DIDN'T, YOU'D BE JOINING THE OTHERS.
NO. WAIT. PLEASE. IT'S MARCH 19.
AND?
IT'S MY BIRTHDAY...
DEET

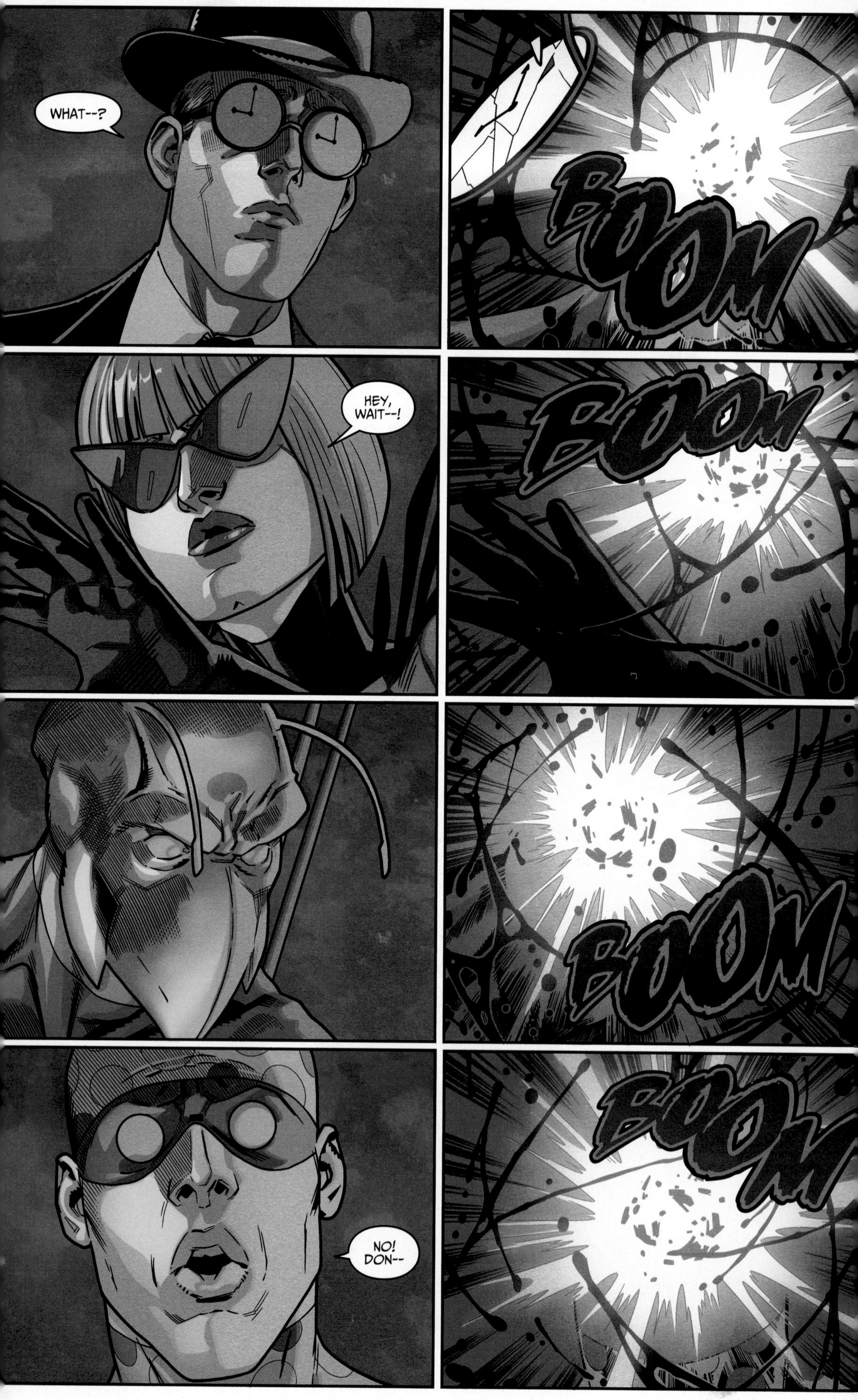
WHAT--?
BOOM
HEY, WAIT--!
BOOM
BOOM
NO! DON--
BOOM

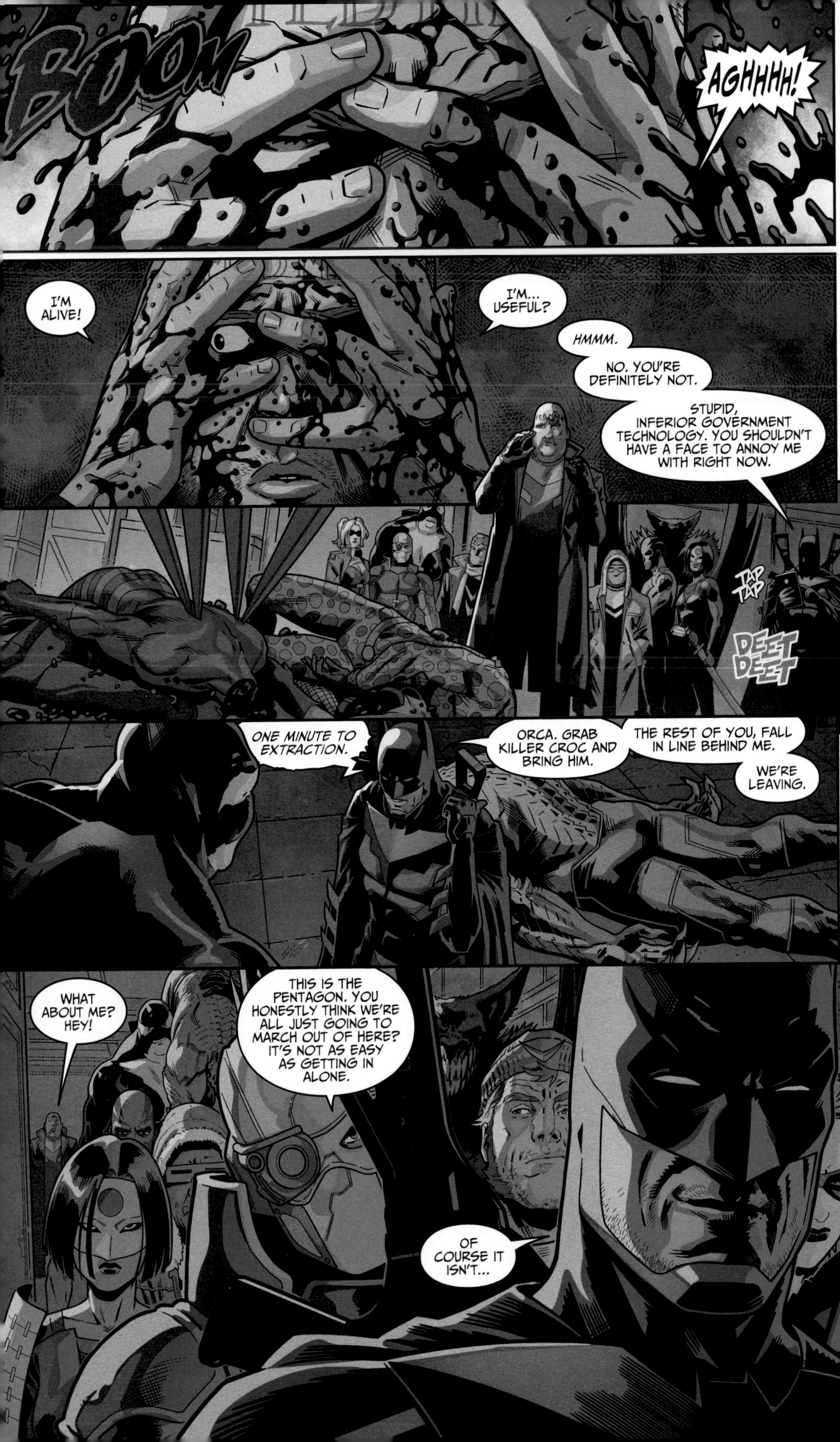
BOOM
AGHHHH!
I'M ALIVE!
I'M... USEFUL?
HMMM.
NO. YOU'RE DEFINITELY NOT.
STUPID, INFERIOR GOVERNMENT TECHNOLOGY. YOU SHOULDN'T HAVE A FACE TO ANNOY ME WITH RIGHT NOW.
TAP TAP
DEET DEET
ONE MINUTE TO EXTRACTION.
ORCA. GRAB KILLER CROC AND BRING HIM.
THE REST OF YOU, FALL IN LINE BEHIND ME.
WE'RE LEAVING.
WHAT ABOUT ME? HEY!
THIS IS THE PENTAGON. YOU HONESTLY THINK WE'RE ALL JUST GOING TO MARCH OUT OF HERE? IT'S NOT AS EASY AS GETTING IN ALONE.
OF COURSE IT ISN'T...

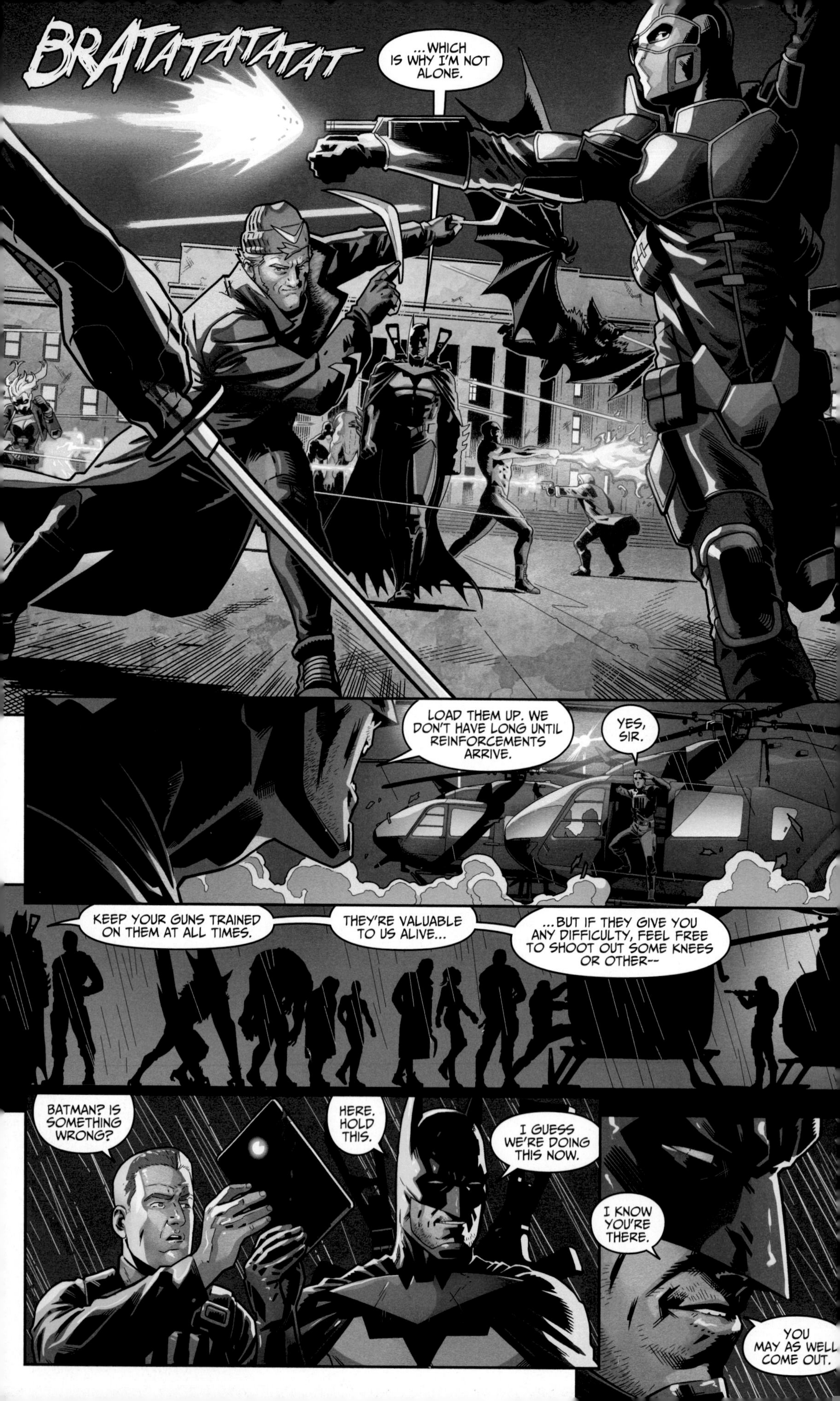
BRATATATATAT
...WHICH IS WHY I'M NOT ALONE.
LOAD THEM UP. WE DON'T HAVE LONG UNTIL REINFORCEMENTS ARRIVE.
YES, SIR.
KEEP YOUR GUNS TRAINED ON THEM AT ALL TIMES.
THEY'RE VALUABLE TO US ALIVE...
...BUT IF THEY GIVE YOU ANY DIFFICULTY, FEEL FREE TO SHOOT OUT SOME KNEES OR OTHER--
BATMAN? IS SOMETHING WRONG?
HERE. HOLD THIS.
I GUESS WE'RE DOING THIS NOW.
I KNOW YOU'RE THERE.
YOU MAY AS WELL COME OUT.

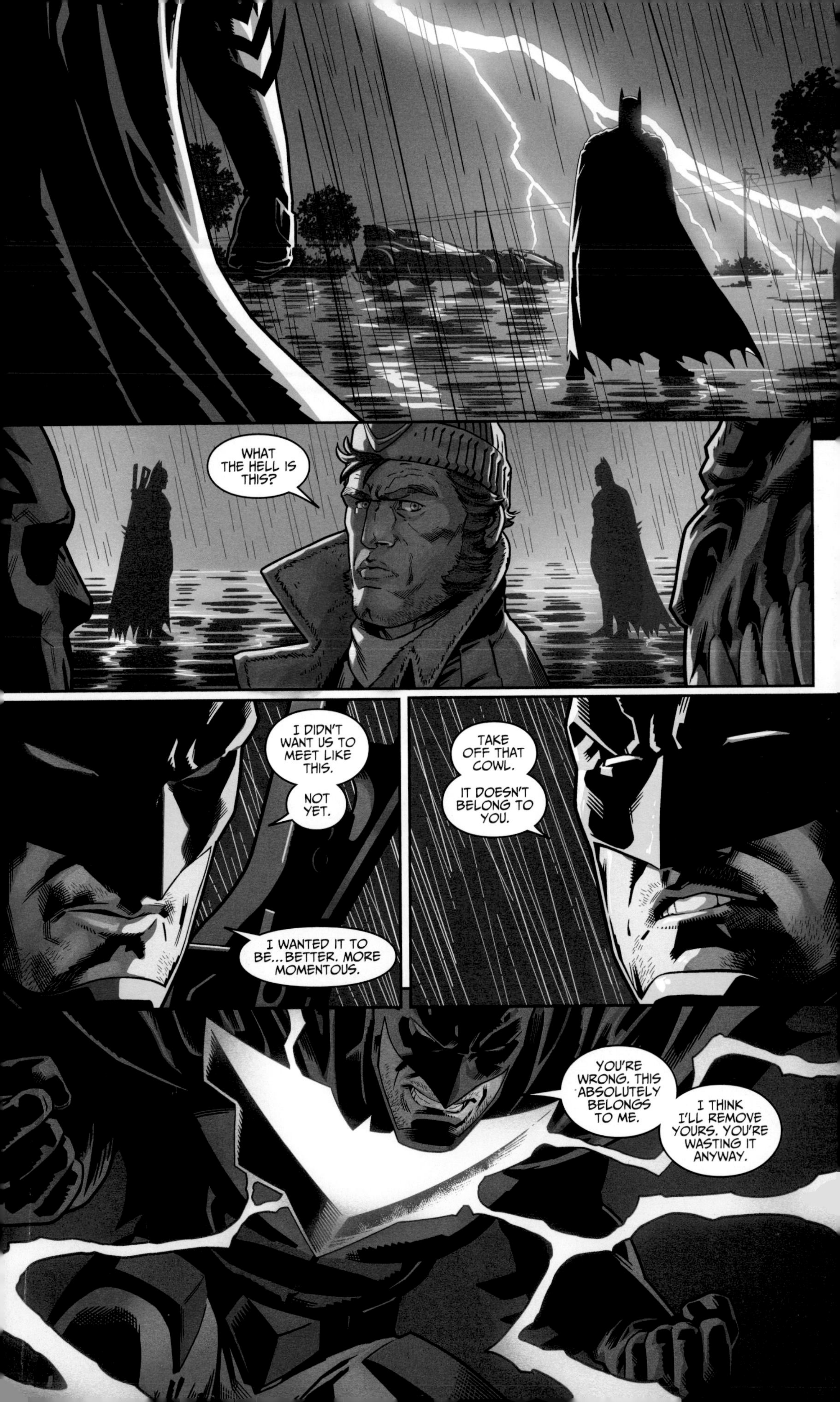
WHAT THE HELL IS THIS?
I DIDN'T WANT US TO MEET LIKE THIS.
NOT YET.
I WANTED IT TO BE...BETTER. MORE MOMENTOUS.
TAKE OFF THAT COWL.
IT DOESN'T BELONG TO YOU.
YOU'RE WRONG. THIS ABSOLUTELY BELONGS TO ME.
I THINK I'LL REMOVE YOURS. YOU'RE WASTING IT ANYWAY.

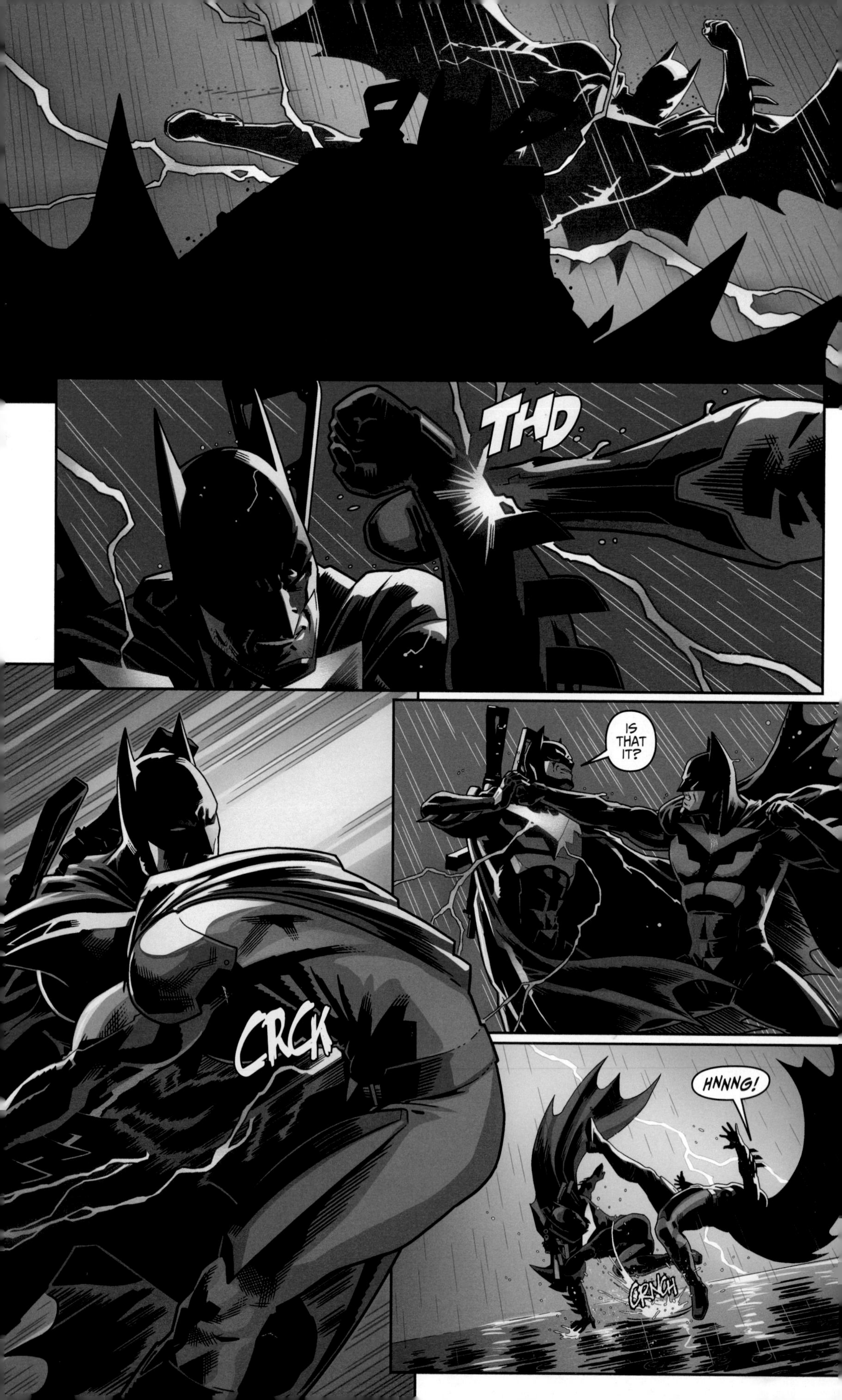
THD
CRCK
IS THAT IT?
HNNNG!
CRNCH

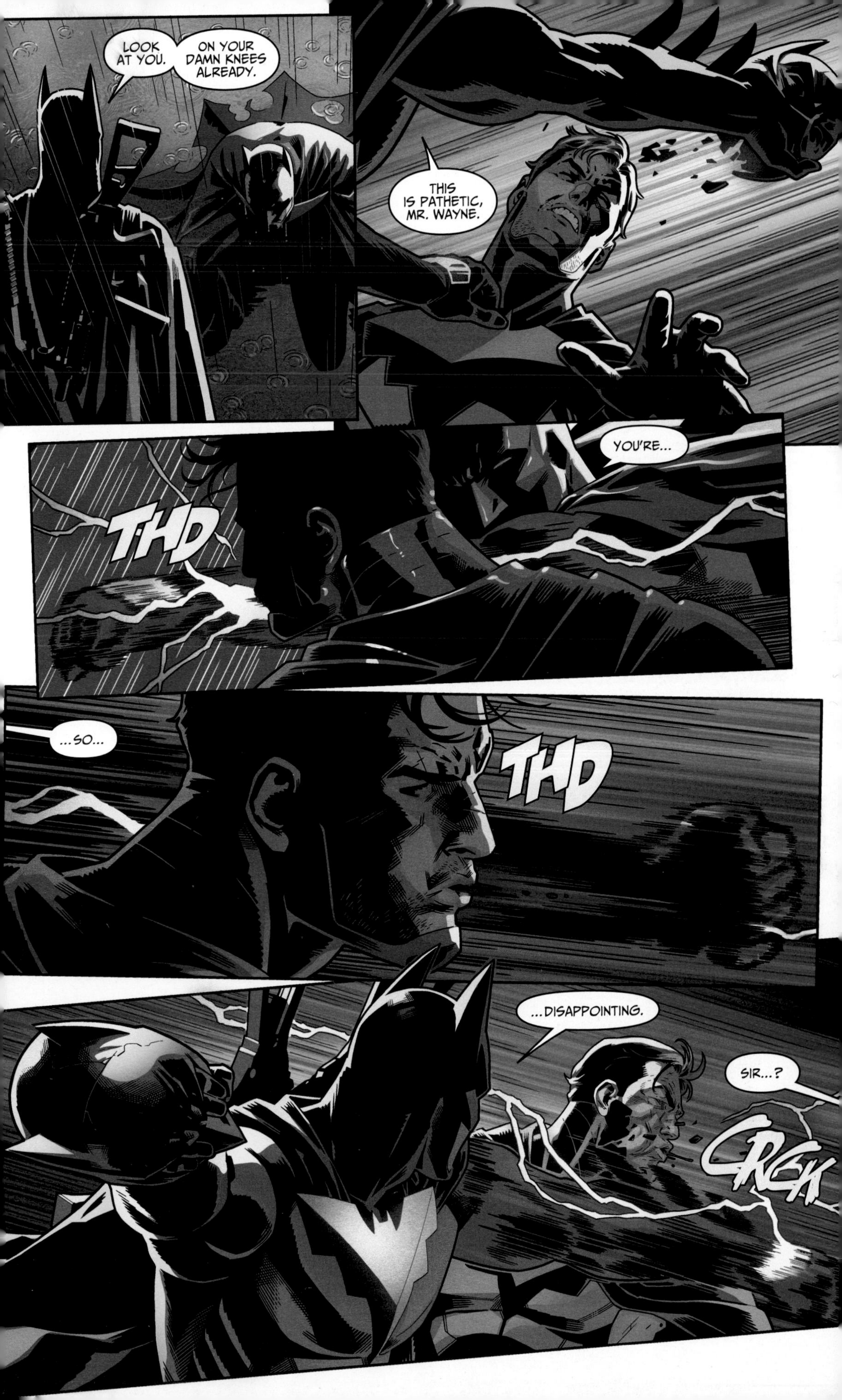
LOOK AT YOU.
ON YOUR DAMN KNEES ALREADY.
THIS IS PATHETIC, MR. WAYNE.
YOU'RE...
THD
...SO...
THD
...DISAPPOINTING.
SIR...?
CRCK

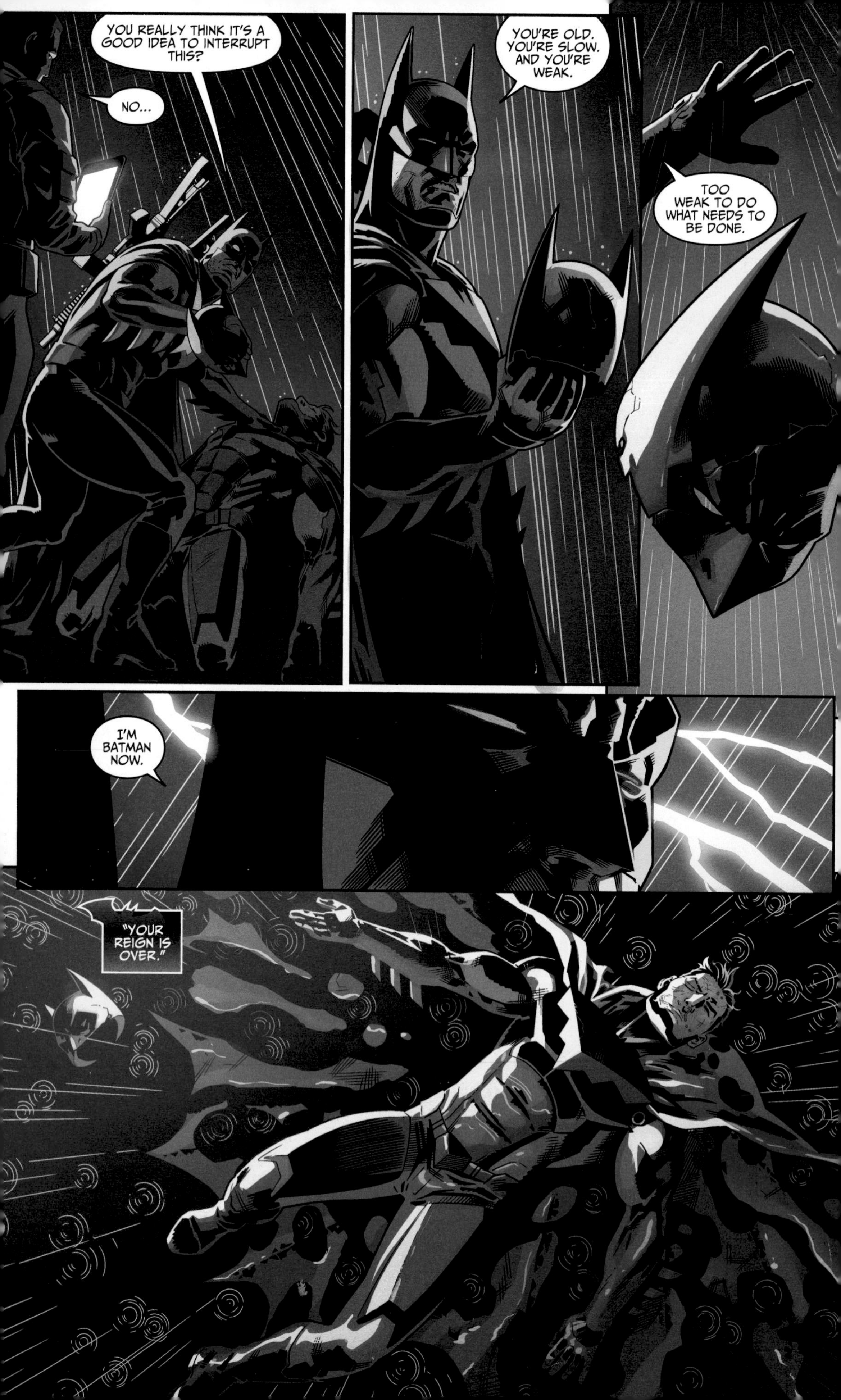

YOU REALLY THINK IT'S A GOOD IDEA TO INTERRUPT THIS?
NO...
YOU'RE OLD. YOU'RE SLOW. AND YOU'RE WEAK.
TOO WEAK TO DO WHAT NEEDS TO BE DONE.
I'M BATMAN NOW.
"YOUR REIGN IS OVER."

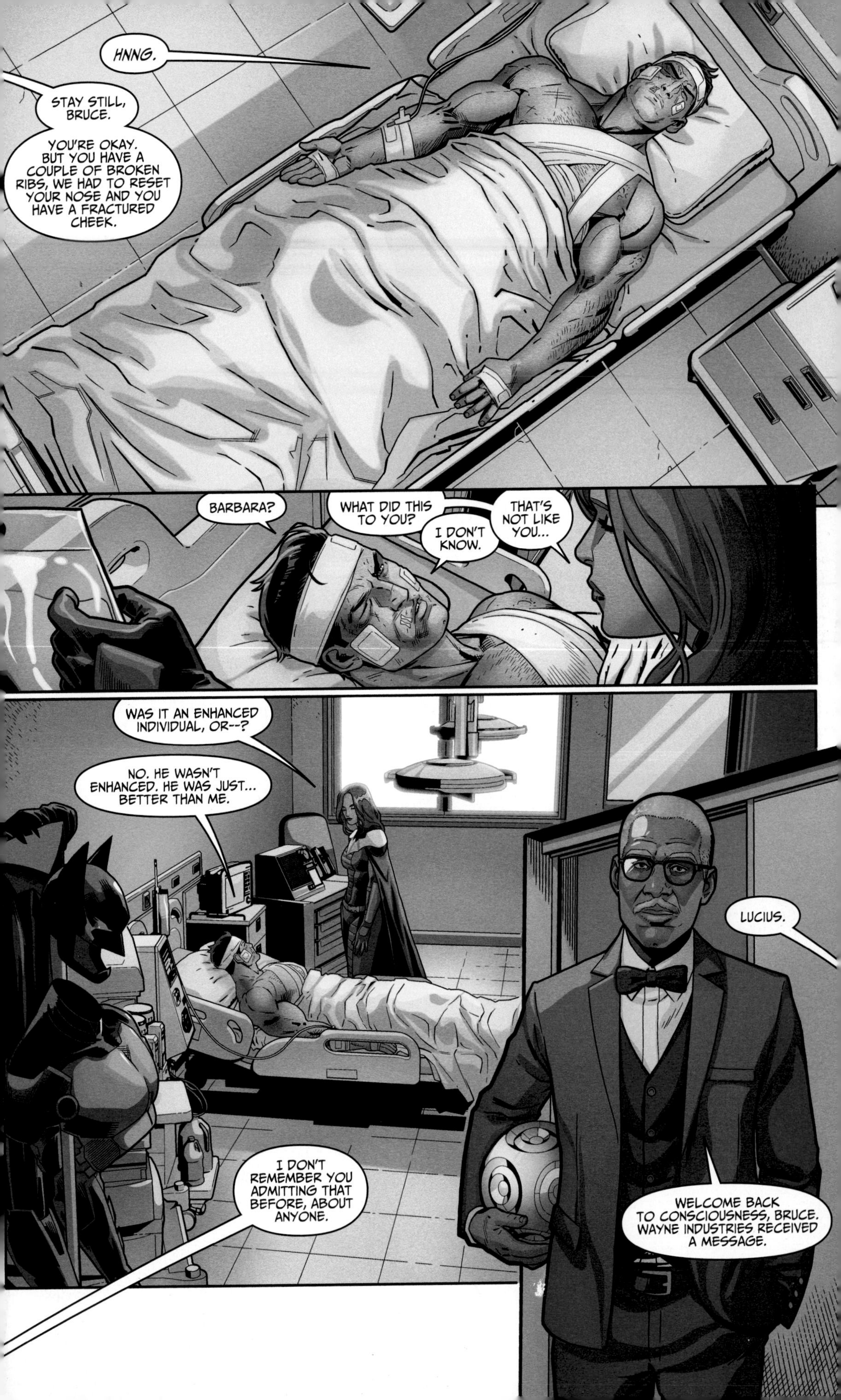

HNNG.
STAY STILL, BRUCE.
YOU'RE OKAY. BUT YOU HAVE A COUPLE OF BROKEN RIBS, WE HAD TO RESET YOUR NOSE AND YOU HAVE A FRACTURED CHEEK.
BARBARA?
WHAT DID THIS TO YOU?
I DON'T KNOW.
THAT'S NOT LIKE YOU...
WAS IT AN ENHANCED INDIVIDUAL, OR--?
NO. HE WASN'T ENHANCED. HE WAS JUST... BETTER THAN ME.
I DON'T REMEMBER YOU ADMITTING THAT BEFORE, ABOUT ANYONE.
LUCIUS.
WELCOME BACK TO CONSCIOUSNESS, BRUCE. WAYNE INDUSTRIES RECEIVED A MESSAGE.

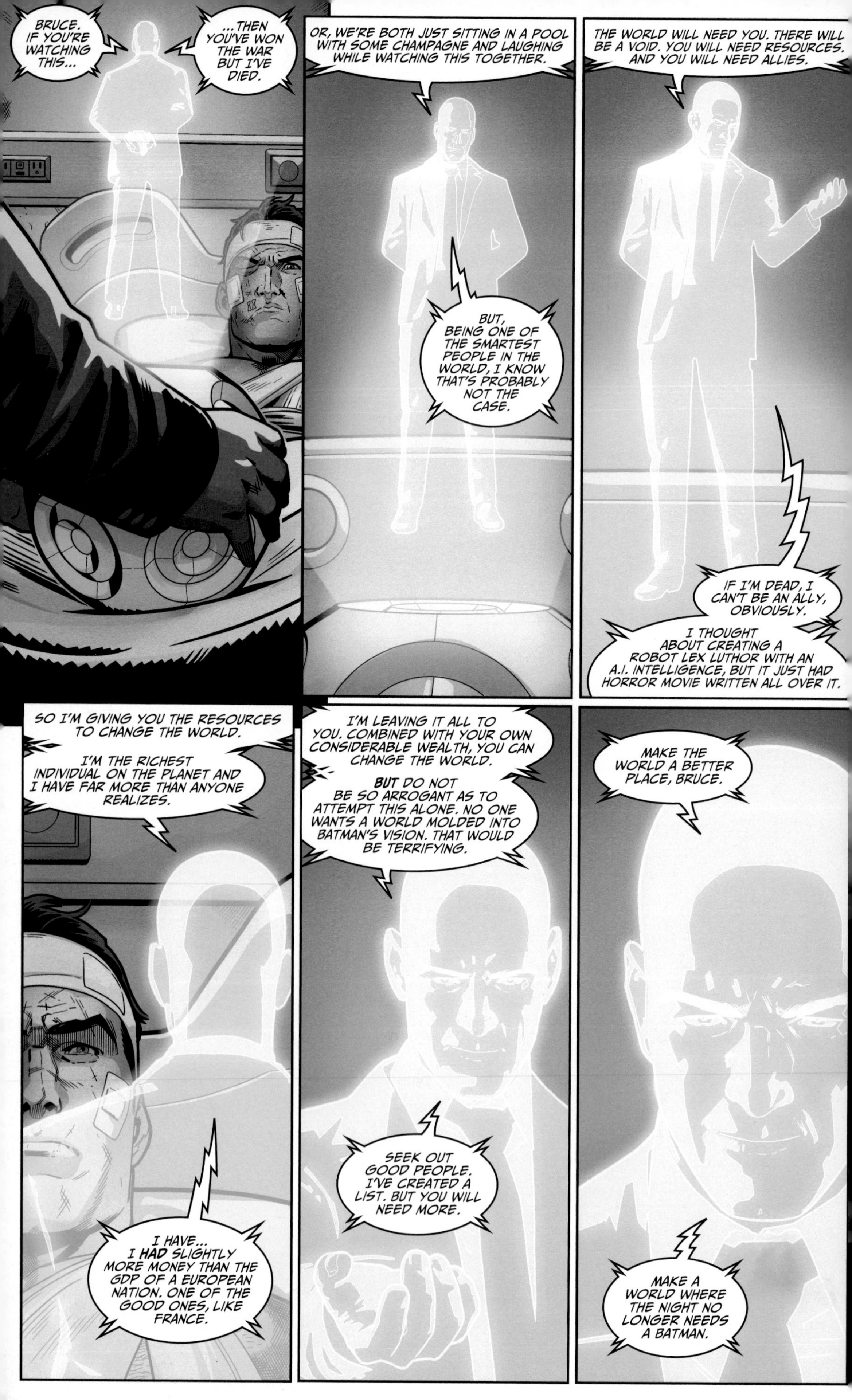
BRUCE. IF YOU'RE WATCHING THIS...
...THEN YOU'VE WON THE WAR BUT I'VE DIED.
OR, WE'RE BOTH JUST SITTING IN A POOL WITH SOME CHAMPAGNE AND LAUGHING WHILE WATCHING THIS TOGETHER.
BUT, BEING ONE OF THE SMARTEST PEOPLE IN THE WORLD, I KNOW THAT'S PROBABLY NOT THE CASE.
THE WORLD WILL NEED YOU. THERE WILL BE A VOID. YOU WILL NEED RESOURCES. AND YOU WILL NEED ALLIES.
IF I'M DEAD, I CAN'T BE AN ALLY, OBVIOUSLY.
I THOUGHT ABOUT CREATING A ROBOT LEX LUTHOR WITH AN A.I. INTELLIGENCE, BUT IT JUST HAD HORROR MOVIE WRITTEN ALL OVER IT.
SO I'M GIVING YOU THE RESOURCES TO CHANGE THE WORLD.
I'M THE RICHEST INDIVIDUAL ON THE PLANET AND I HAVE FAR MORE THAN ANYONE REALIZES.
I HAVE... I **HAD** SLIGHTLY MORE MONEY THAN THE GDP OF A EUROPEAN NATION. ONE OF THE GOOD ONES, LIKE FRANCE.
I'M LEAVING IT ALL TO YOU. COMBINED WITH YOUR OWN CONSIDERABLE WEALTH, YOU CAN CHANGE THE WORLD.
BUT DO NOT BE SO ARROGANT AS TO ATTEMPT THIS ALONE. NO ONE WANTS A WORLD MOLDED INTO BATMAN'S VISION. THAT WOULD BE TERRIFYING.
SEEK OUT GOOD PEOPLE. I'VE CREATED A LIST. BUT YOU WILL NEED MORE.
MAKE THE WORLD A BETTER PLACE, BRUCE.
MAKE A WORLD WHERE THE NIGHT NO LONGER NEEDS A BATMAN.

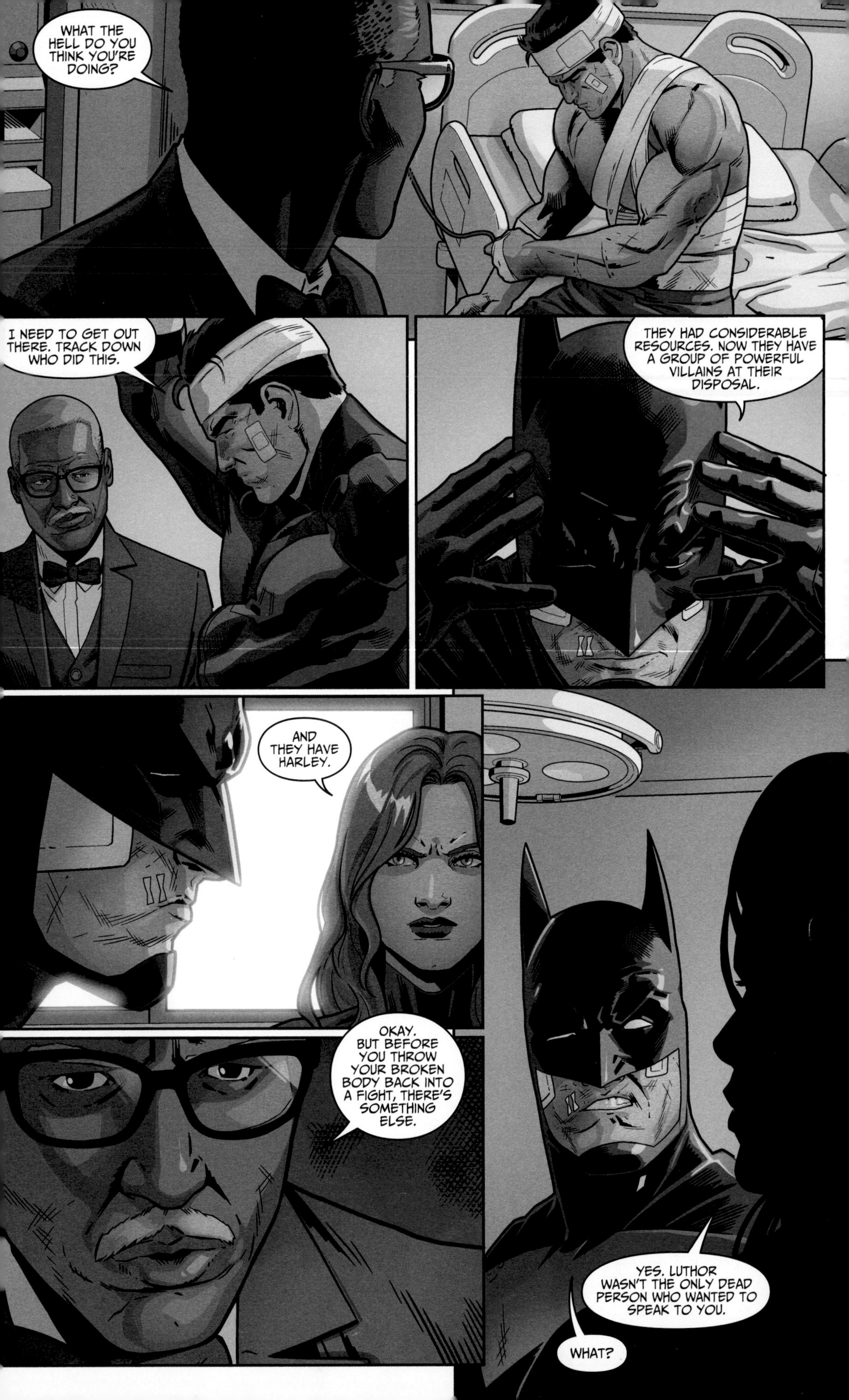
WHAT THE HELL DO YOU THINK YOU'RE DOING?
I NEED TO GET OUT THERE. TRACK DOWN WHO DID THIS.
THEY HAD CONSIDERABLE RESOURCES. NOW THEY HAVE A GROUP OF POWERFUL VILLAINS AT THEIR DISPOSAL.
AND THEY HAVE HARLEY.
OKAY. BUT BEFORE YOU THROW YOUR BROKEN BODY BACK INTO A FIGHT, THERE'S SOMETHING ELSE.
YES. LUTHOR WASN'T THE ONLY DEAD PERSON WHO WANTED TO SPEAK TO YOU.
WHAT?

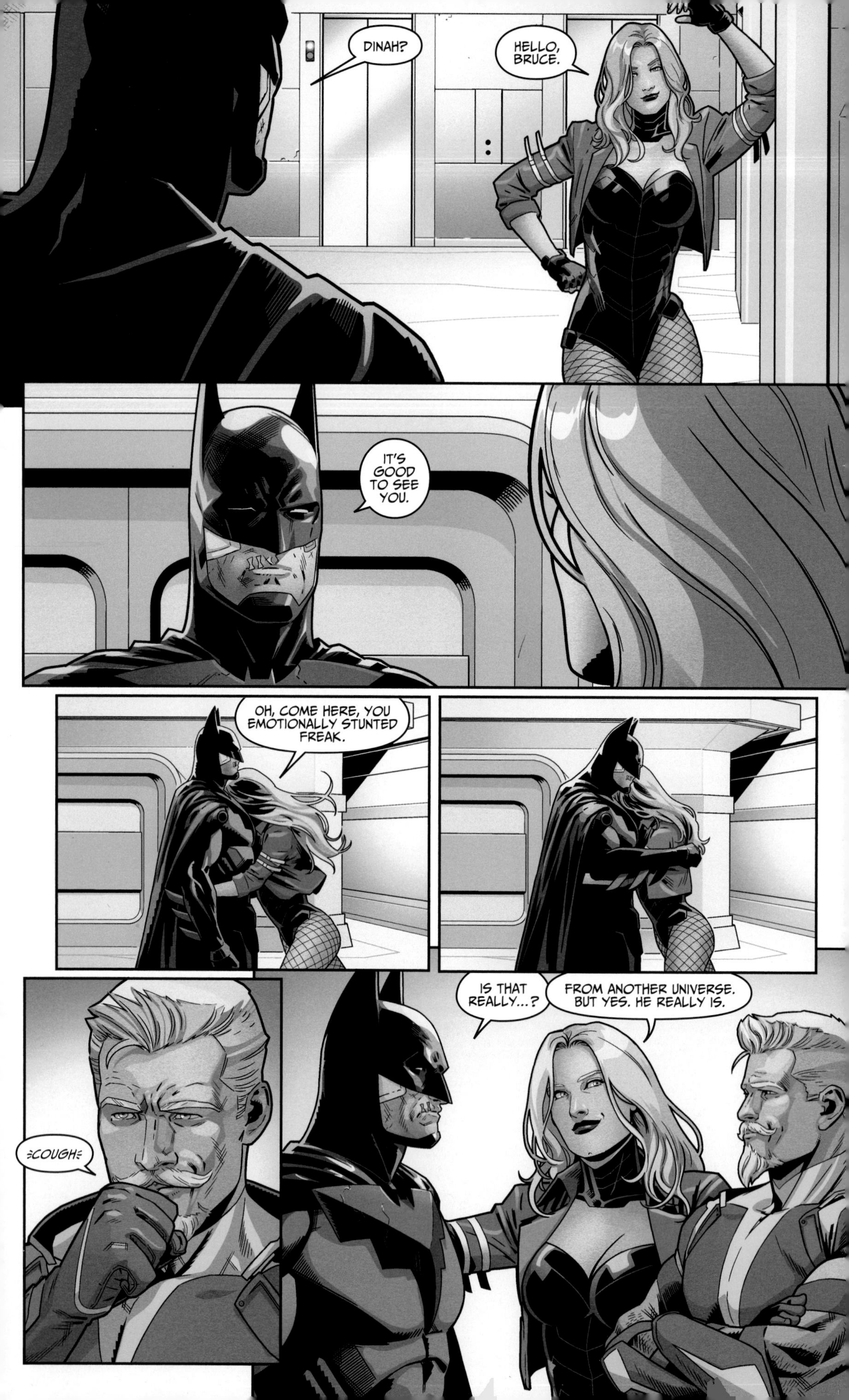
DINAH?
HELLO, BRUCE.
IT'S GOOD TO SEE YOU.
OH, COME HERE, YOU EMOTIONALLY STUNTED FREAK.
≡COUGH≡
IS THAT REALLY...?
FROM ANOTHER UNIVERSE. BUT YES. HE REALLY IS.

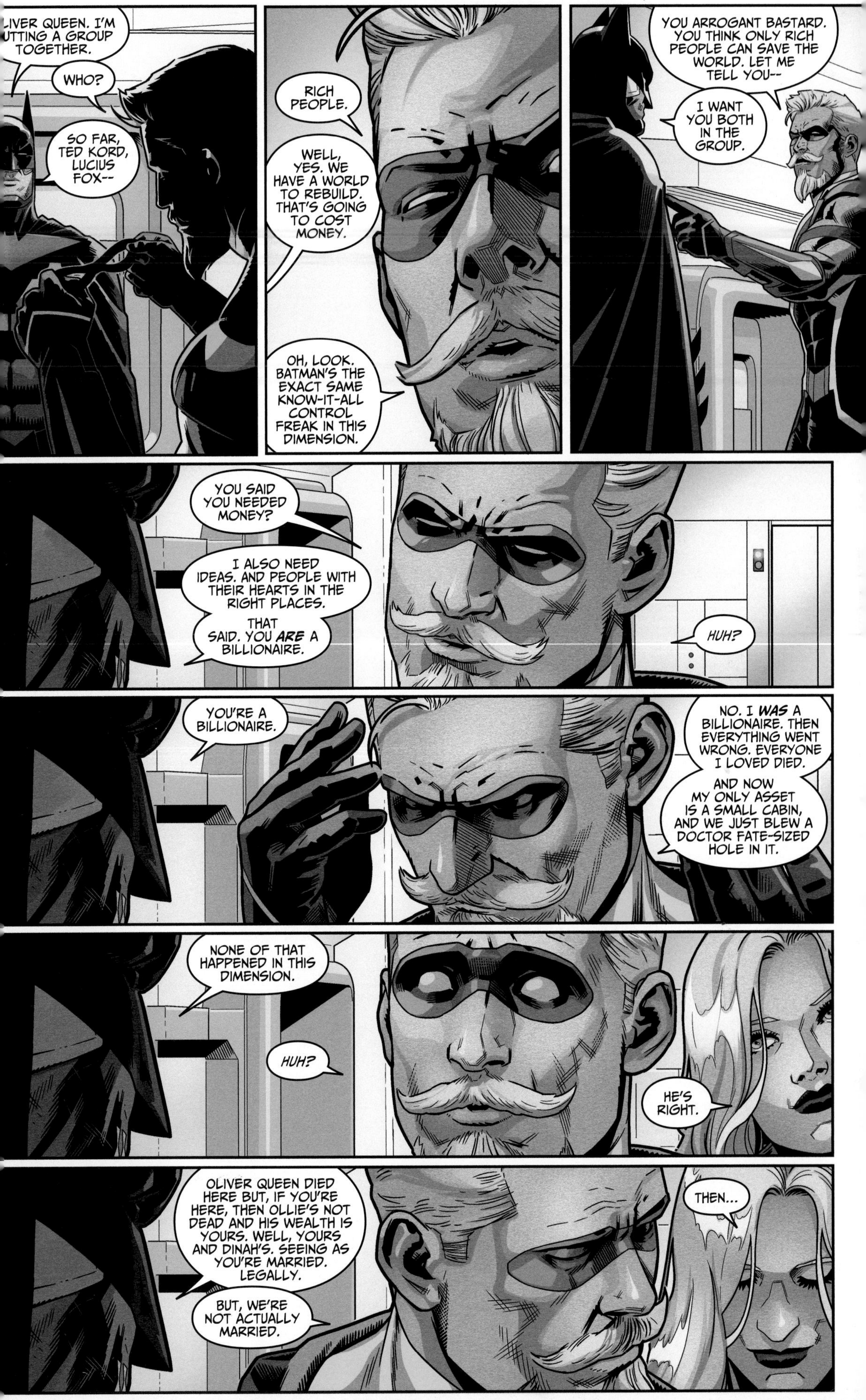

LIVER QUEEN. I'M
UTTING A GROUP TOGETHER.
WHO?
SO FAR, TED KORD, LUCIUS FOX--
RICH PEOPLE.
WELL, YES. WE HAVE A WORLD TO REBUILD. THAT'S GOING TO COST MONEY.
OH, LOOK. BATMAN'S THE EXACT SAME KNOW-IT-ALL CONTROL FREAK IN THIS DIMENSION.
YOU ARROGANT BASTARD. YOU THINK ONLY RICH PEOPLE CAN SAVE THE WORLD. LET ME TELL YOU--
I WANT YOU BOTH IN THE GROUP.
YOU SAID YOU NEEDED MONEY?
I ALSO NEED IDEAS. AND PEOPLE WITH THEIR HEARTS IN THE RIGHT PLACES.
THAT SAID. YOU ARE A BILLIONAIRE.
HUH?
YOU'RE A BILLIONAIRE.
NO. I WAS A BILLIONAIRE. THEN EVERYTHING WENT WRONG. EVERYONE I LOVED DIED.
AND NOW MY ONLY ASSET IS A SMALL CABIN, AND WE JUST BLEW A DOCTOR FATE-SIZED HOLE IN IT.
NONE OF THAT HAPPENED IN THIS DIMENSION.
HUH?
HE'S RIGHT.
OLIVER QUEEN DIED HERE BUT, IF YOU'RE HERE, THEN OLLIE'S NOT DEAD AND HIS WEALTH IS YOURS. WELL, YOURS AND DINAH'S. SEEING AS YOU'RE MARRIED. LEGALLY.
THEN...
BUT, WE'RE NOT ACTUALLY MARRIED.

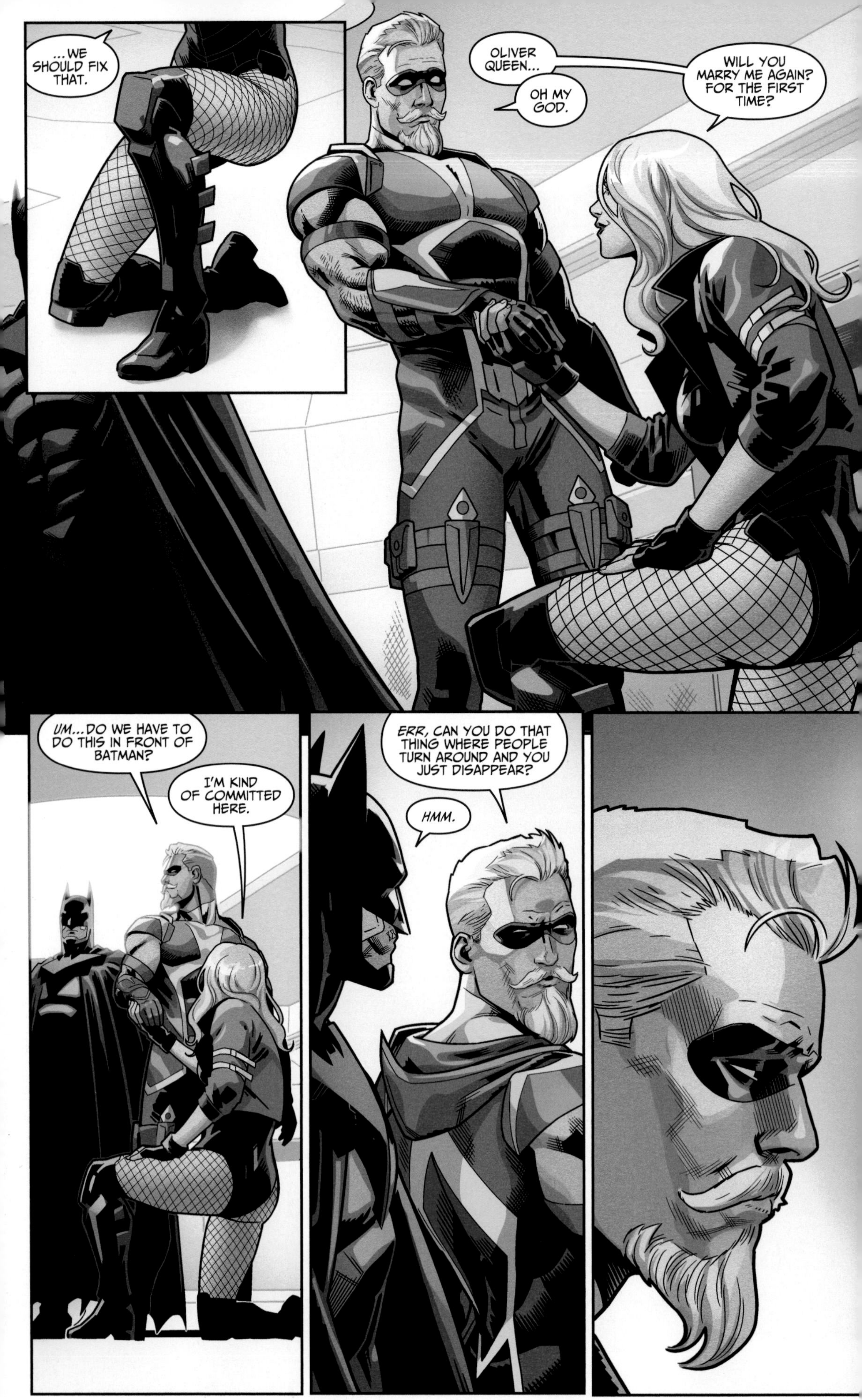
...WE SHOULD FIX THAT.
OLIVER QUEEN...
OH MY GOD.
WILL YOU MARRY ME AGAIN? FOR THE FIRST TIME?
UM...DO WE HAVE TO DO THIS IN FRONT OF BATMAN?
I'M KIND OF COMMITTED HERE.
ERR, CAN YOU DO THAT THING WHERE PEOPLE TURN AROUND AND YOU JUST DISAPPEAR?
HMM.

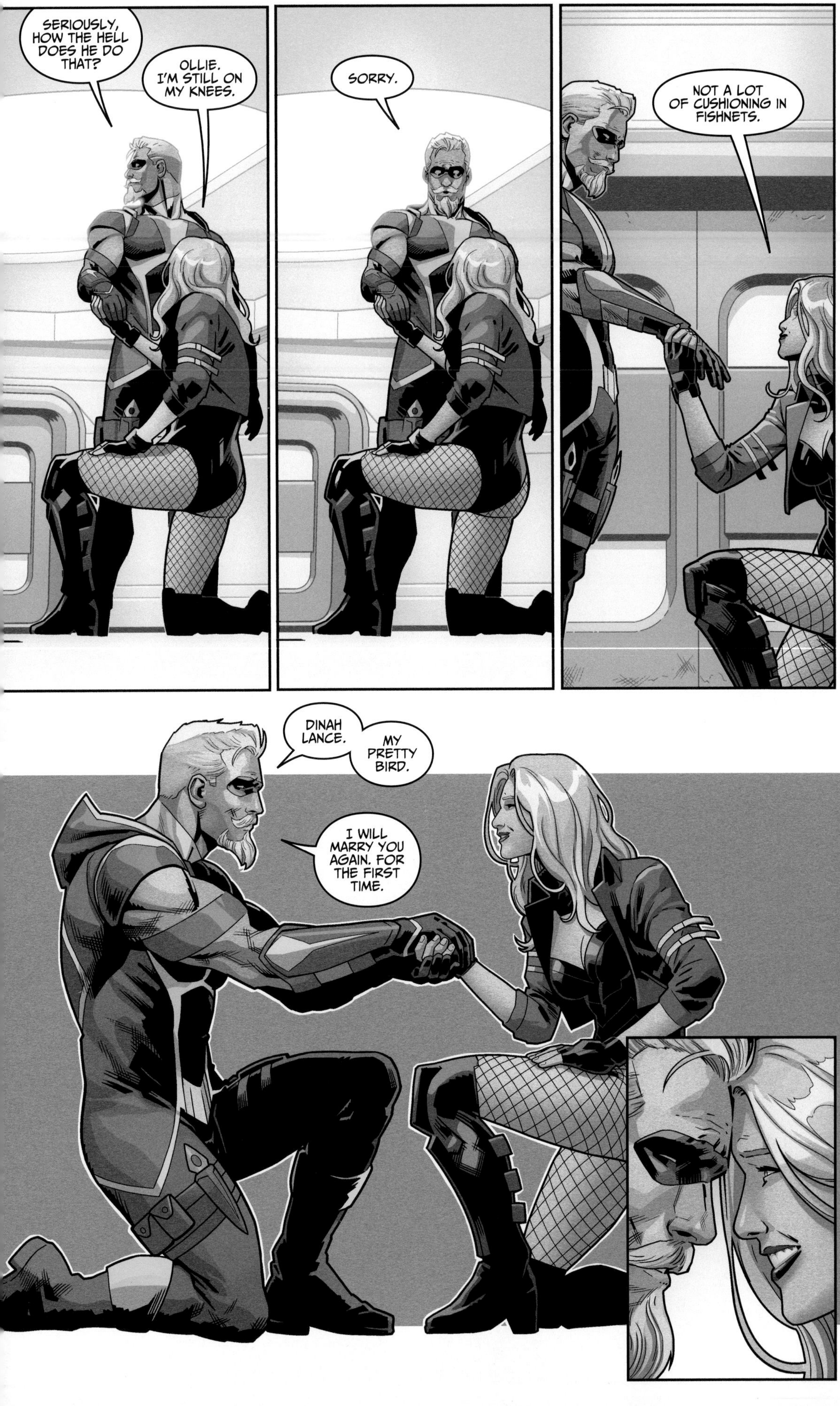
SERIOUSLY, HOW THE HELL DOES HE DO THAT?
OLLIE. I'M STILL ON MY KNEES.
SORRY.
NOT A LOT OF CUSHIONING IN FISHNETS.
DINAH LANCE.
MY PRETTY BIRD.
I WILL MARRY YOU AGAIN. FOR THE FIRST TIME.

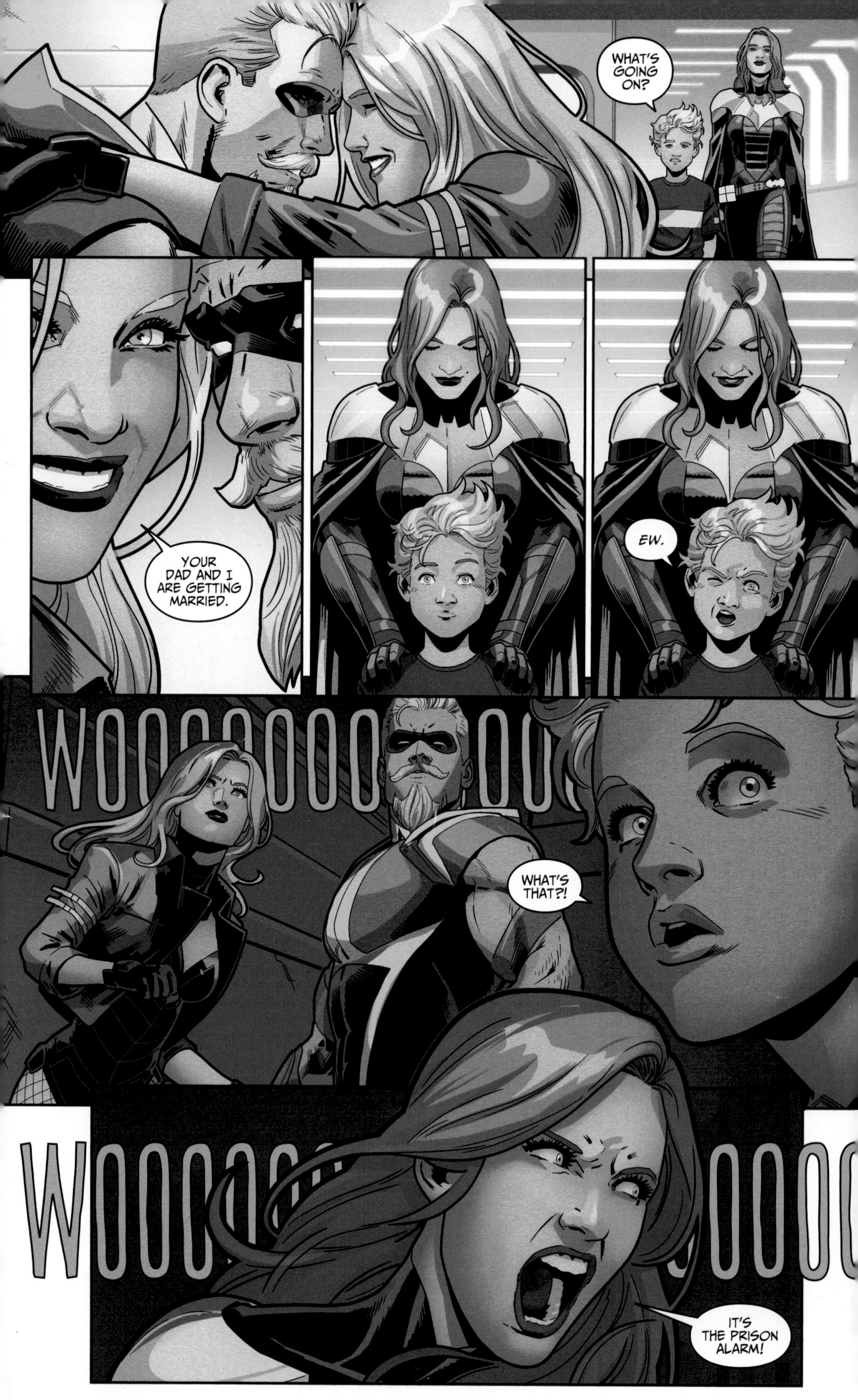
WHAT'S GOING ON?
YOUR DAD AND I ARE GETTING MARRIED.
EW.
WHAT'S THAT?!
IT'S THE PRISON ALARM!

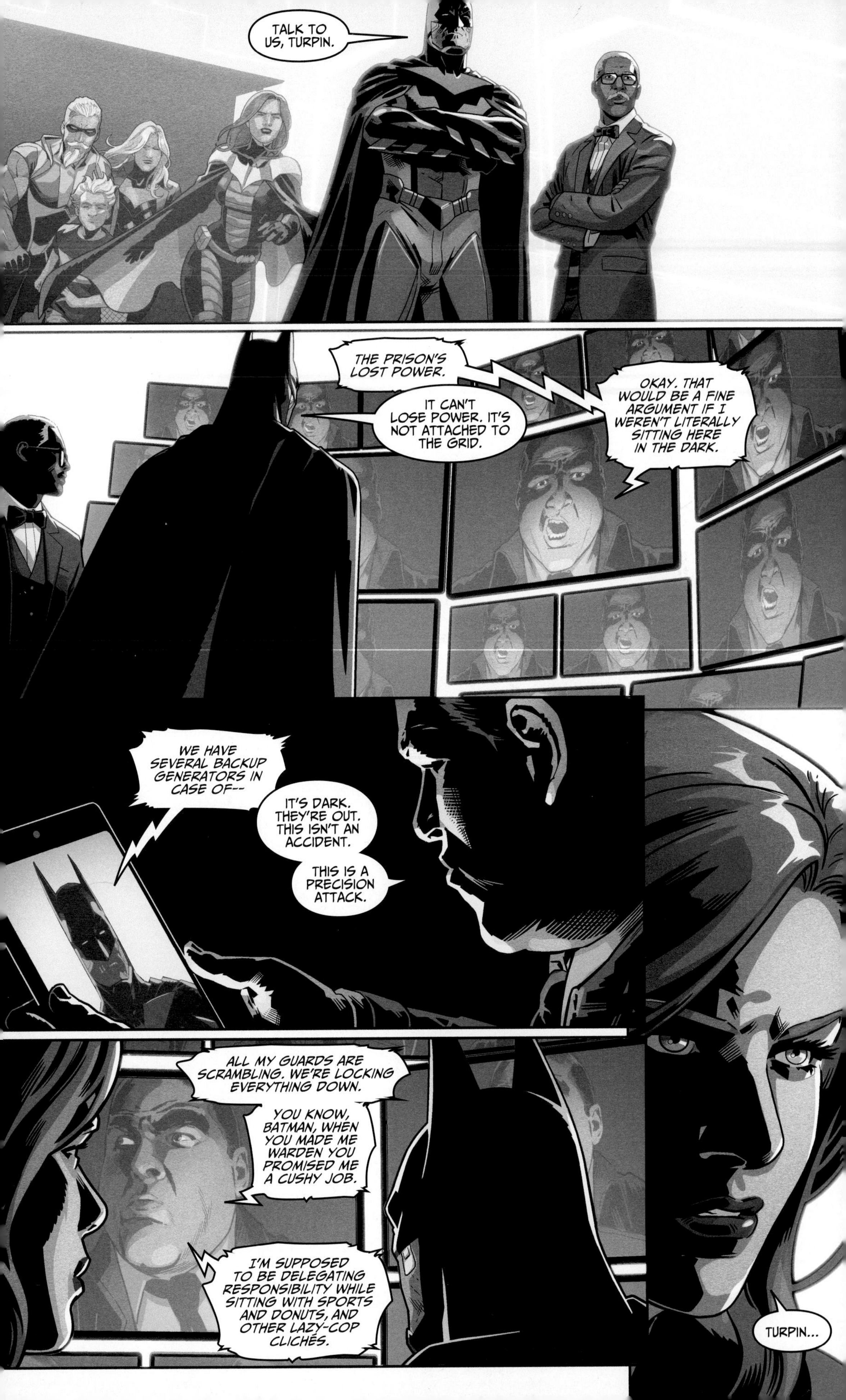
TALK TO US, TURPIN.
THE PRISON'S LOST POWER.
IT CAN'T LOSE POWER. IT'S NOT ATTACHED TO THE GRID.
OKAY. THAT WOULD BE A FINE ARGUMENT IF I WEREN'T LITERALLY SITTING HERE IN THE DARK.
WE HAVE SEVERAL BACKUP GENERATORS IN CASE OF--
IT'S DARK. THEY'RE OUT. THIS ISN'T AN ACCIDENT.
THIS IS A PRECISION ATTACK.
ALL MY GUARDS ARE SCRAMBLING. WE'RE LOCKING EVERYTHING DOWN.
YOU KNOW, BATMAN, WHEN YOU MADE ME WARDEN YOU PROMISED ME A CUSHY JOB.
I'M SUPPOSED TO BE DELEGATING RESPONSIBILITY WHILE SITTING WITH SPORTS AND DONUTS, AND OTHER LAZY-COP CLICHÉS.
TURPIN...

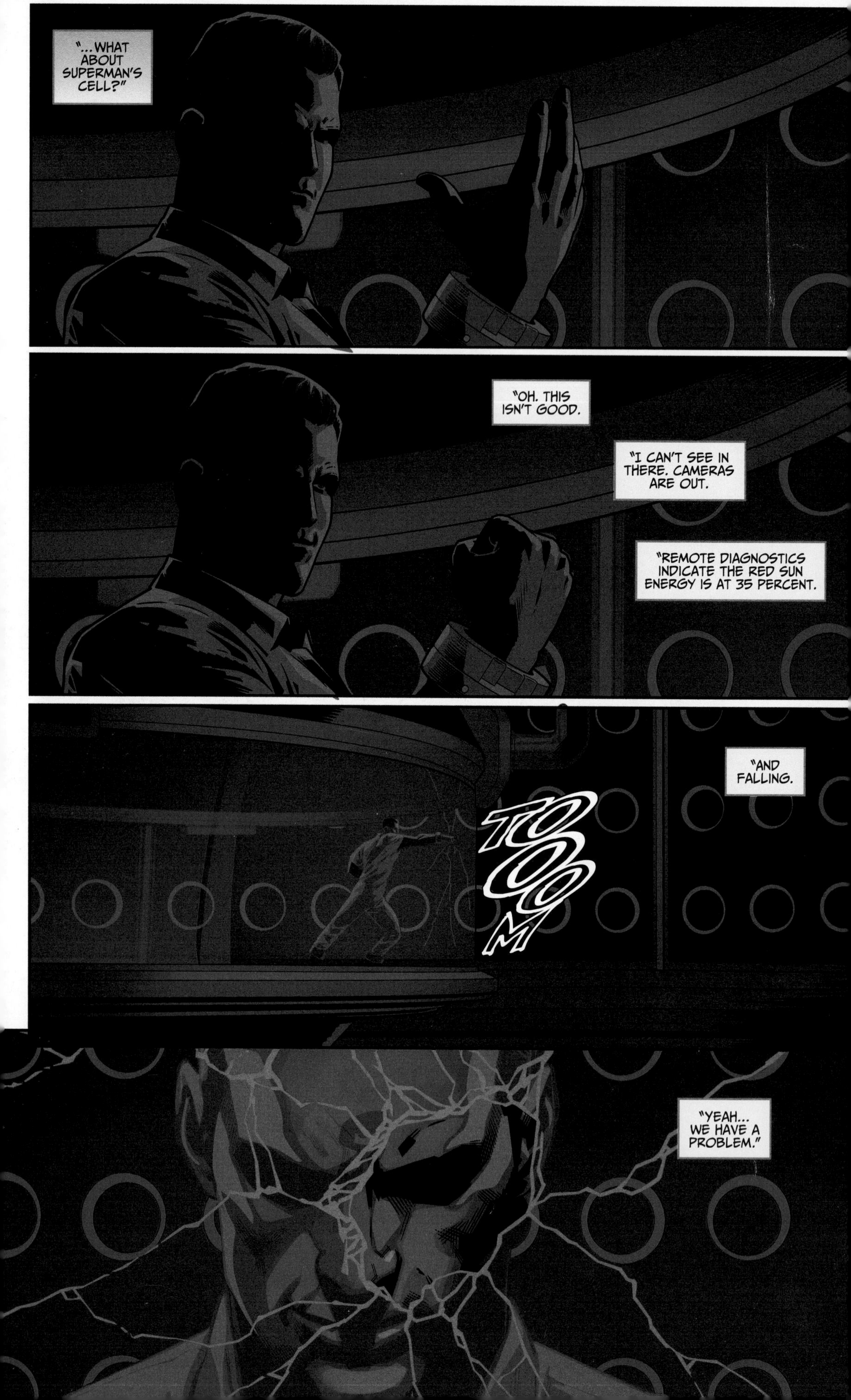
"...WHAT ABOUT SUPERMAN'S CELL?"
"OH. THIS ISN'T GOOD.
"I CAN'T SEE IN THERE. CAMERAS ARE OUT.
"REMOTE DIAGNOSTICS INDICATE THE RED SUN ENERGY IS AT 35 PERCENT.
"AND FALLING.
TOOOOM
"YEAH... WE HAVE A PROBLEM."

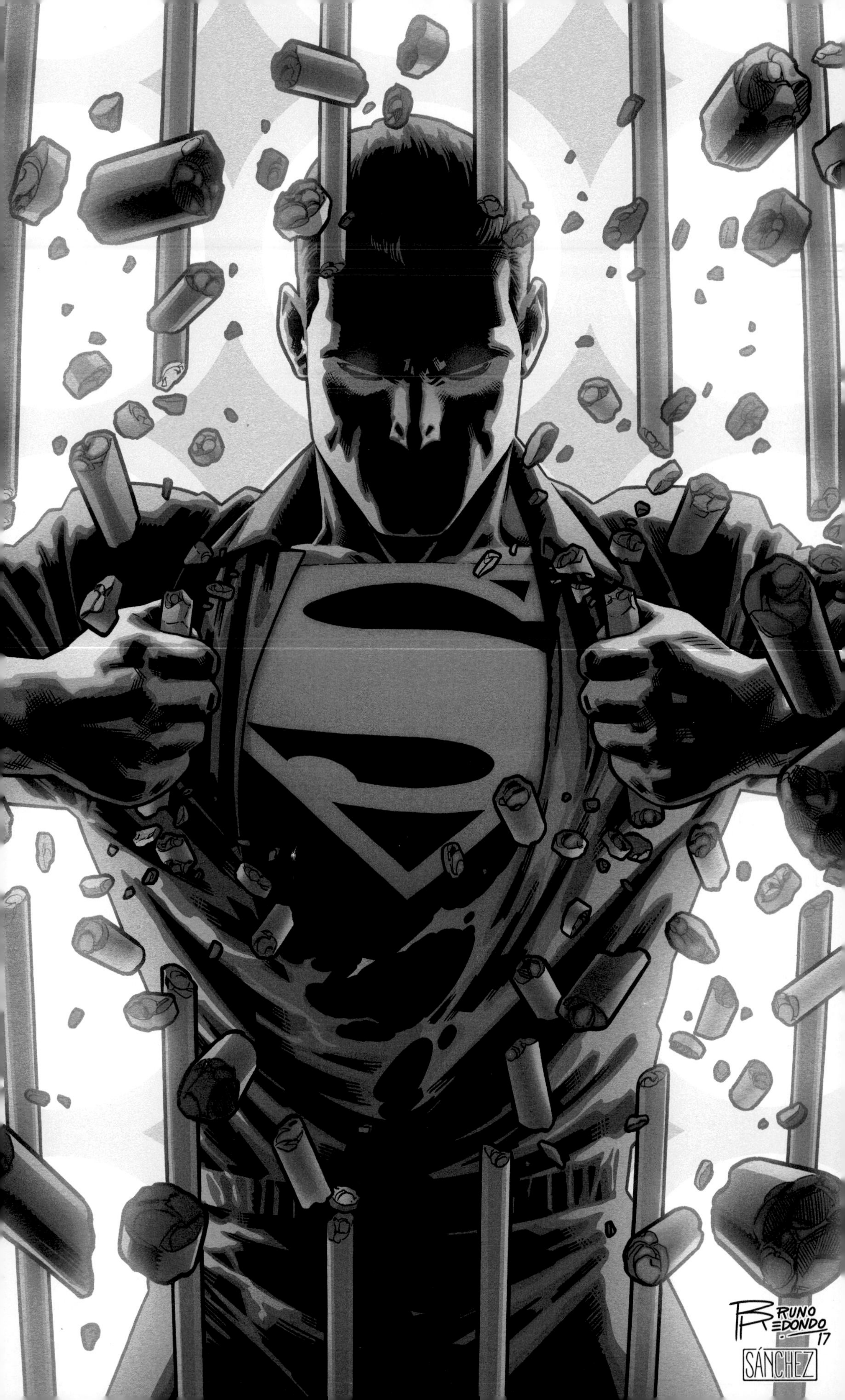
BRUNO REDONDO 17
SÁNCHEZ

"Contingency"

Daniel Sampere Penciller **Juan Albarran** Inker

Rex Lokus Colorist Cover art by **Bruno Redondo** and **Alejandro Sanchez**

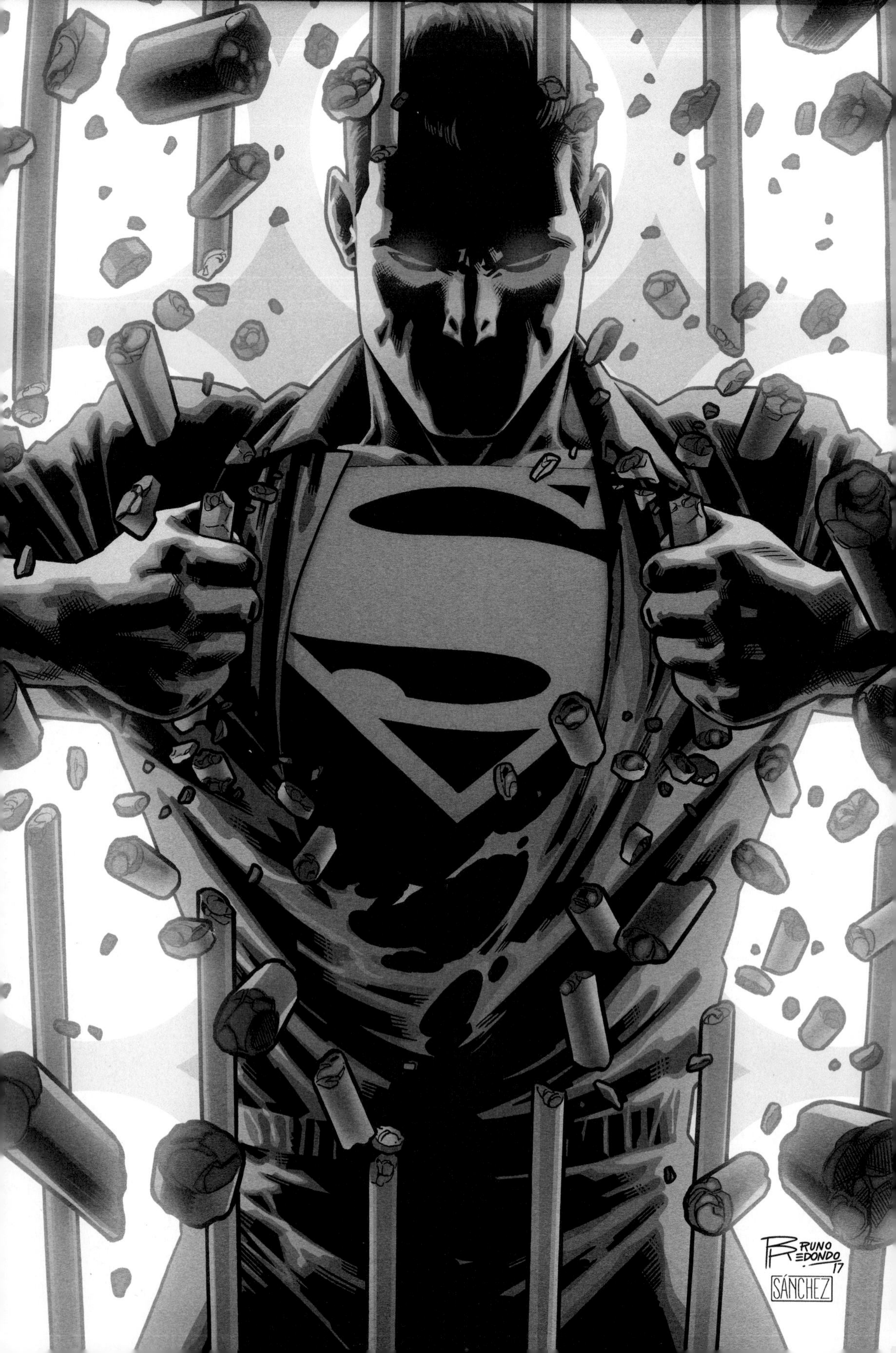
BRUNO REDONDO 17
SÁNCHEZ

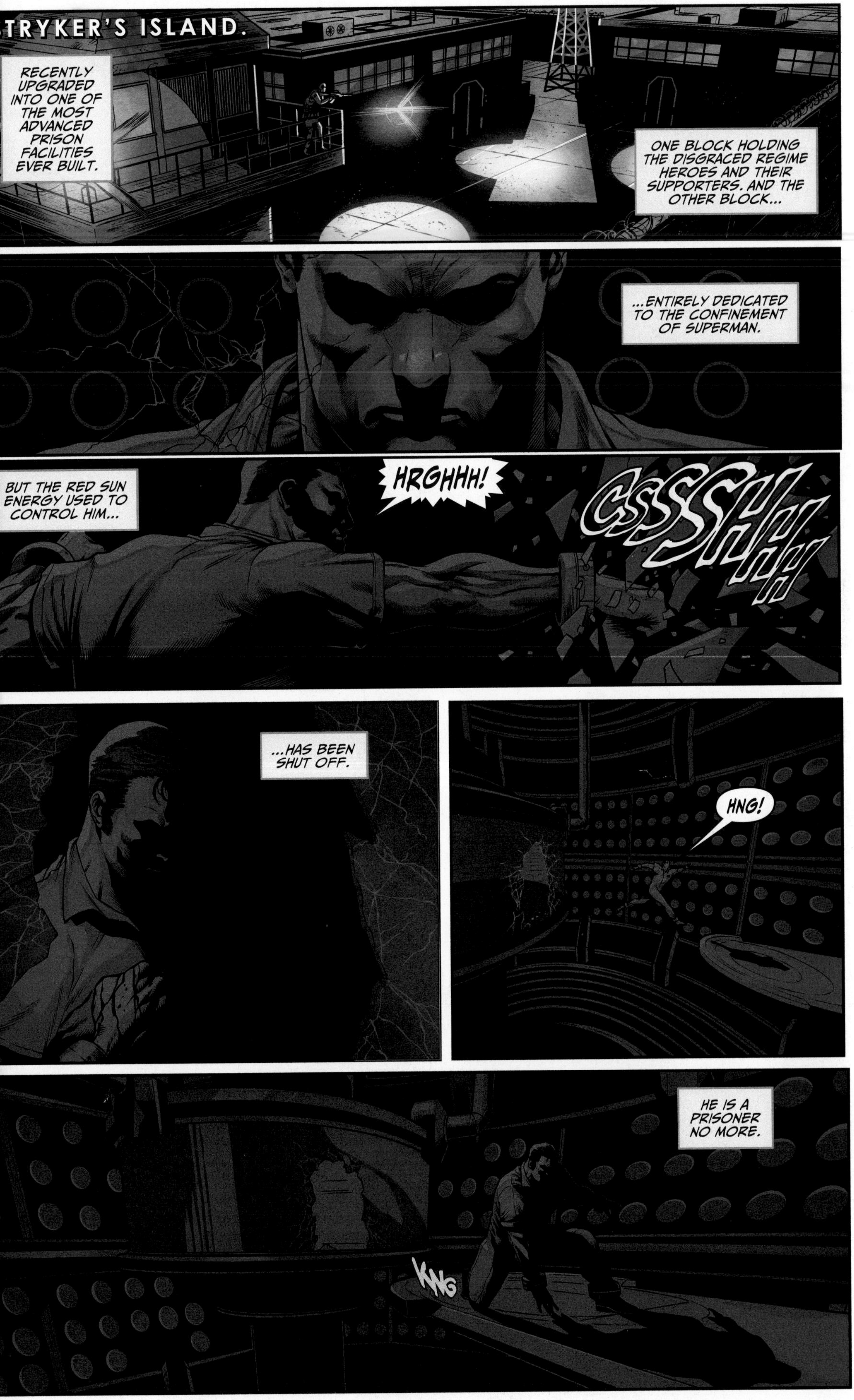
TRYKER'S ISLAND.
RECENTLY UPGRADED INTO ONE OF THE MOST ADVANCED PRISON FACILITIES EVER BUILT.
ONE BLOCK HOLDING THE DISGRACED REGIME HEROES AND THEIR SUPPORTERS. AND THE OTHER BLOCK...
...ENTIRELY DEDICATED TO THE CONFINEMENT OF SUPERMAN.
BUT THE RED SUN ENERGY USED TO CONTROL HIM...
HRGHHH!
CSSSSHHHH
...HAS BEEN SHUT OFF.
HNG!
HE IS A PRISONER NO MORE.
KNG

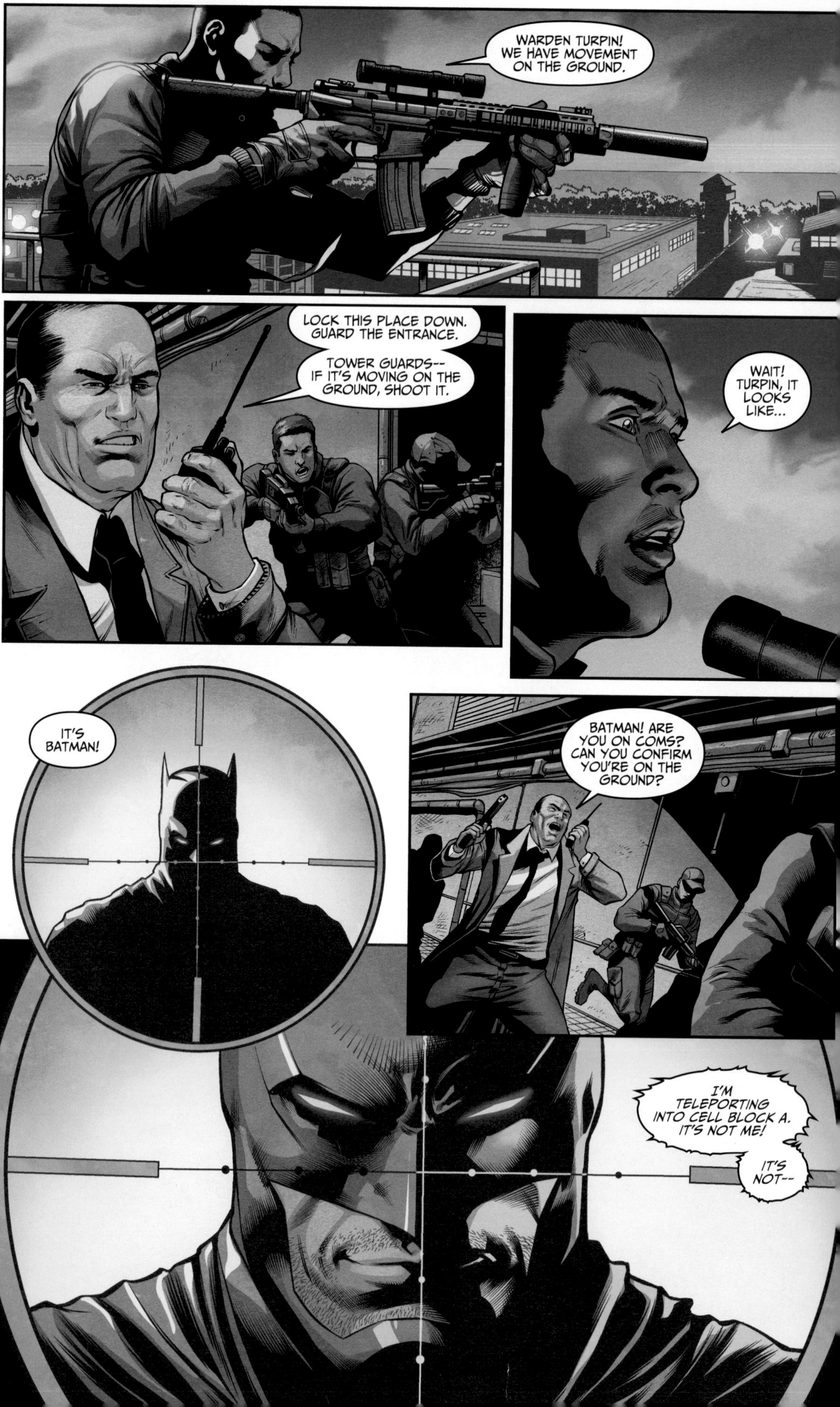
WARDEN TURPIN! WE HAVE MOVEMENT ON THE GROUND.
LOCK THIS PLACE DOWN. GUARD THE ENTRANCE.
TOWER GUARDS-- IF IT'S MOVING ON THE GROUND, SHOOT IT.
WAIT! TURPIN, IT LOOKS LIKE...
IT'S BATMAN!
BATMAN! ARE YOU ON COMS? CAN YOU CONFIRM YOU'RE ON THE GROUND?
I'M TELEPORTING INTO CELL BLOCK A. IT'S NOT ME!
IT'S NOT--

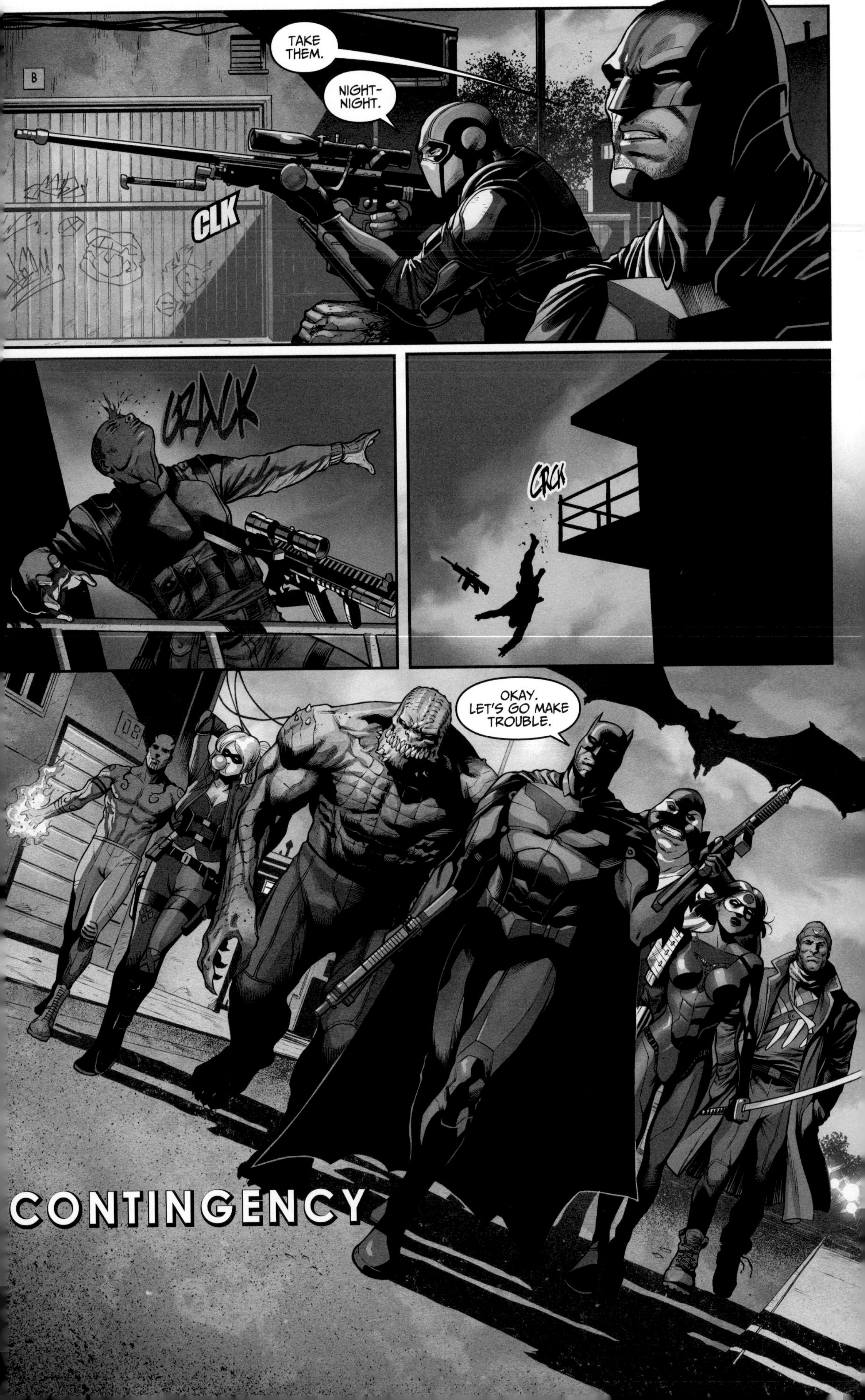
B
TAKE THEM.
NIGHT-NIGHT.
CLK
CRACK
CRCK
80
OKAY. LET'S GO MAKE TROUBLE.
CONTINGENCY

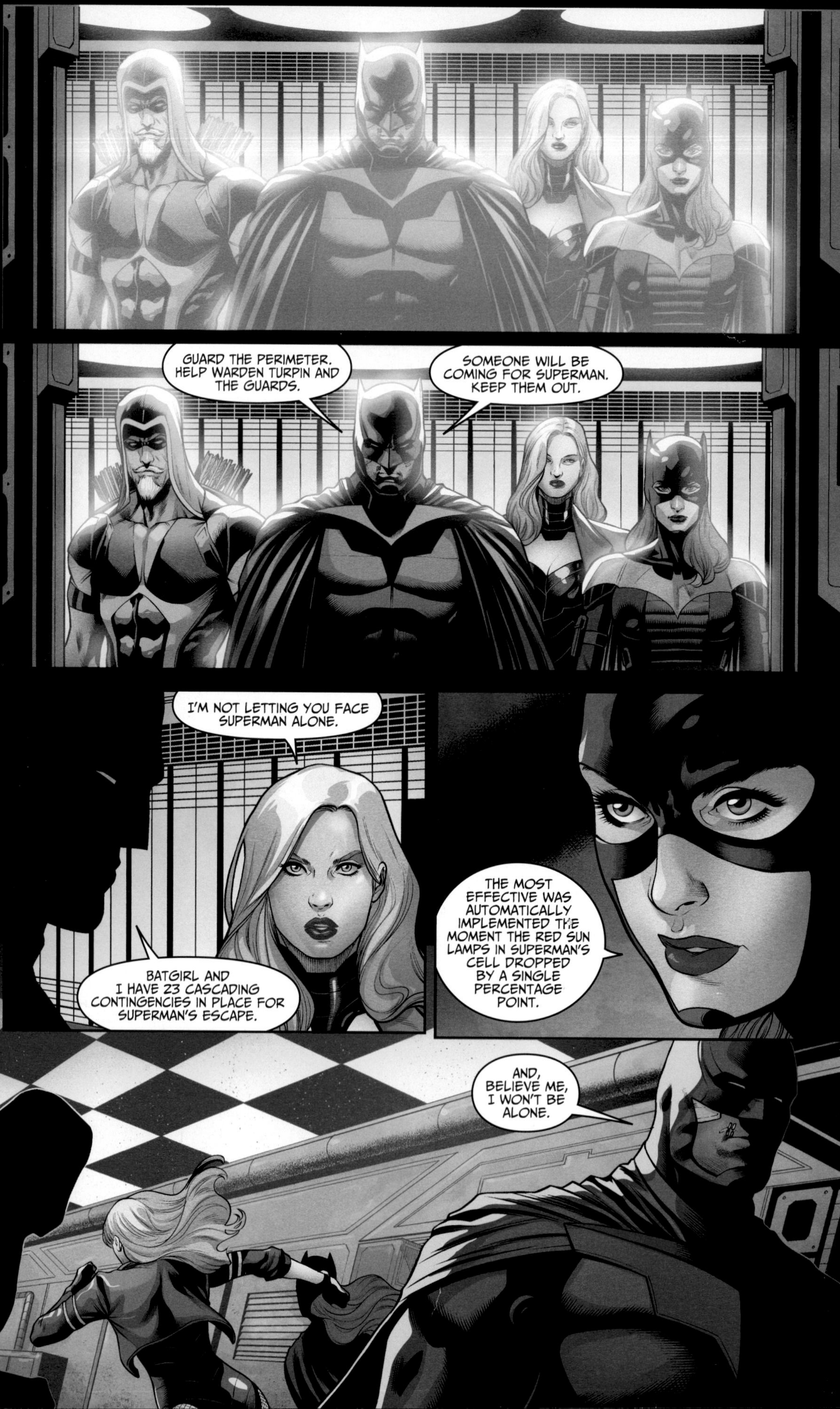
GUARD THE PERIMETER. HELP WARDEN TURPIN AND THE GUARDS.
SOMEONE WILL BE COMING FOR SUPERMAN. KEEP THEM OUT.
I'M NOT LETTING YOU FACE SUPERMAN ALONE.
BATGIRL AND I HAVE 23 CASCADING CONTINGENCIES IN PLACE FOR SUPERMAN'S ESCAPE.
THE MOST EFFECTIVE WAS AUTOMATICALLY IMPLEMENTED THE MOMENT THE RED SUN LAMPS IN SUPERMAN'S CELL DROPPED BY A SINGLE PERCENTAGE POINT.
AND, BELIEVE ME, I WON'T BE ALONE.

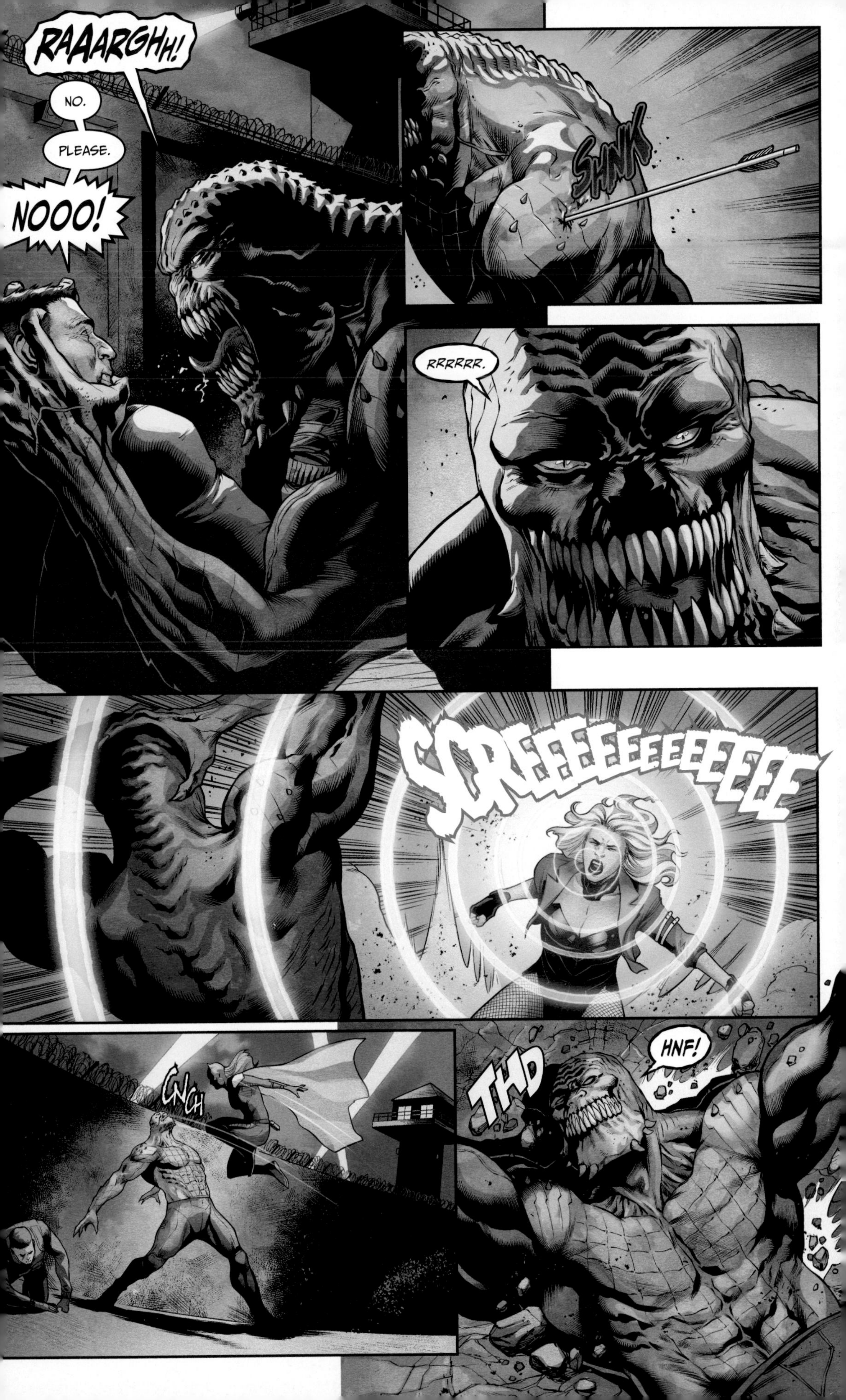
RAAARGHH!
NO.
PLEASE.
NOOO!
SHNK
RRRRRR.
SCREEEEEEEEEEEEE
CNCH
THD
HNF!

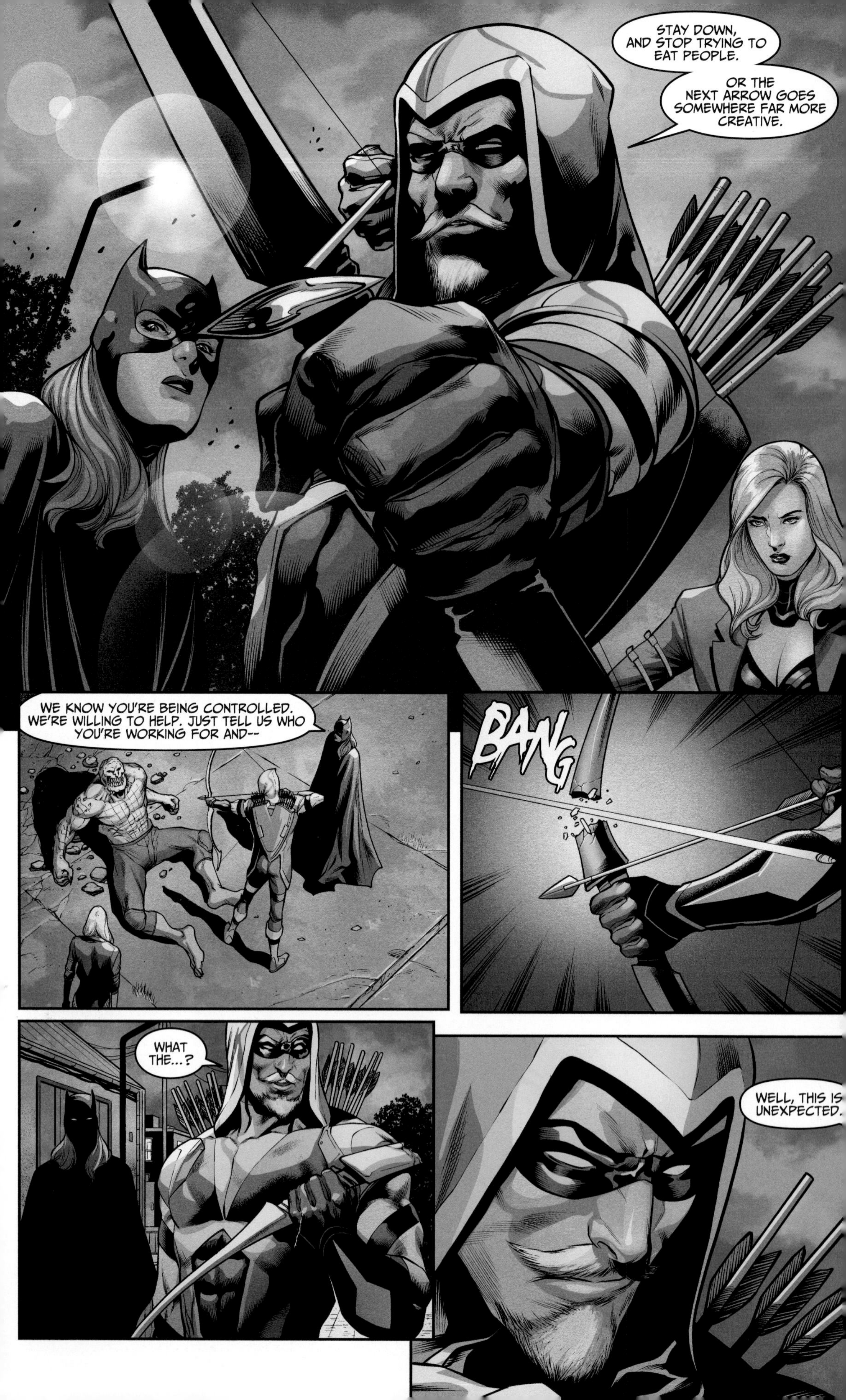
STAY DOWN, AND STOP TRYING TO EAT PEOPLE.
OR THE NEXT ARROW GOES SOMEWHERE FAR MORE CREATIVE.
WE KNOW YOU'RE BEING CONTROLLED. WE'RE WILLING TO HELP. JUST TELL US WHO YOU'RE WORKING FOR AND--
BANG
WHAT THE...?
WELL, THIS IS UNEXPECTED.

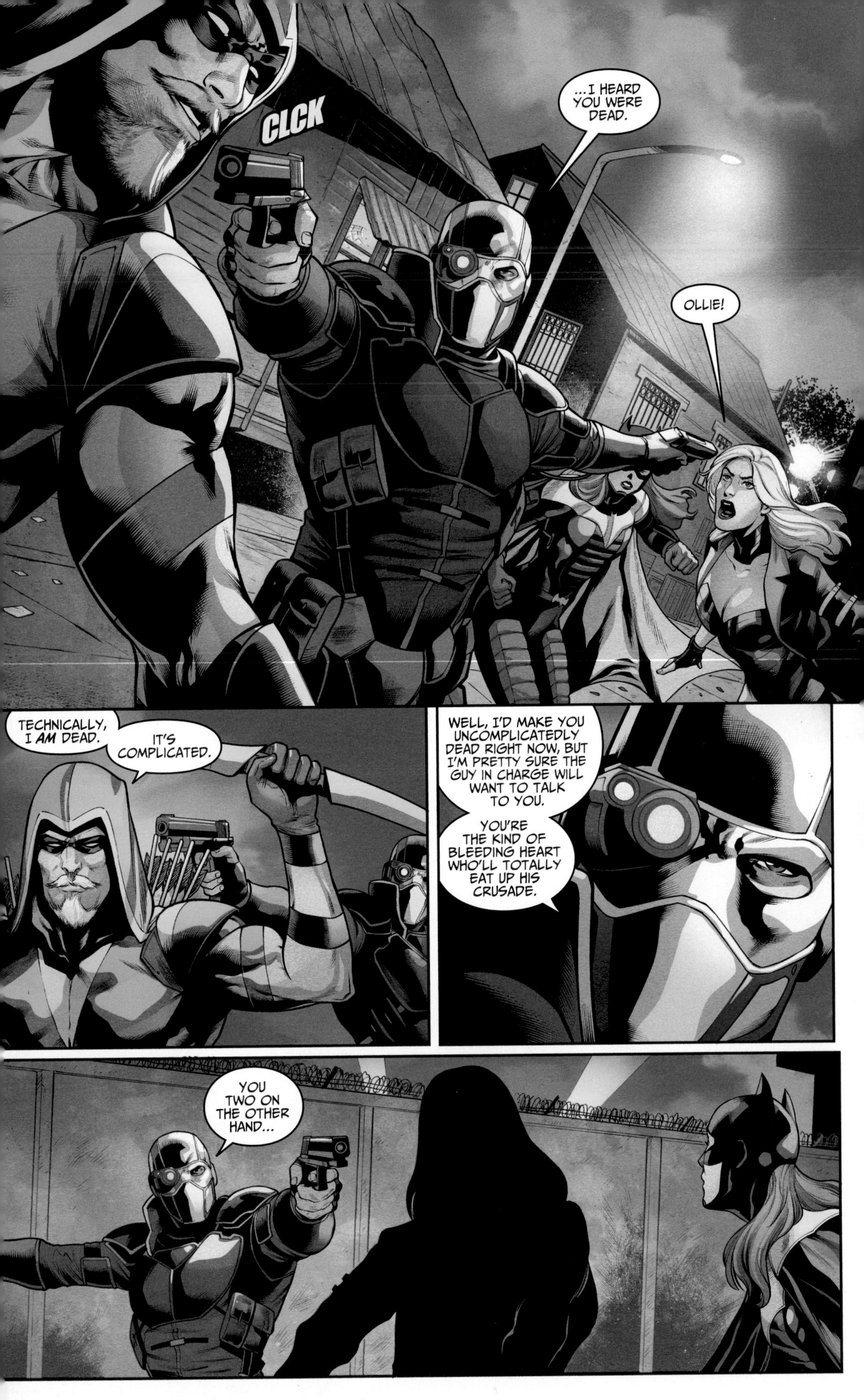
CLCK
...I HEARD YOU WERE DEAD.
OLLIE!
TECHNICALLY, I AM DEAD.
IT'S COMPLICATED.
WELL, I'D MAKE YOU UNCOMPLICATEDLY DEAD RIGHT NOW, BUT I'M PRETTY SURE THE GUY IN CHARGE WILL WANT TO TALK TO YOU.
YOU'RE THE KIND OF BLEEDING HEART WHO'LL TOTALLY EAT UP HIS CRUSADE.
YOU TWO ON THE OTHER HAND...

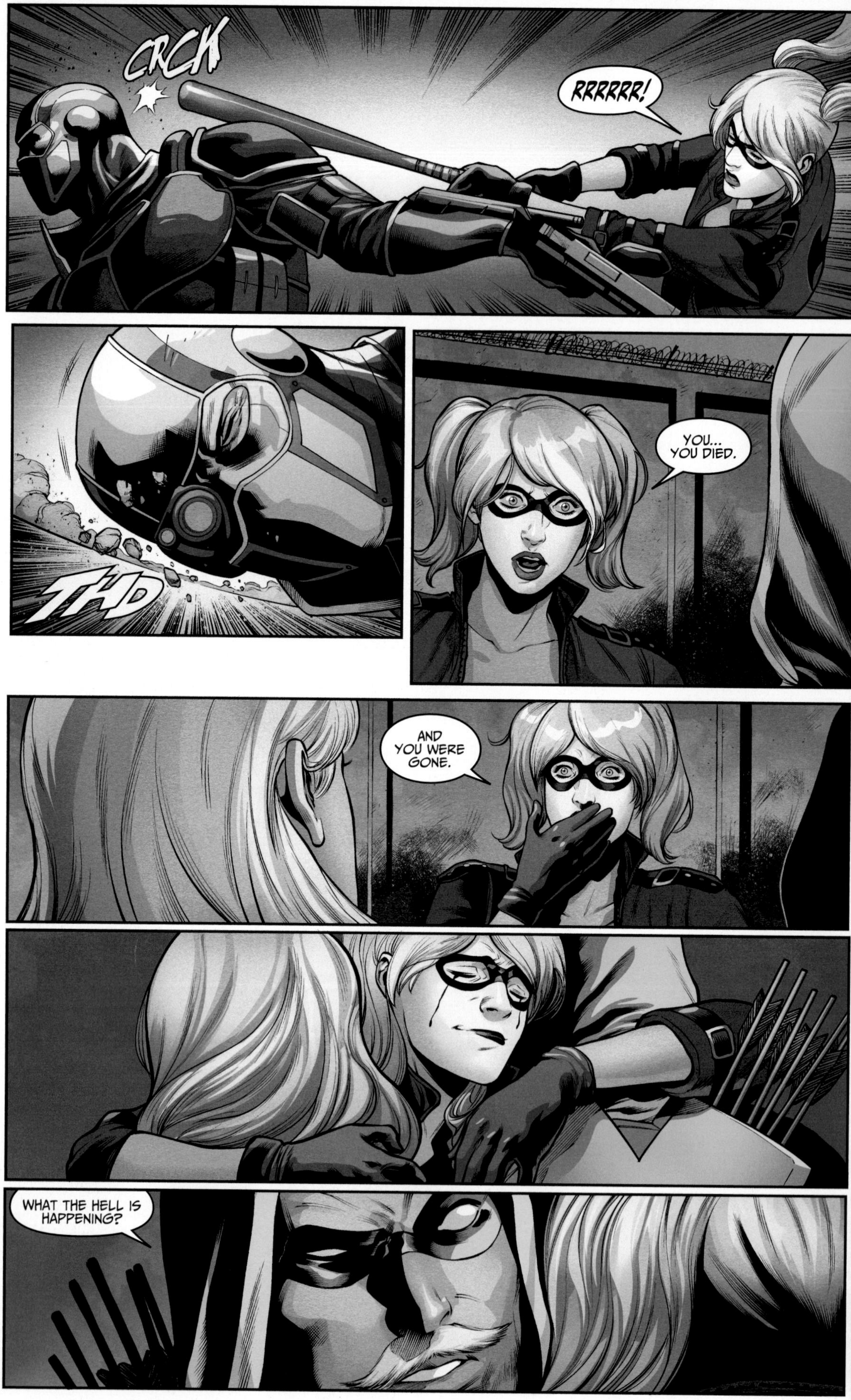
CRCK
RRRRRR!
THD
YOU... YOU DIED.
AND YOU WERE GONE.
WHAT THE HELL IS HAPPENING?

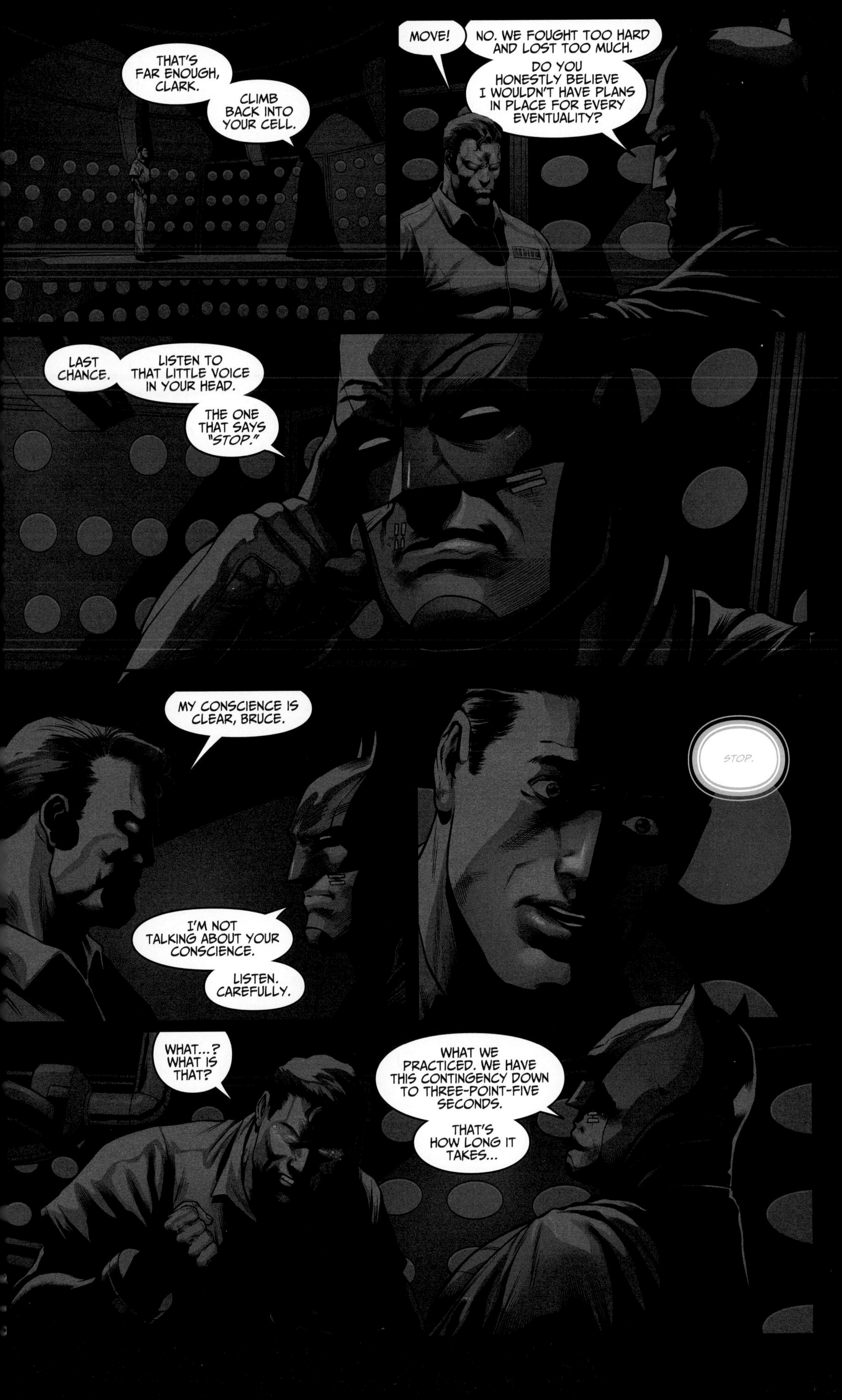

THAT'S FAR ENOUGH, CLARK.
CLIMB BACK INTO YOUR CELL.
MOVE!
NO. WE FOUGHT TOO HARD AND LOST TOO MUCH.
DO YOU HONESTLY BELIEVE I WOULDN'T HAVE PLANS IN PLACE FOR EVERY EVENTUALITY?
LAST CHANCE.
LISTEN TO THAT LITTLE VOICE IN YOUR HEAD.
THE ONE THAT SAYS "STOP."
MY CONSCIENCE IS CLEAR, BRUCE.
I'M NOT TALKING ABOUT YOUR CONSCIENCE.
LISTEN. CAREFULLY.
STOP.
WHAT...? WHAT IS THAT?
WHAT WE PRACTICED. WE HAVE THIS CONTINGENCY DOWN TO THREE-POINT-FIVE SECONDS.
THAT'S HOW LONG IT TAKES...

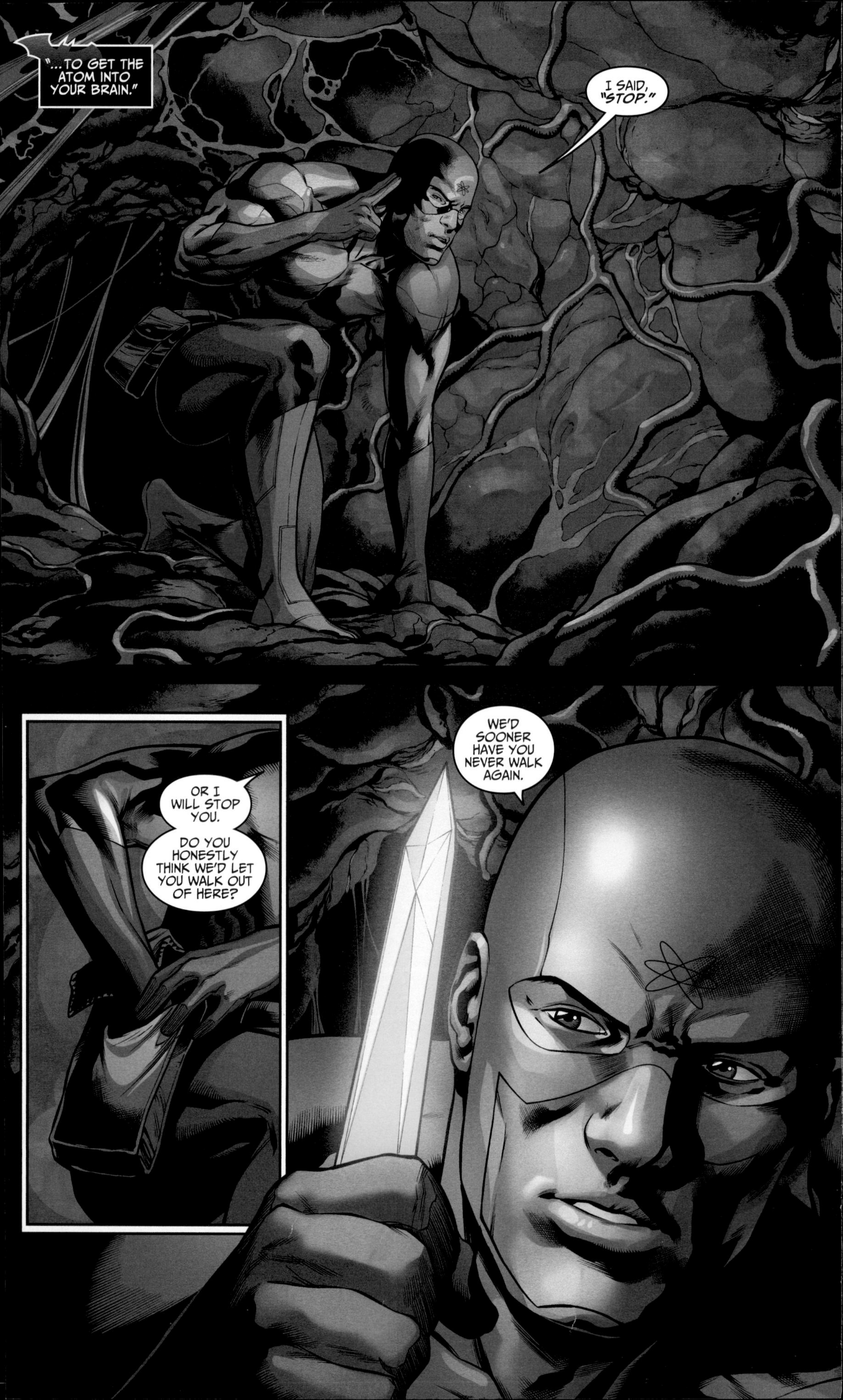
"...TO GET THE ATOM INTO YOUR BRAIN."
I SAID, "STOP."
WE'D SOONER HAVE YOU NEVER WALK AGAIN.
OR I WILL STOP YOU.
DO YOU HONESTLY THINK WE'D LET YOU WALK OUT OF HERE?

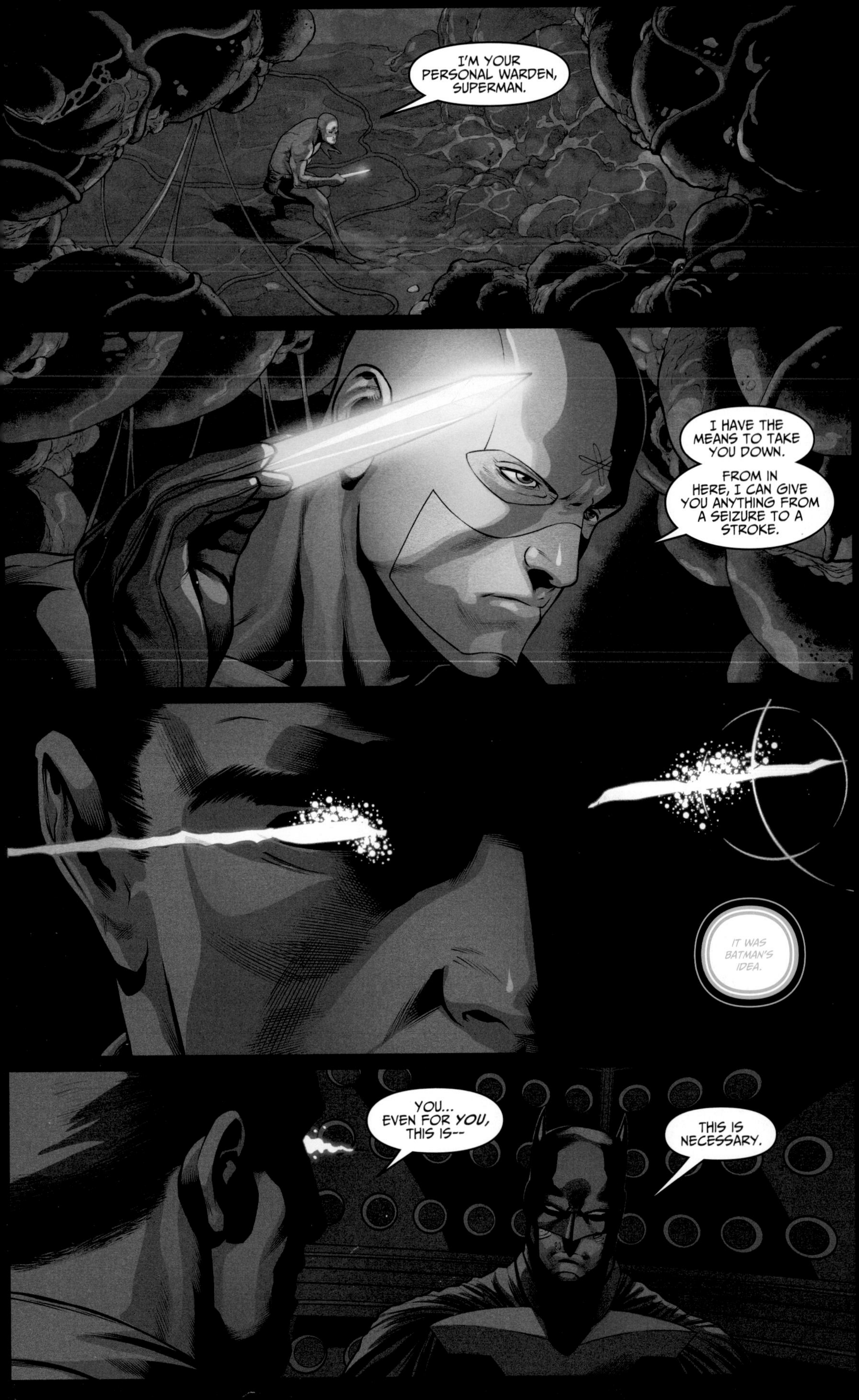
I'M YOUR PERSONAL WARDEN, SUPERMAN.
I HAVE THE MEANS TO TAKE YOU DOWN.
FROM IN HERE, I CAN GIVE YOU ANYTHING FROM A SEIZURE TO A STROKE.
IT WAS BATMAN'S IDEA.
YOU... EVEN FOR *YOU*, THIS IS--
THIS IS NECESSARY.

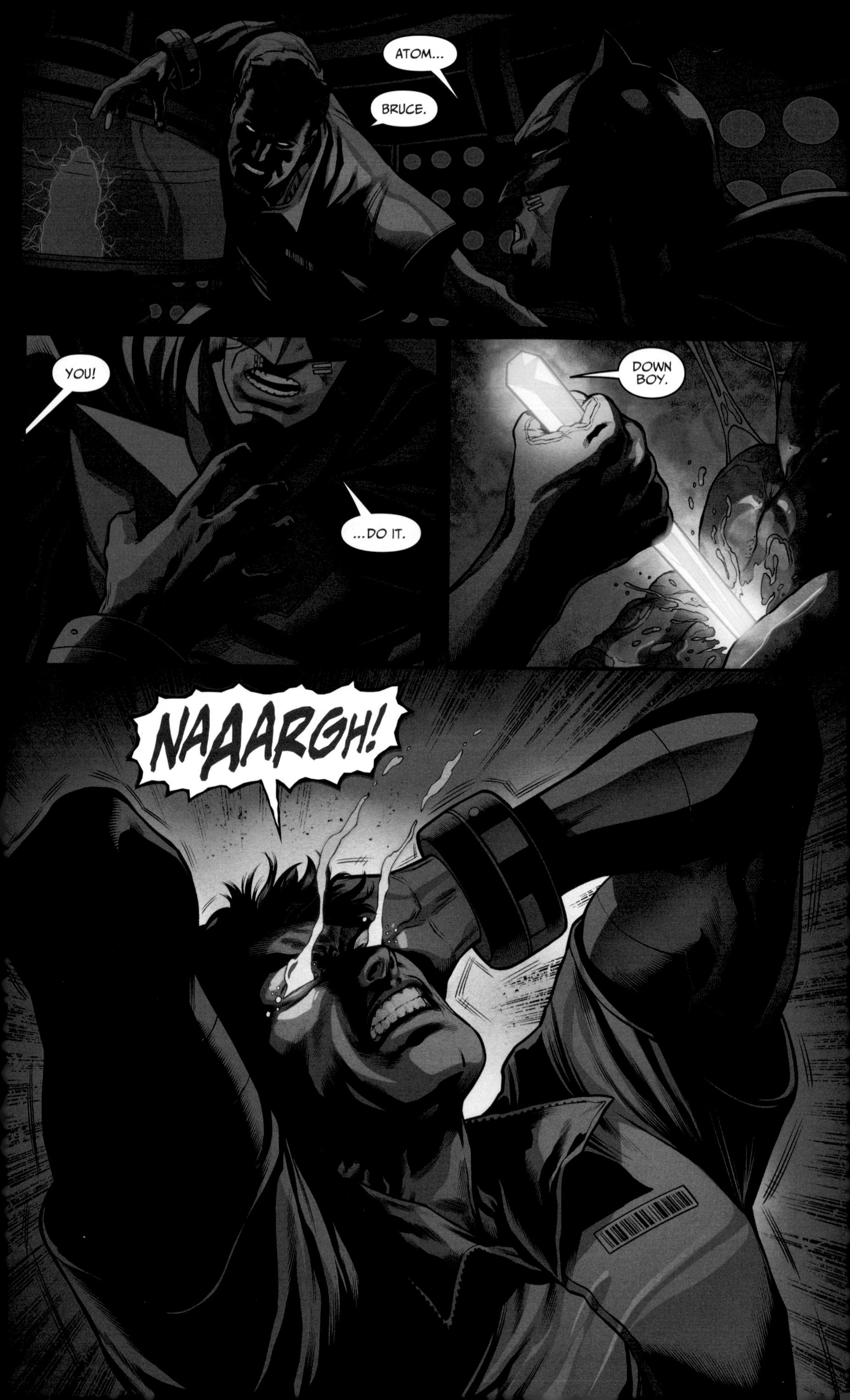
ATOM...
BRUCE.
YOU!
...DO IT.
DOWN BOY.
NAAARGH!

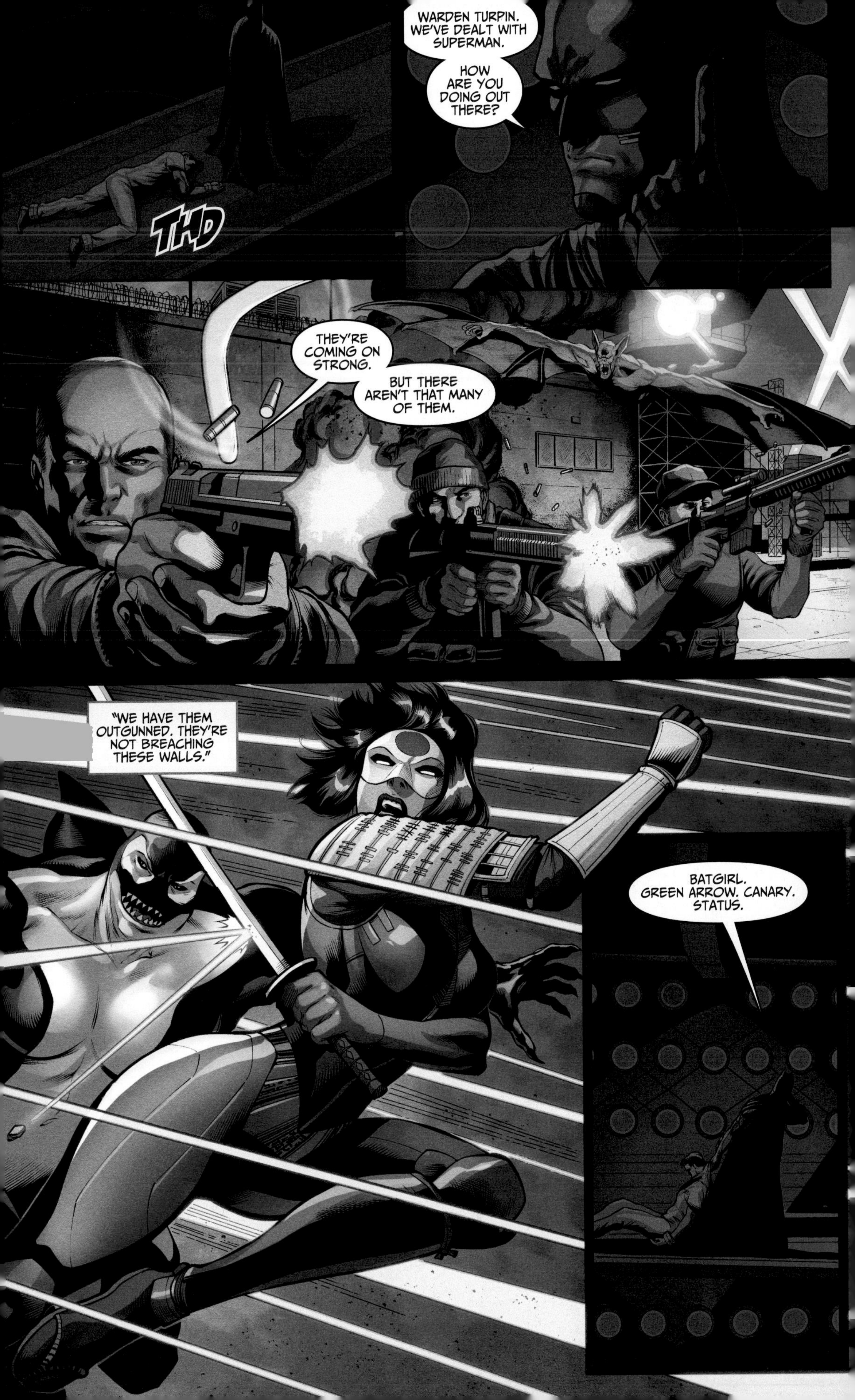

THD
WARDEN TURPIN. WE'VE DEALT WITH SUPERMAN.
HOW ARE YOU DOING OUT THERE?
THEY'RE COMING ON STRONG.
BUT THERE AREN'T THAT MANY OF THEM.
"WE HAVE THEM OUTGUNNED. THEY'RE NOT BREACHING THESE WALLS."
BATGIRL. GREEN ARROW. CANARY. STATUS.

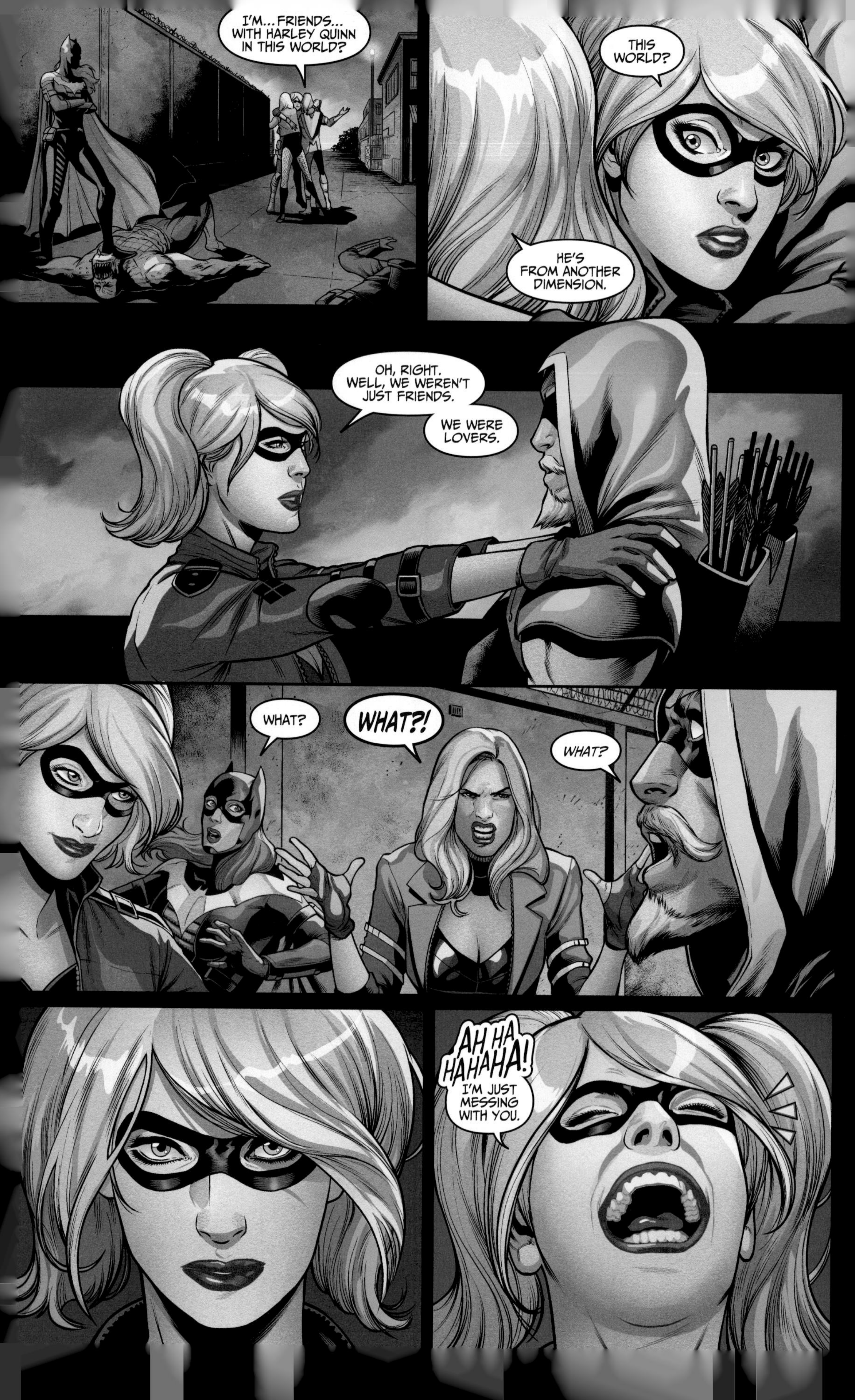
I'M... FRIENDS... WITH HARLEY QUINN IN THIS WORLD?
THIS WORLD?
HE'S FROM ANOTHER DIMENSION.
OH, RIGHT. WELL, WE WEREN'T JUST FRIENDS.
WE WERE LOVERS.
WHAT?
WHAT?!
WHAT?
AH HA HAHAHA!
I'M JUST MESSING WITH YOU.

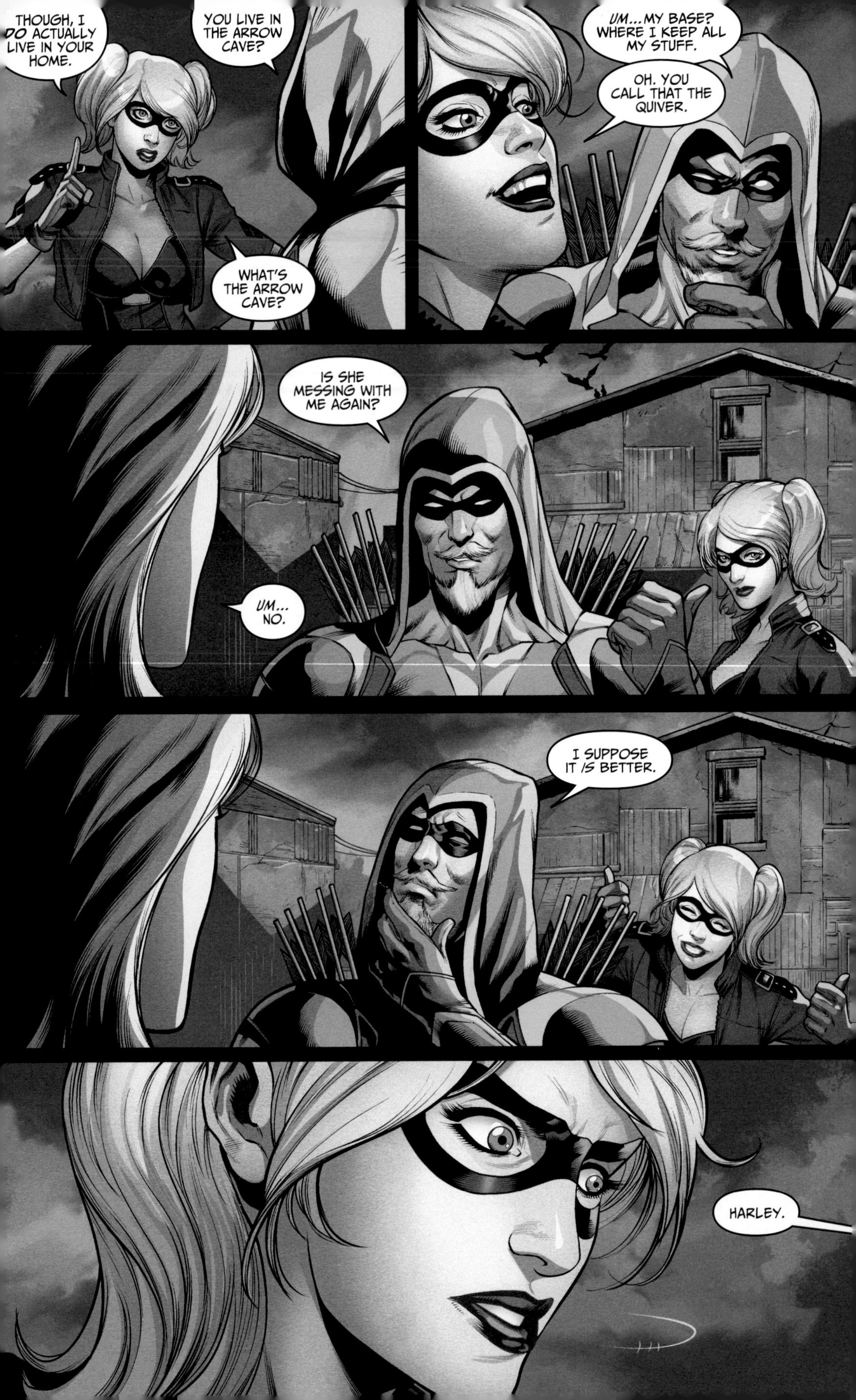
THOUGH, I *DO* ACTUALLY LIVE IN YOUR HOME.
YOU LIVE IN THE ARROW CAVE?
WHAT'S THE ARROW CAVE?
UM... MY BASE? WHERE I KEEP ALL MY STUFF.
OH. YOU CALL THAT THE QUIVER.
IS SHE MESSING WITH ME AGAIN?
UM... NO.
I SUPPOSE IT *IS* BETTER.
HARLEY.

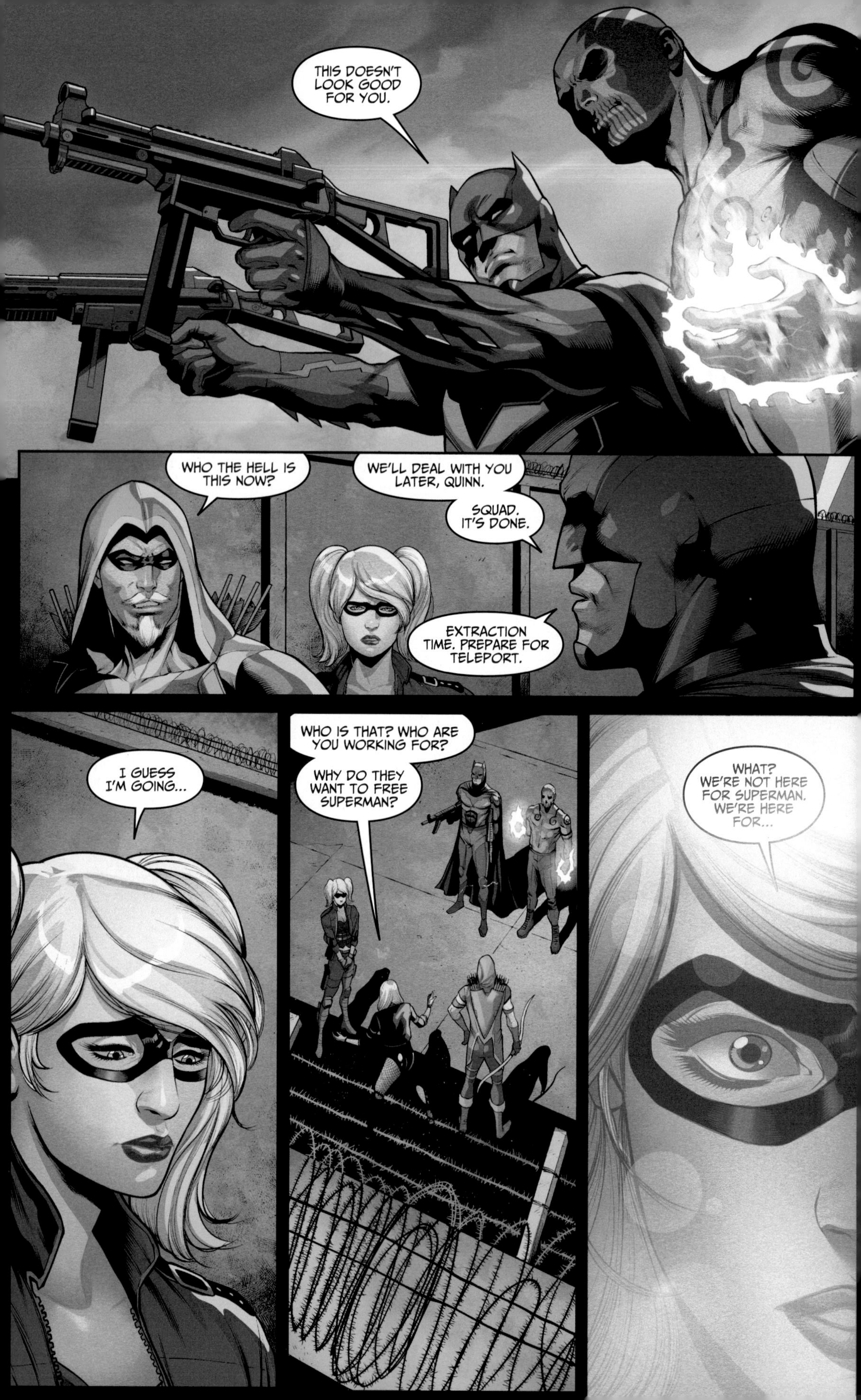

THIS DOESN'T LOOK GOOD FOR YOU.
WHO THE HELL IS THIS NOW?
WE'LL DEAL WITH YOU LATER, QUINN.
SQUAD. IT'S DONE.
EXTRACTION TIME. PREPARE FOR TELEPORT.
I GUESS I'M GOING...
WHO IS THAT? WHO ARE YOU WORKING FOR?
WHY DO THEY WANT TO FREE SUPERMAN?
WHAT? WE'RE NOT HERE FOR SUPERMAN. WE'RE HERE FOR...

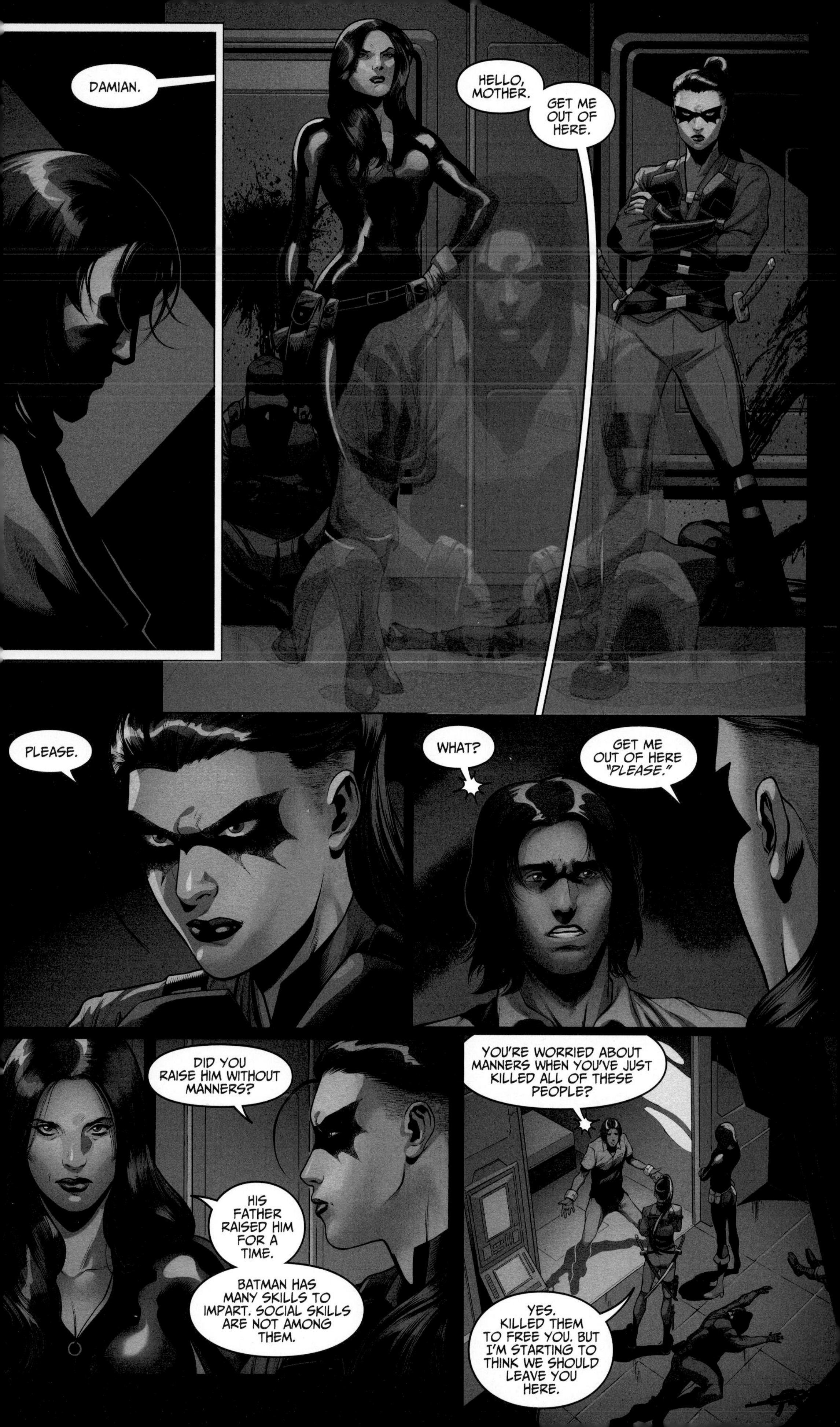
DAMIAN.
HELLO, MOTHER.
GET ME OUT OF HERE.
PLEASE.
WHAT?
GET ME OUT OF HERE *"PLEASE."*
DID YOU RAISE HIM WITHOUT MANNERS?
HIS FATHER RAISED HIM FOR A TIME.
BATMAN HAS MANY SKILLS TO IMPART. SOCIAL SKILLS ARE NOT AMONG THEM.
YOU'RE WORRIED ABOUT MANNERS WHEN YOU'VE JUST KILLED ALL OF THESE PEOPLE?
YES. KILLED THEM TO FREE YOU. BUT I'M STARTING TO THINK WE SHOULD LEAVE YOU HERE.

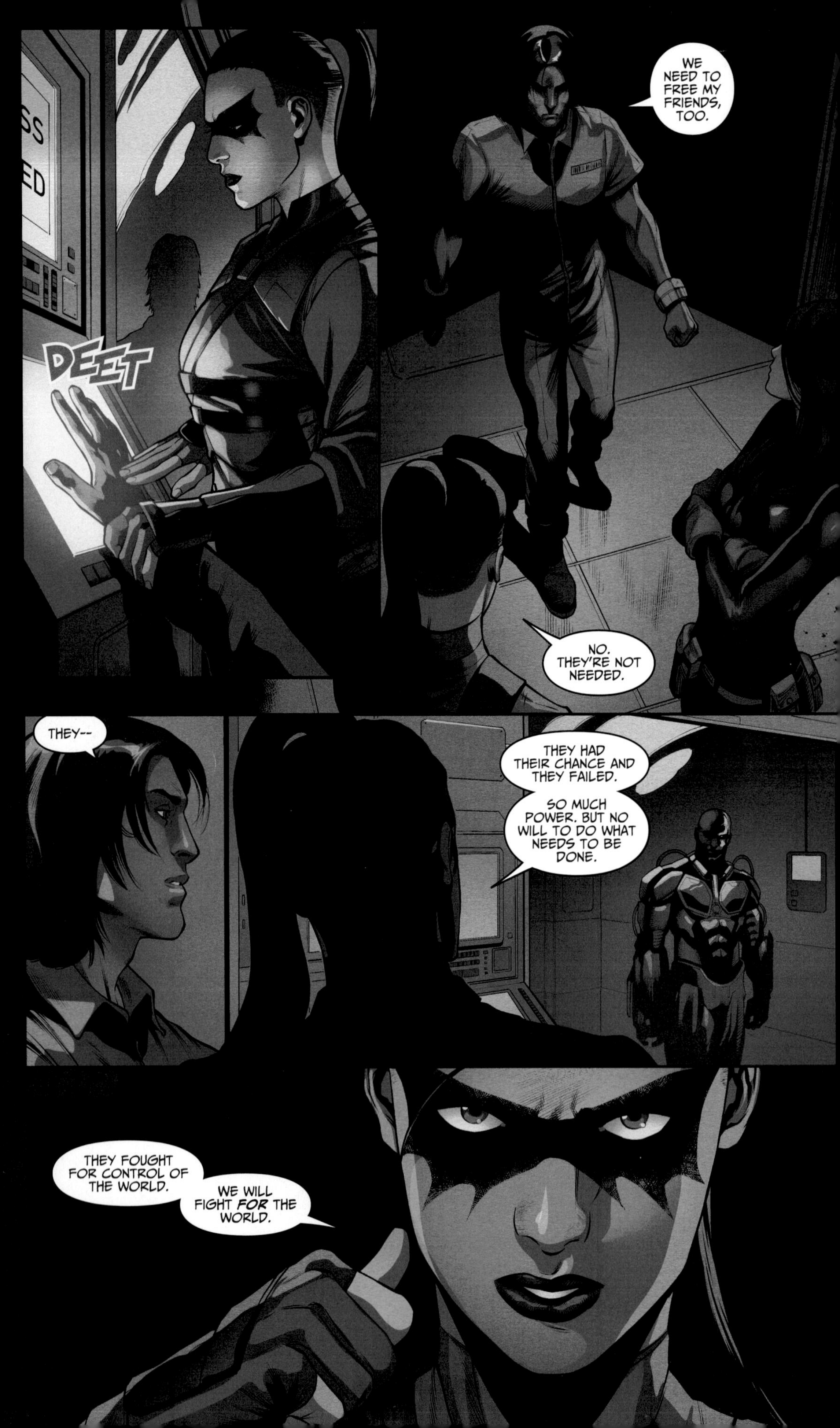
SS
ED
DEET
WE NEED TO FREE MY FRIENDS, TOO.
NO. THEY'RE NOT NEEDED.
THEY--
THEY HAD THEIR CHANCE AND THEY FAILED.
SO MUCH POWER. BUT NO WILL TO DO WHAT NEEDS TO BE DONE.
THEY FOUGHT FOR CONTROL OF THE WORLD.
WE WILL FIGHT *FOR* THE WORLD.

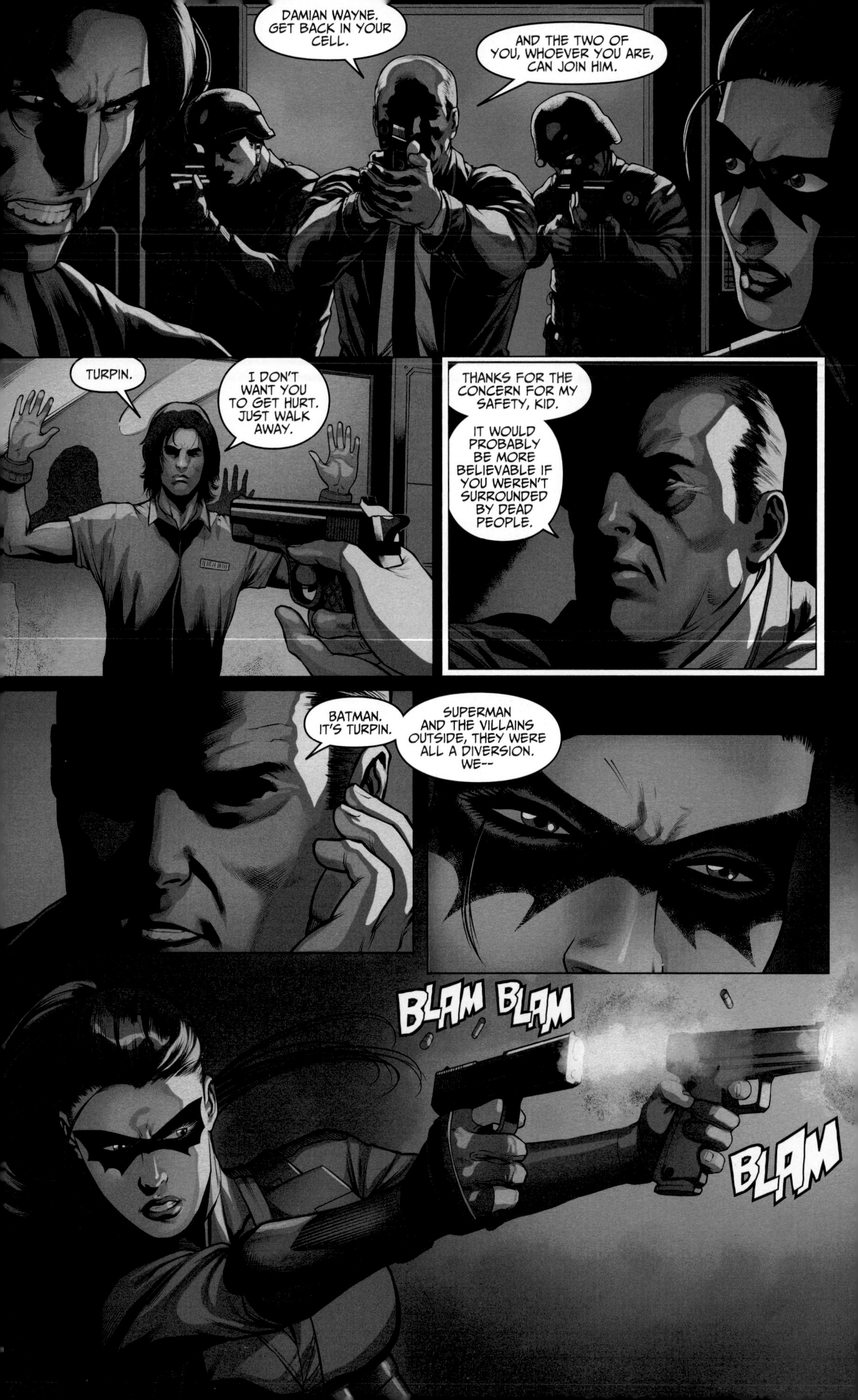
DAMIAN WAYNE. GET BACK IN YOUR CELL.
AND THE TWO OF YOU, WHOEVER YOU ARE, CAN JOIN HIM.
TURPIN.
I DON'T WANT YOU TO GET HURT. JUST WALK AWAY.
THANKS FOR THE CONCERN FOR MY SAFETY, KID.
IT WOULD PROBABLY BE MORE BELIEVABLE IF YOU WEREN'T SURROUNDED BY DEAD PEOPLE.
BATMAN. IT'S TURPIN.
SUPERMAN AND THE VILLAINS OUTSIDE, THEY WERE ALL A DIVERSION. WE--
BLAM BLAM
BLAM

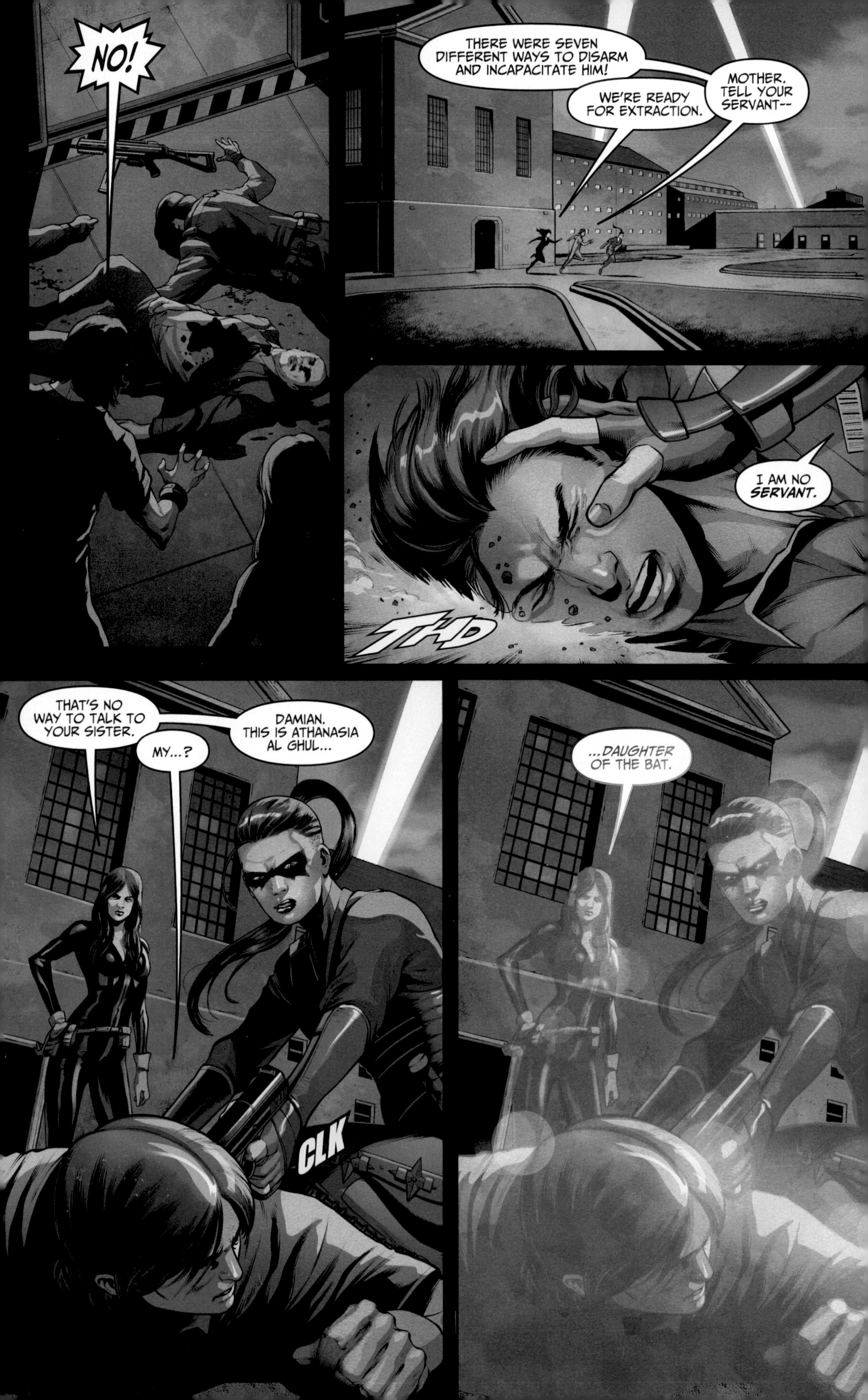
NO!
THERE WERE SEVEN DIFFERENT WAYS TO DISARM AND INCAPACITATE HIM!
WE'RE READY FOR EXTRACTION.
MOTHER. TELL YOUR SERVANT--
I AM NO SERVANT.
THD
THAT'S NO WAY TO TALK TO YOUR SISTER.
MY...?
DAMIAN. THIS IS ATHANASIA AL GHUL...
CLK
...DAUGHTER OF THE BAT.

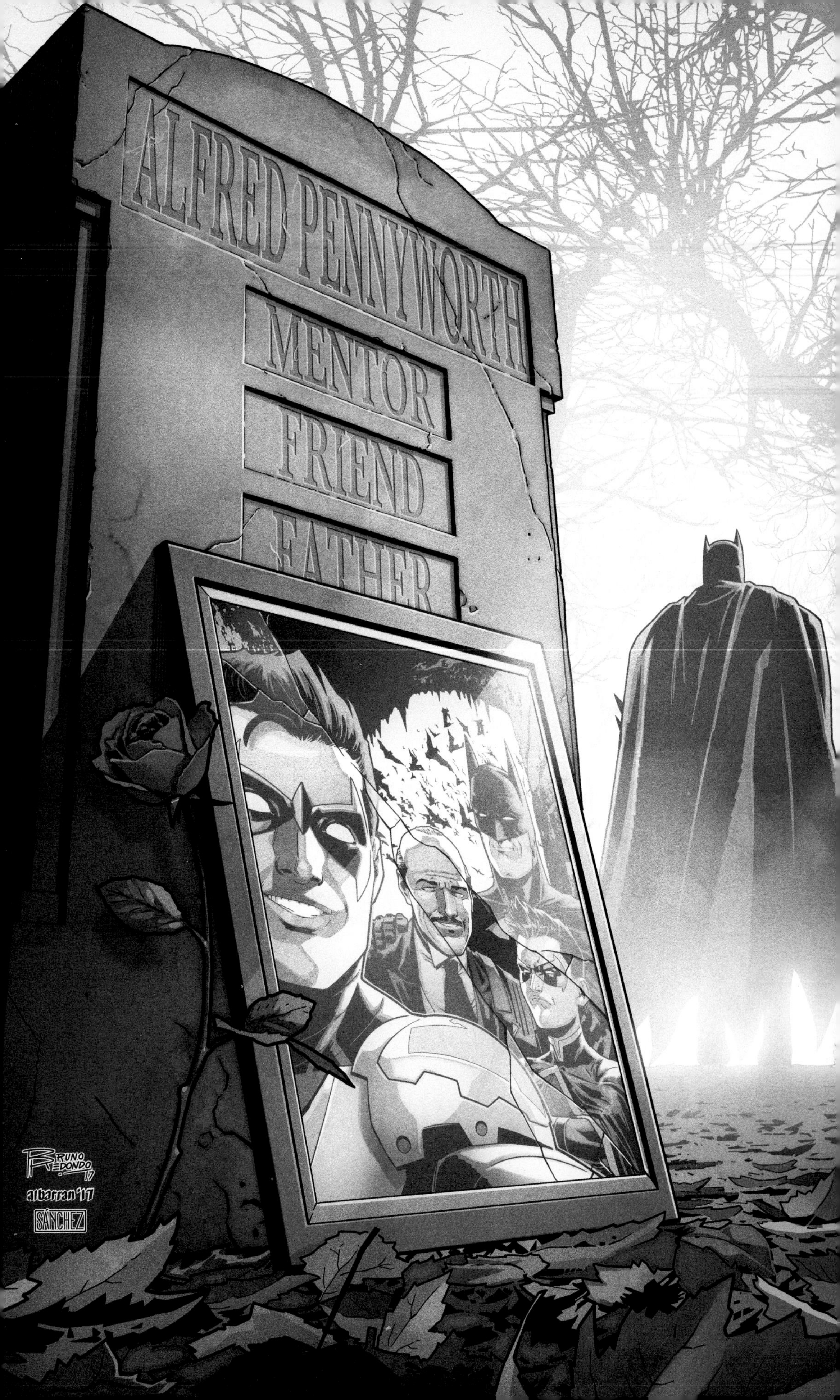
ALFRED PENNYWORTH
MENTOR
FRIEND
FATHER
BRUNO REDONDO '17
albarran '17
SÁNCHEZ

"The Person in Charge"

Daniel Sampere Penciller **Juan Albarran** Inker
Rex Lokus Colorist Cover art by **Bruno Redondo** and **Alejandro Sanchez**

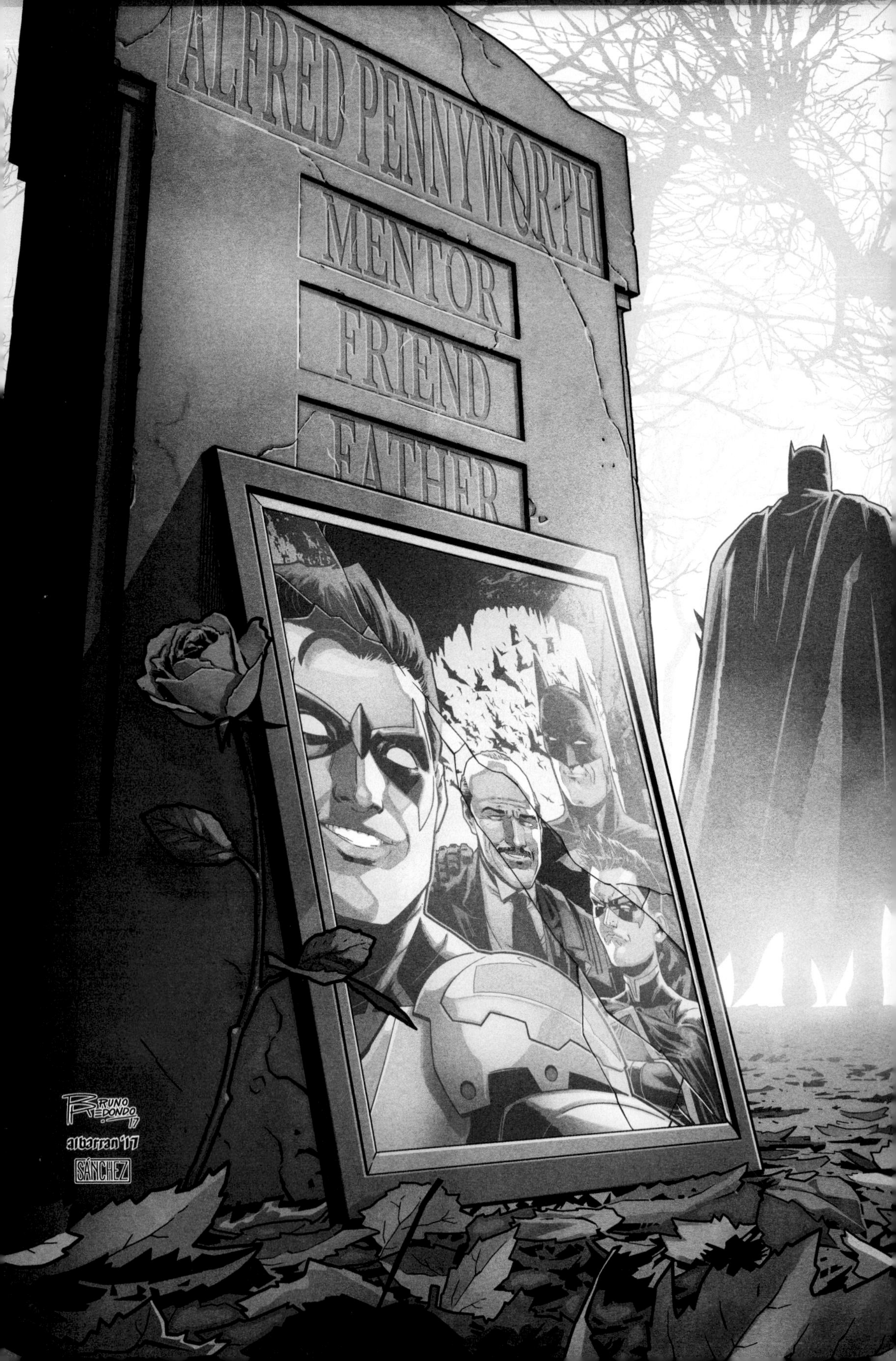
ALFRED PENNYWORTH
MENTOR
FRIEND
FATHER
BRUNO REDONDO '17
albarran '17
SÁNCHEZ

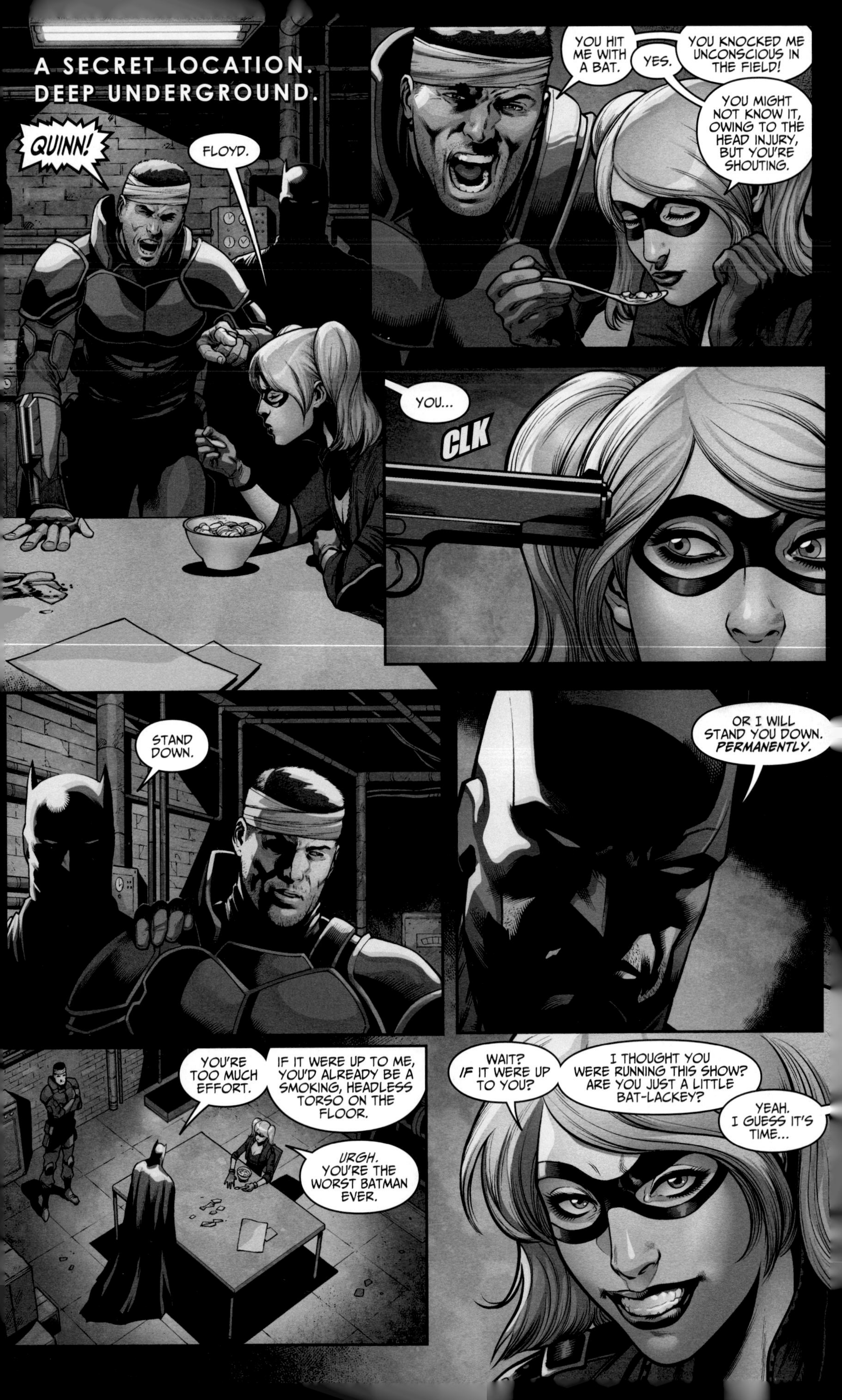

A SECRET LOCATION. DEEP UNDERGROUND.
QUINN!
FLOYD.
YOU HIT ME WITH A BAT.
YES.
YOU KNOCKED ME UNCONSCIOUS IN THE FIELD!
YOU MIGHT NOT KNOW IT, OWING TO THE HEAD INJURY, BUT YOU'RE SHOUTING.
YOU...
CLK
STAND DOWN.
OR I WILL STAND YOU DOWN. PERMANENTLY.
YOU'RE TOO MUCH EFFORT.
IF IT WERE UP TO ME, YOU'D ALREADY BE A SMOKING, HEADLESS TORSO ON THE FLOOR.
URGH. YOU'RE THE WORST BATMAN EVER.
WAIT? IF IT WERE UP TO YOU?
I THOUGHT YOU WERE RUNNING THIS SHOW? ARE YOU JUST A LITTLE BAT-LACKEY?
YEAH. I GUESS IT'S TIME...

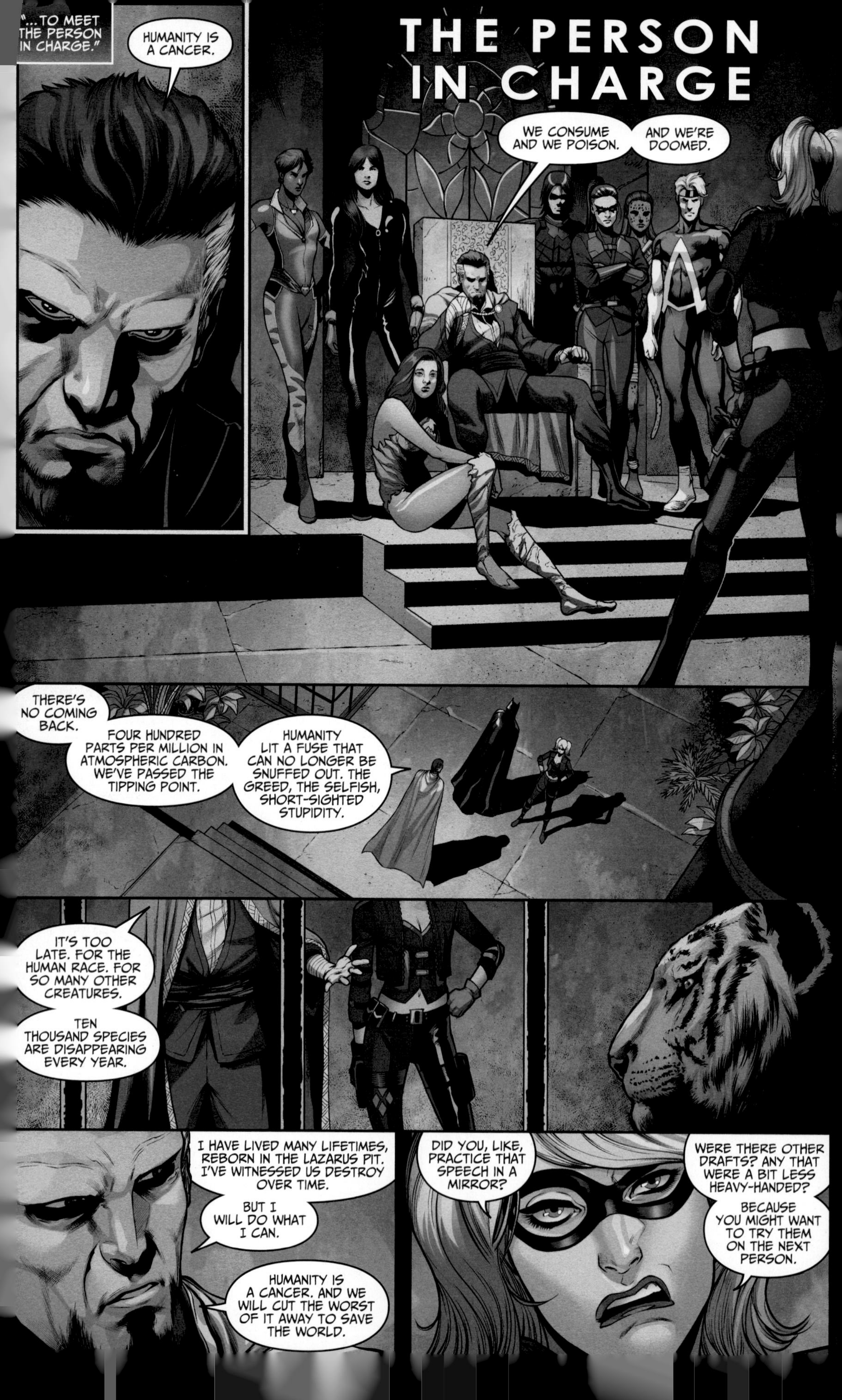

"...TO MEET THE PERSON IN CHARGE."
HUMANITY IS A CANCER.
THE PERSON IN CHARGE
WE CONSUME AND WE POISON.
AND WE'RE DOOMED.
THERE'S NO COMING BACK.
FOUR HUNDRED PARTS PER MILLION IN ATMOSPHERIC CARBON. WE'VE PASSED THE TIPPING POINT.
HUMANITY LIT A FUSE THAT CAN NO LONGER BE SNUFFED OUT. THE GREED, THE SELFISH, SHORT-SIGHTED STUPIDITY.
IT'S TOO LATE. FOR THE HUMAN RACE. FOR SO MANY OTHER CREATURES.
TEN THOUSAND SPECIES ARE DISAPPEARING EVERY YEAR.
I HAVE LIVED MANY LIFETIMES, REBORN IN THE LAZARUS PIT. I'VE WITNESSED US DESTROY OVER TIME.
BUT I WILL DO WHAT I CAN.
HUMANITY IS A CANCER. AND WE WILL CUT THE WORST OF IT AWAY TO SAVE THE WORLD.
DID YOU, LIKE, PRACTICE THAT SPEECH IN A MIRROR?
WERE THERE OTHER DRAFTS? ANY THAT WERE A BIT LESS HEAVY-HANDED?
BECAUSE YOU MIGHT WANT TO TRY THEM ON THE NEXT PERSON.

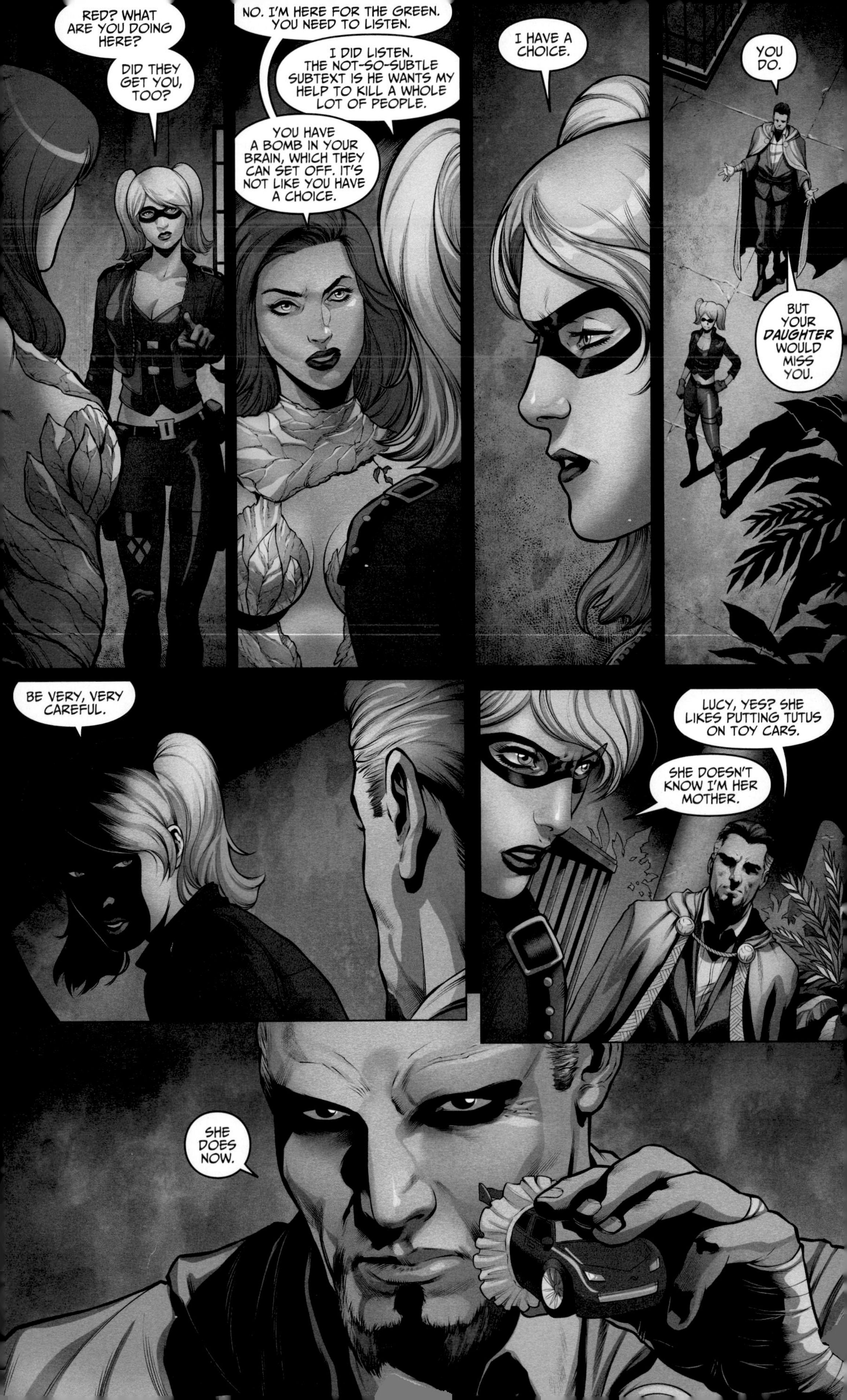

RED? WHAT ARE YOU DOING HERE?
DID THEY GET YOU, TOO?
NO. I'M HERE FOR THE GREEN. YOU NEED TO LISTEN.
I DID LISTEN. THE NOT-SO-SUBTLE SUBTEXT IS HE WANTS MY HELP TO KILL A WHOLE LOT OF PEOPLE.
YOU HAVE A BOMB IN YOUR BRAIN, WHICH THEY CAN SET OFF. IT'S NOT LIKE YOU HAVE A CHOICE.
I HAVE A CHOICE.
YOU DO.
BUT YOUR *DAUGHTER* WOULD MISS YOU.
BE VERY, VERY CAREFUL.
LUCY, YES? SHE LIKES PUTTING TUTUS ON TOY CARS.
SHE DOESN'T KNOW I'M HER MOTHER.
SHE DOES NOW.

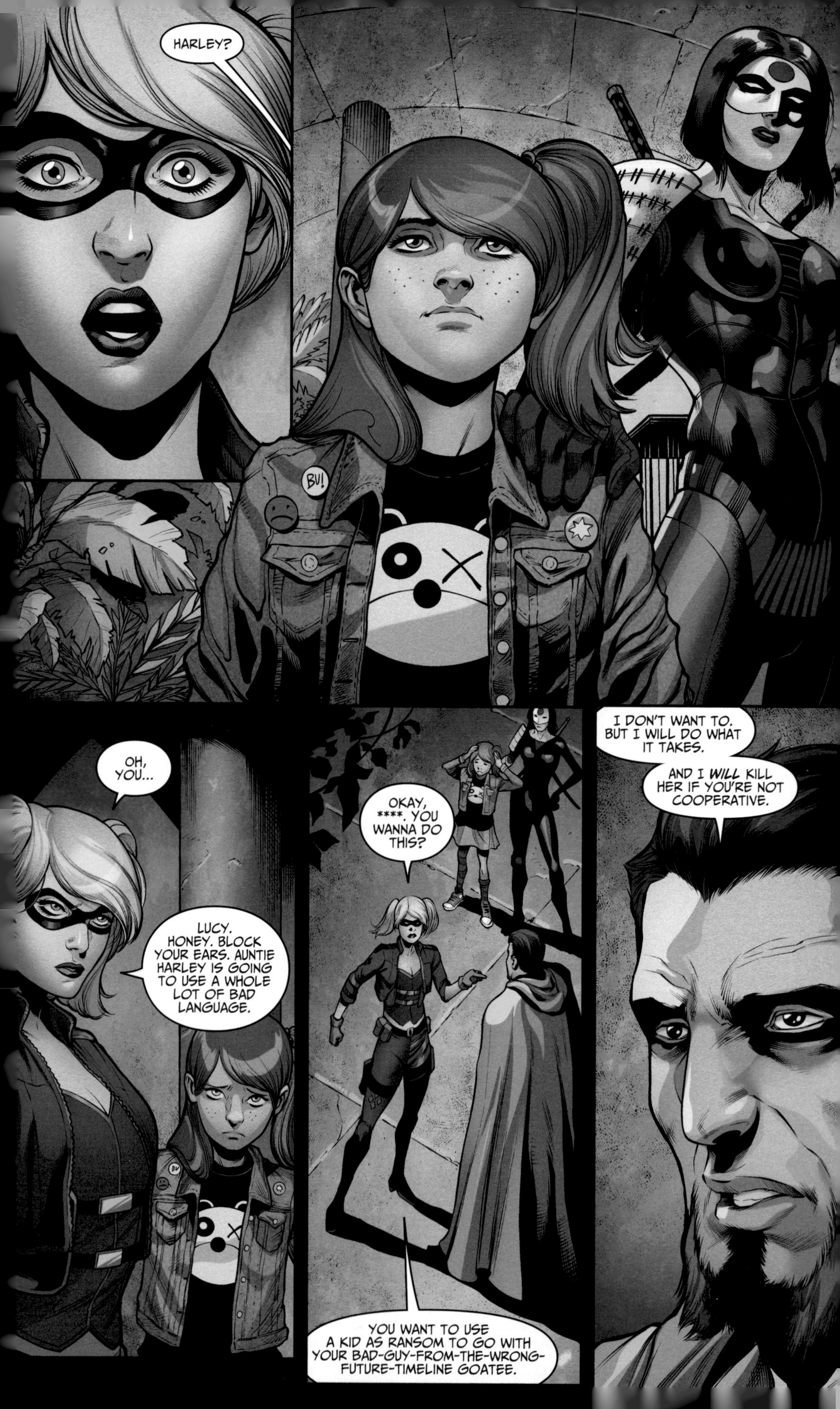
HARLEY?
BU!
OH, YOU...
LUCY. HONEY. BLOCK YOUR EARS. AUNTIE HARLEY IS GOING TO USE A WHOLE LOT OF BAD LANGUAGE.
OKAY, ****. YOU WANNA DO THIS?
YOU WANT TO USE A KID AS RANSOM TO GO WITH YOUR BAD-GUY-FROM-THE-WRONG-FUTURE-TIMELINE GOATEE.
I DON'T WANT TO. BUT I WILL DO WHAT IT TAKES.
AND I WILL KILL HER IF YOU'RE NOT COOPERATIVE.

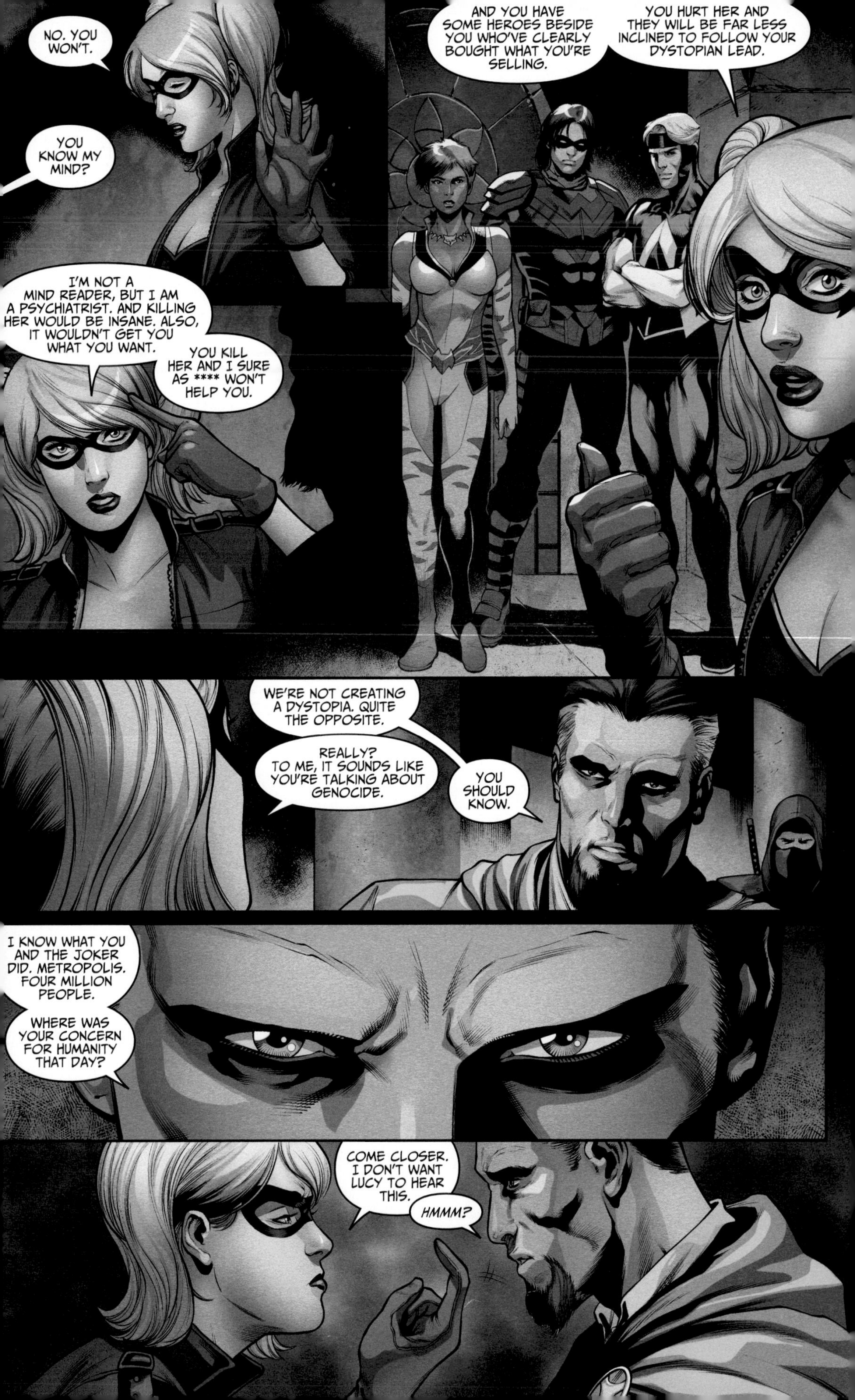
NO. YOU WON'T.
YOU KNOW MY MIND?
I'M NOT A MIND READER, BUT I AM A PSYCHIATRIST. AND KILLING HER WOULD BE INSANE. ALSO, IT WOULDN'T GET YOU WHAT YOU WANT.
YOU KILL HER AND I SURE AS **** WON'T HELP YOU.
AND YOU HAVE SOME HEROES BESIDE YOU WHO'VE CLEARLY BOUGHT WHAT YOU'RE SELLING.
YOU HURT HER AND THEY WILL BE FAR LESS INCLINED TO FOLLOW YOUR DYSTOPIAN LEAD.
WE'RE NOT CREATING A DYSTOPIA. QUITE THE OPPOSITE.
REALLY? TO ME, IT SOUNDS LIKE YOU'RE TALKING ABOUT GENOCIDE.
YOU SHOULD KNOW.
I KNOW WHAT YOU AND THE JOKER DID. METROPOLIS. FOUR MILLION PEOPLE.
WHERE WAS YOUR CONCERN FOR HUMANITY THAT DAY?
COME CLOSER. I DON'T WANT LUCY TO HEAR THIS.
HMMM?

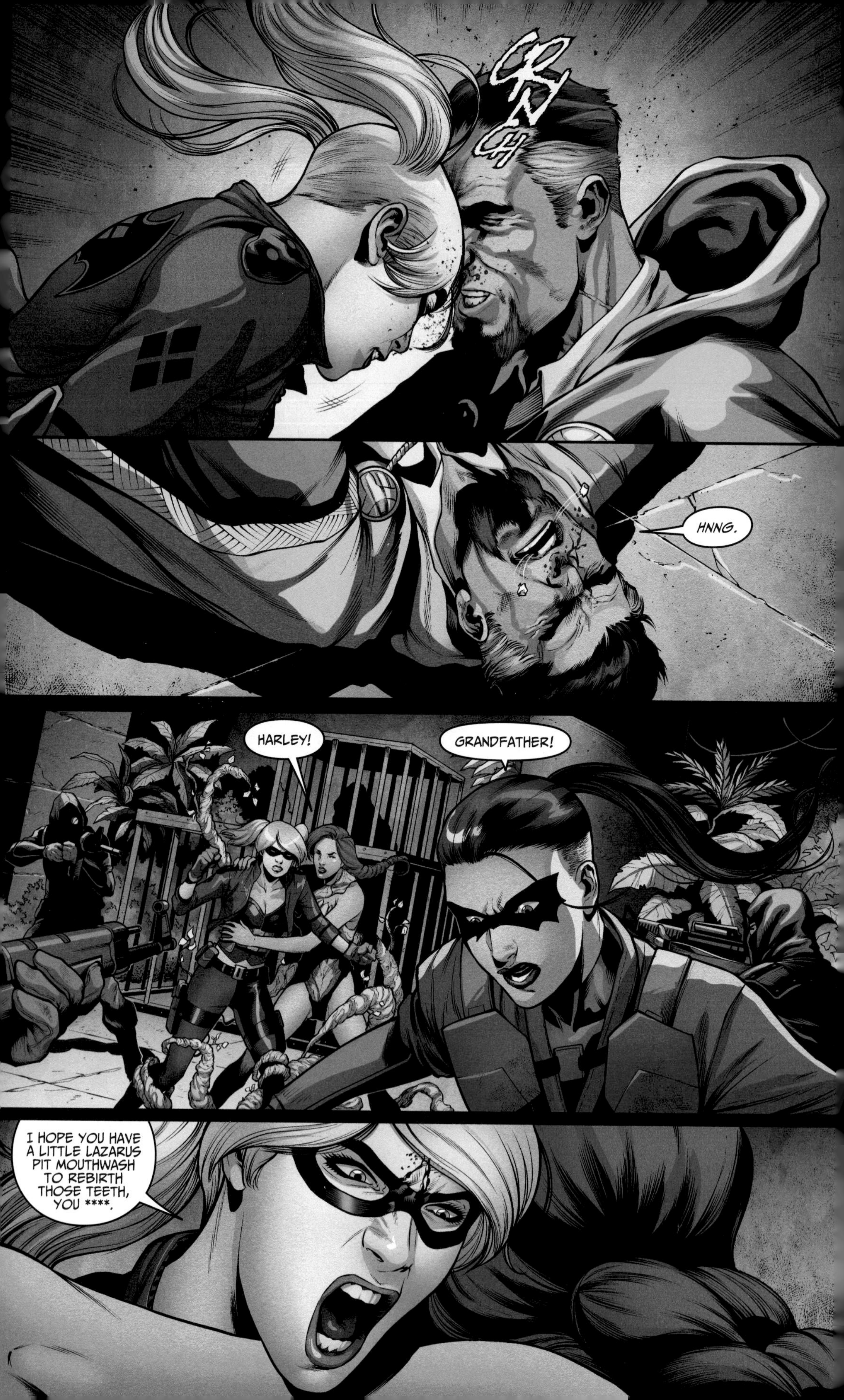
CRUNCH
HNNG.
HARLEY!
GRANDFATHER!
I HOPE YOU HAVE A LITTLE LAZARUS PIT MOUTHWASH TO REBIRTH THOSE TEETH, YOU ****.

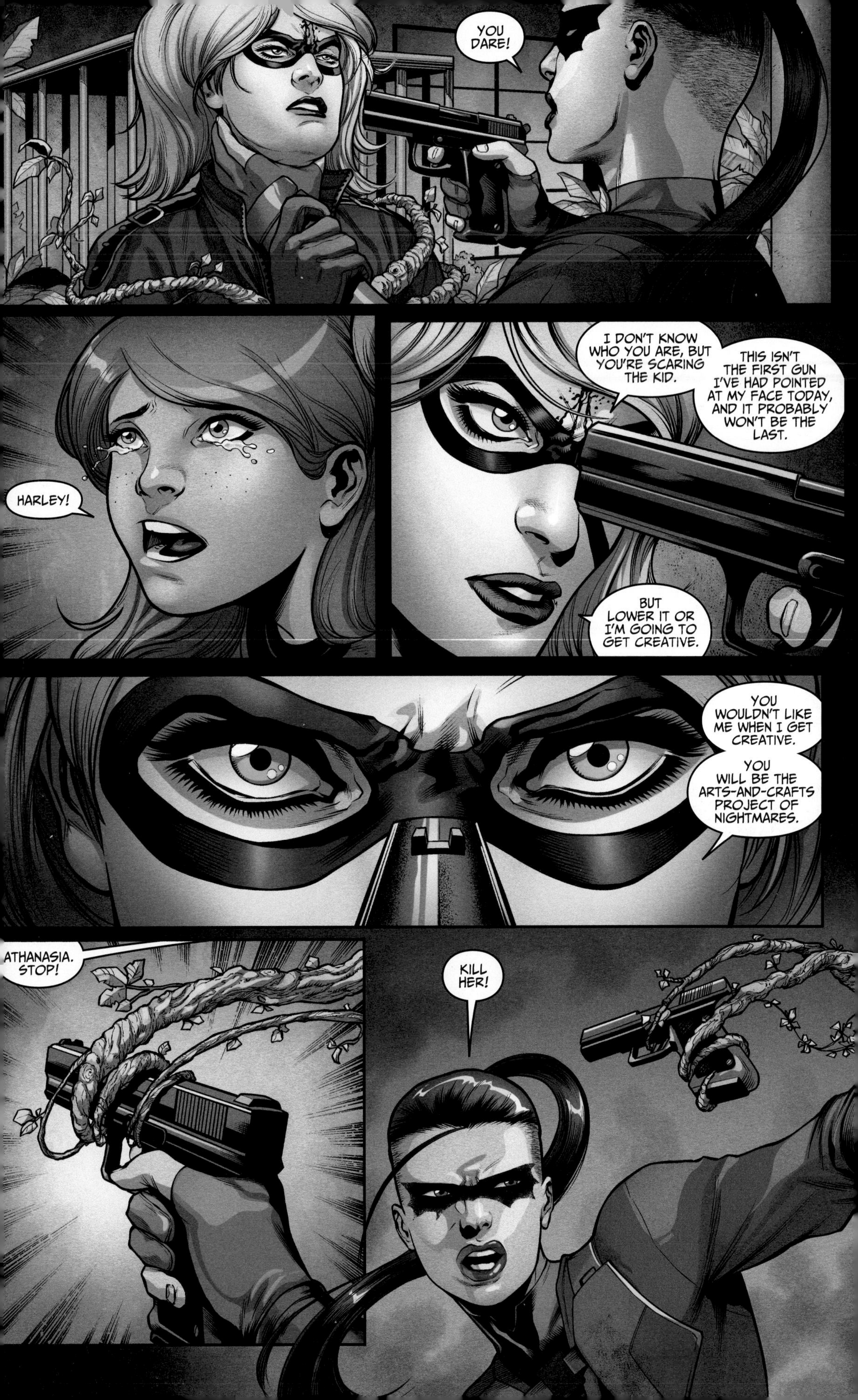
YOU DARE!
HARLEY!
I DON'T KNOW WHO YOU ARE, BUT YOU'RE SCARING THE KID.
THIS ISN'T THE FIRST GUN I'VE HAD POINTED AT MY FACE TODAY, AND IT PROBABLY WON'T BE THE LAST.
BUT LOWER IT OR I'M GOING TO GET CREATIVE.
YOU WOULDN'T LIKE ME WHEN I GET CREATIVE.
YOU WILL BE THE ARTS-AND-CRAFTS PROJECT OF NIGHTMARES.
ATHANASIA. STOP!
KILL HER!

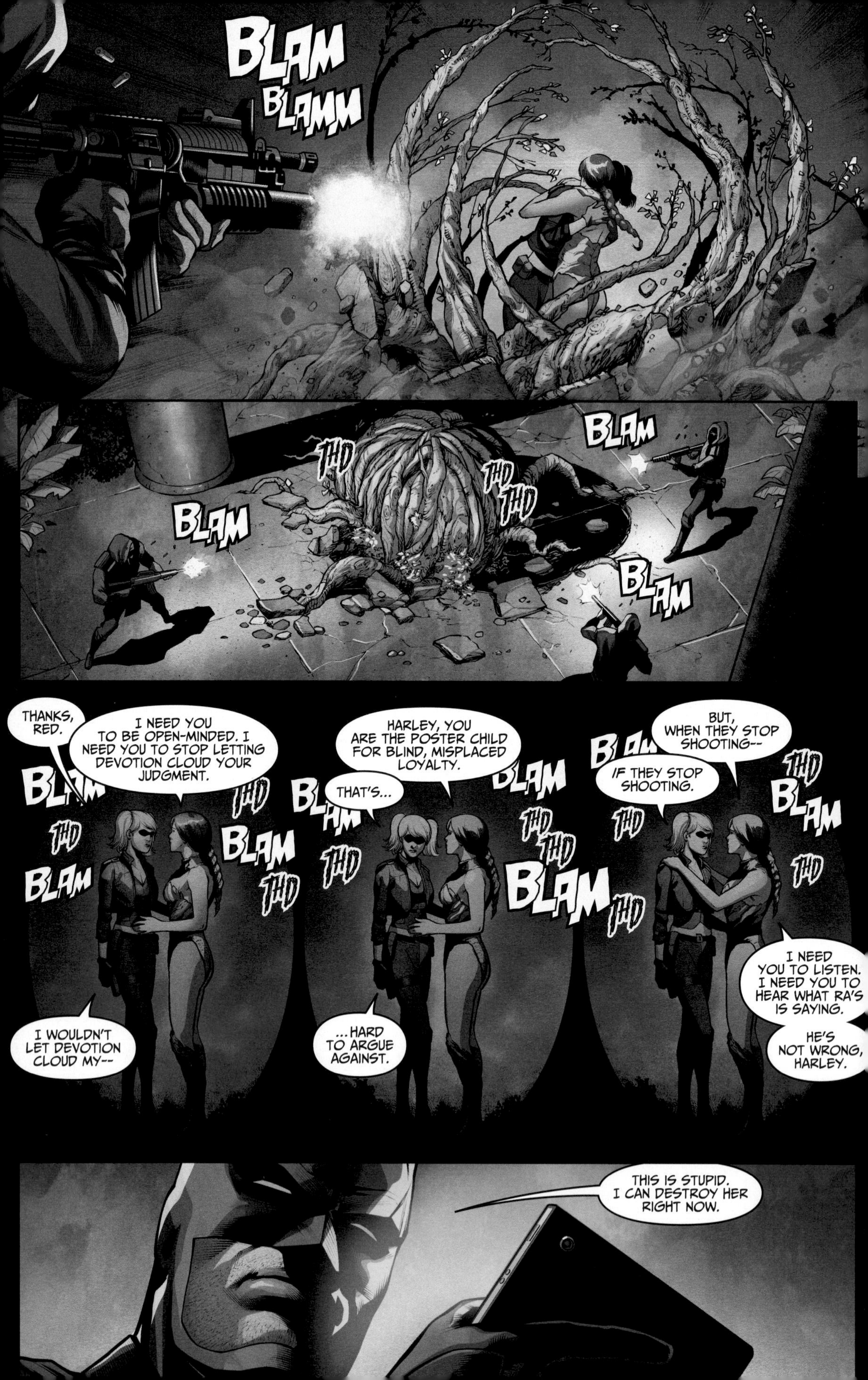
BLAM
BLAMM
THD
BLAM
THD THD
BLAM
BLAM
THANKS, RED.
I NEED YOU TO BE OPEN-MINDED. I NEED YOU TO STOP LETTING DEVOTION CLOUD YOUR JUDGMENT.
BLAM
THD
BLAM
THD
BLAM
THD
I WOULDN'T LET DEVOTION CLOUD MY--
HARLEY, YOU ARE THE POSTER CHILD FOR BLIND, MISPLACED LOYALTY.
THAT'S...
BLAM
THD
BLAM
THD
THD
BLAM
THD
...HARD TO ARGUE AGAINST.
BUT, WHEN THEY STOP SHOOTING--
IF THEY STOP SHOOTING.
THD
THD
BLAM
THD
I NEED YOU TO LISTEN. I NEED YOU TO HEAR WHAT RA'S IS SAYING.
HE'S NOT WRONG, HARLEY.
THIS IS STUPID. I CAN DESTROY HER RIGHT NOW.

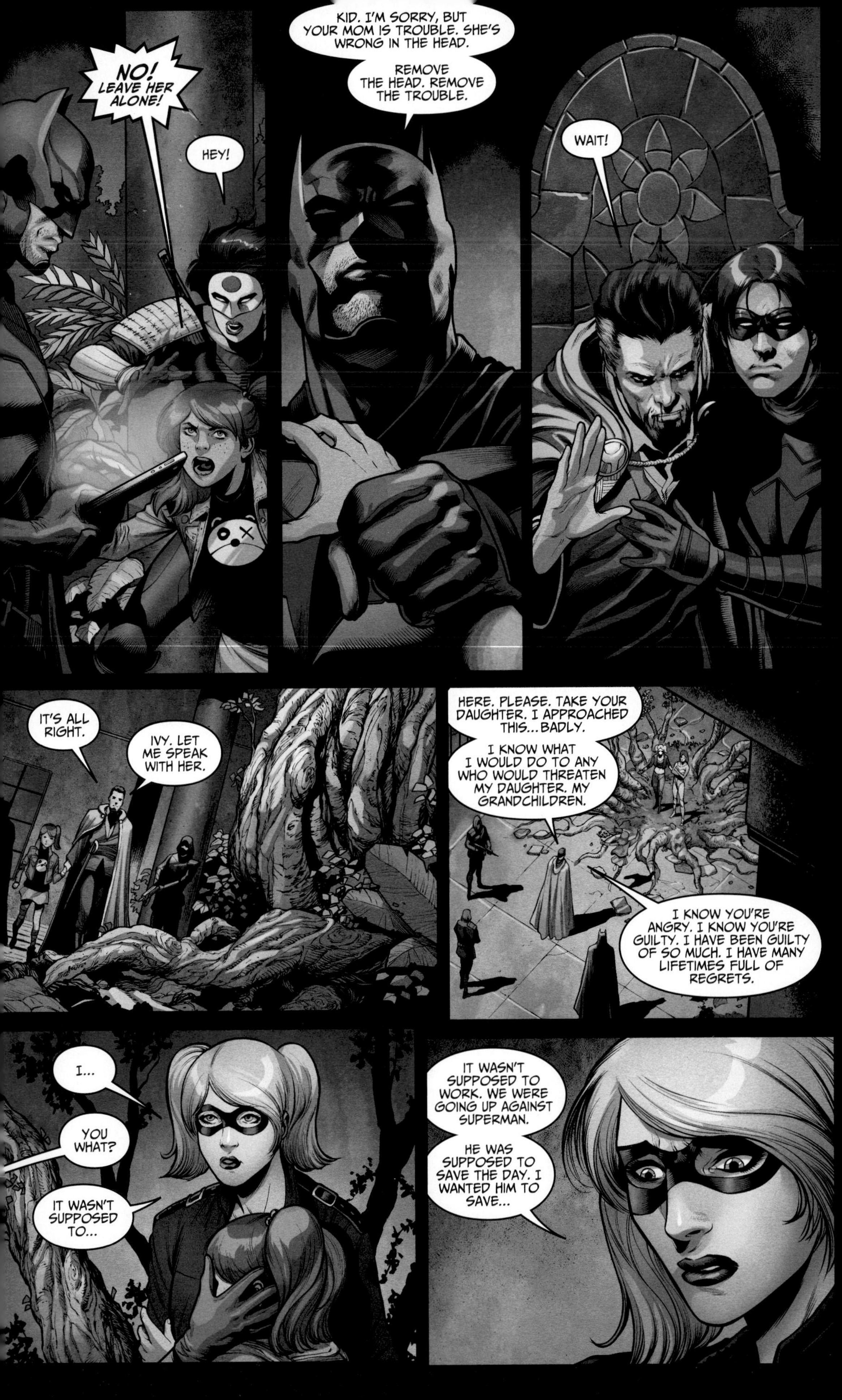
NO! LEAVE HER ALONE!
HEY!
KID. I'M SORRY, BUT YOUR MOM IS TROUBLE. SHE'S WRONG IN THE HEAD.
REMOVE THE HEAD. REMOVE THE TROUBLE.
WAIT!
IT'S ALL RIGHT.
IVY. LET ME SPEAK WITH HER.
HERE. PLEASE. TAKE YOUR DAUGHTER. I APPROACHED THIS... BADLY.
I KNOW WHAT I WOULD DO TO ANY WHO WOULD THREATEN MY DAUGHTER. MY GRANDCHILDREN.
I KNOW YOU'RE ANGRY. I KNOW YOU'RE GUILTY. I HAVE BEEN GUILTY OF SO MUCH. I HAVE MANY LIFETIMES FULL OF REGRETS.
I...
YOU WHAT?
IT WASN'T SUPPOSED TO...
IT WASN'T SUPPOSED TO WORK. WE WERE GOING UP AGAINST SUPERMAN.
HE WAS SUPPOSED TO SAVE THE DAY. I WANTED HIM TO SAVE...

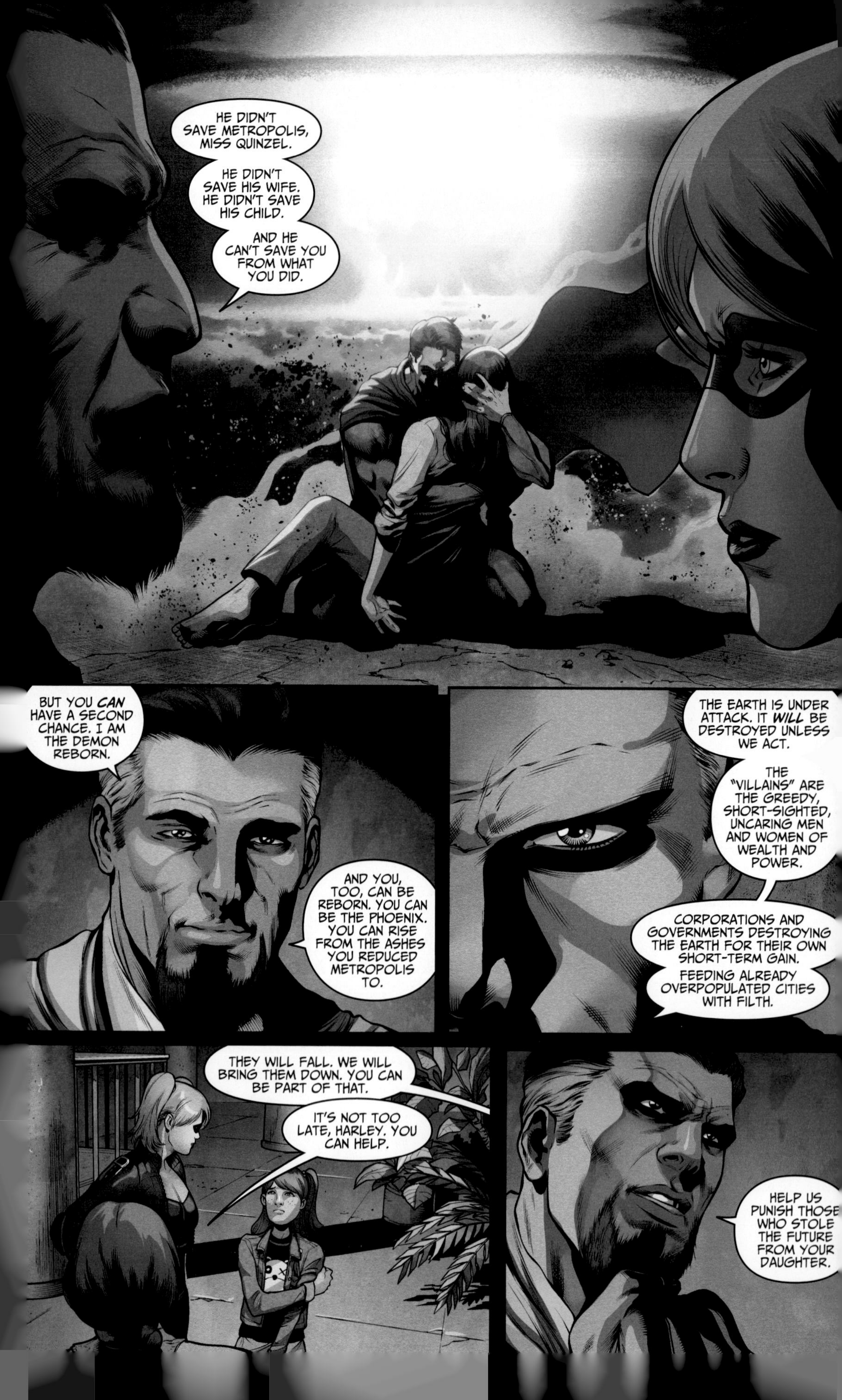
HE DIDN'T SAVE METROPOLIS, MISS QUINZEL.
HE DIDN'T SAVE HIS WIFE. HE DIDN'T SAVE HIS CHILD.
AND HE CAN'T SAVE YOU FROM WHAT YOU DID.
BUT YOU CAN HAVE A SECOND CHANCE. I AM THE DEMON REBORN.
AND YOU, TOO, CAN BE REBORN. YOU CAN BE THE PHOENIX. YOU CAN RISE FROM THE ASHES YOU REDUCED METROPOLIS TO.
THE EARTH IS UNDER ATTACK. IT WILL BE DESTROYED UNLESS WE ACT.
THE "VILLAINS" ARE THE GREEDY, SHORT-SIGHTED, UNCARING MEN AND WOMEN OF WEALTH AND POWER.
CORPORATIONS AND GOVERNMENTS DESTROYING THE EARTH FOR THEIR OWN SHORT-TERM GAIN.
FEEDING ALREADY OVERPOPULATED CITIES WITH FILTH.
THEY WILL FALL. WE WILL BRING THEM DOWN. YOU CAN BE PART OF THAT.
IT'S NOT TOO LATE, HARLEY. YOU CAN HELP.
HELP US PUNISH THOSE WHO STOLE THE FUTURE FROM YOUR DAUGHTER.

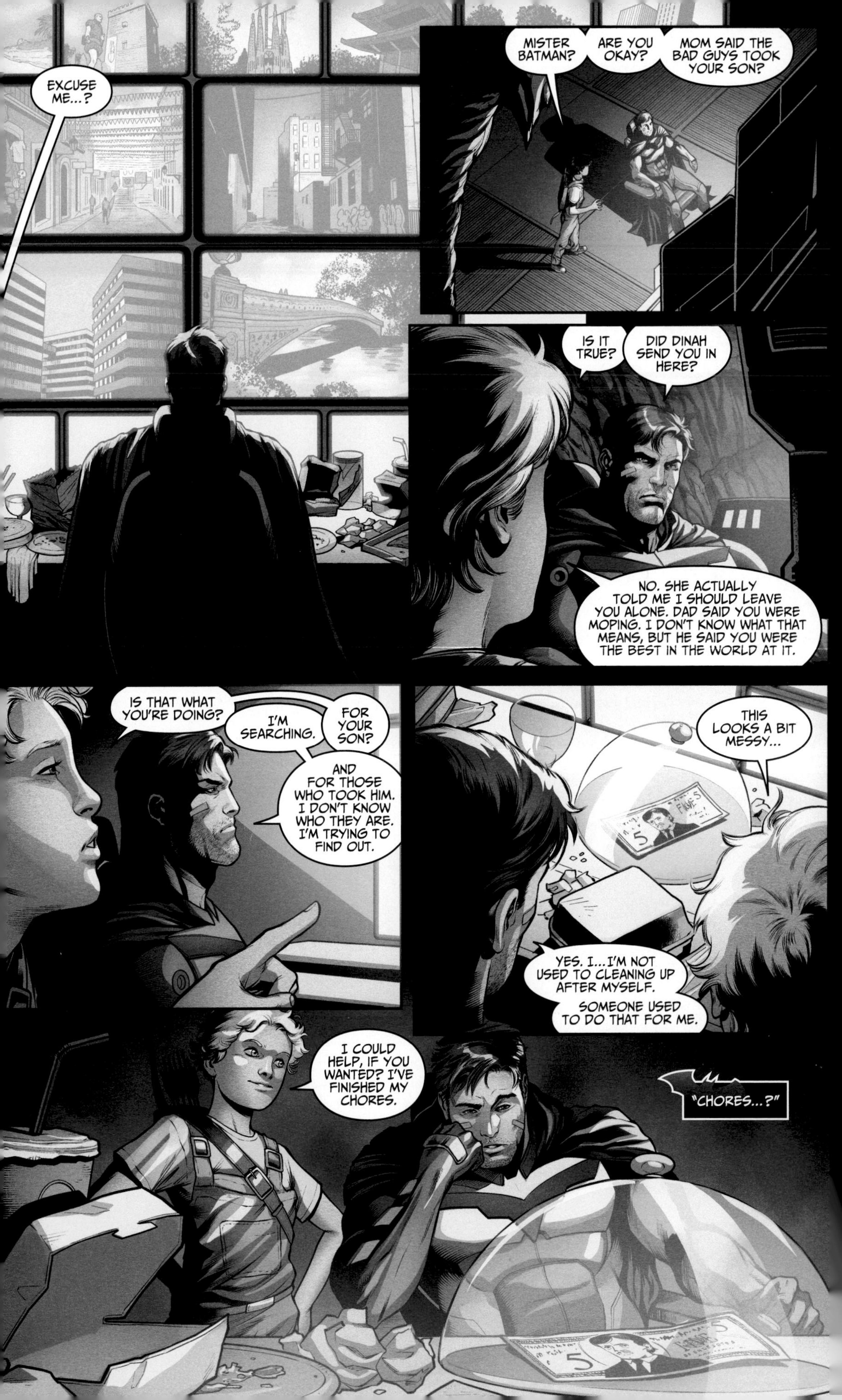

EXCUSE ME...?
MISTER BATMAN?
ARE YOU OKAY?
MOM SAID THE BAD GUYS TOOK YOUR SON?
IS IT TRUE?
DID DINAH SEND YOU IN HERE?
NO. SHE ACTUALLY TOLD ME I SHOULD LEAVE YOU ALONE. DAD SAID YOU WERE MOPING. I DON'T KNOW WHAT THAT MEANS, BUT HE SAID YOU WERE THE BEST IN THE WORLD AT IT.
IS THAT WHAT YOU'RE DOING?
I'M SEARCHING.
FOR YOUR SON?
AND FOR THOSE WHO TOOK HIM. I DON'T KNOW WHO THEY ARE. I'M TRYING TO FIND OUT.
THIS LOOKS A BIT MESSY...
YES. I...I'M NOT USED TO CLEANING UP AFTER MYSELF.
SOMEONE USED TO DO THAT FOR ME.
I COULD HELP, IF YOU WANTED? I'VE FINISHED MY CHORES.
"CHORES...?"

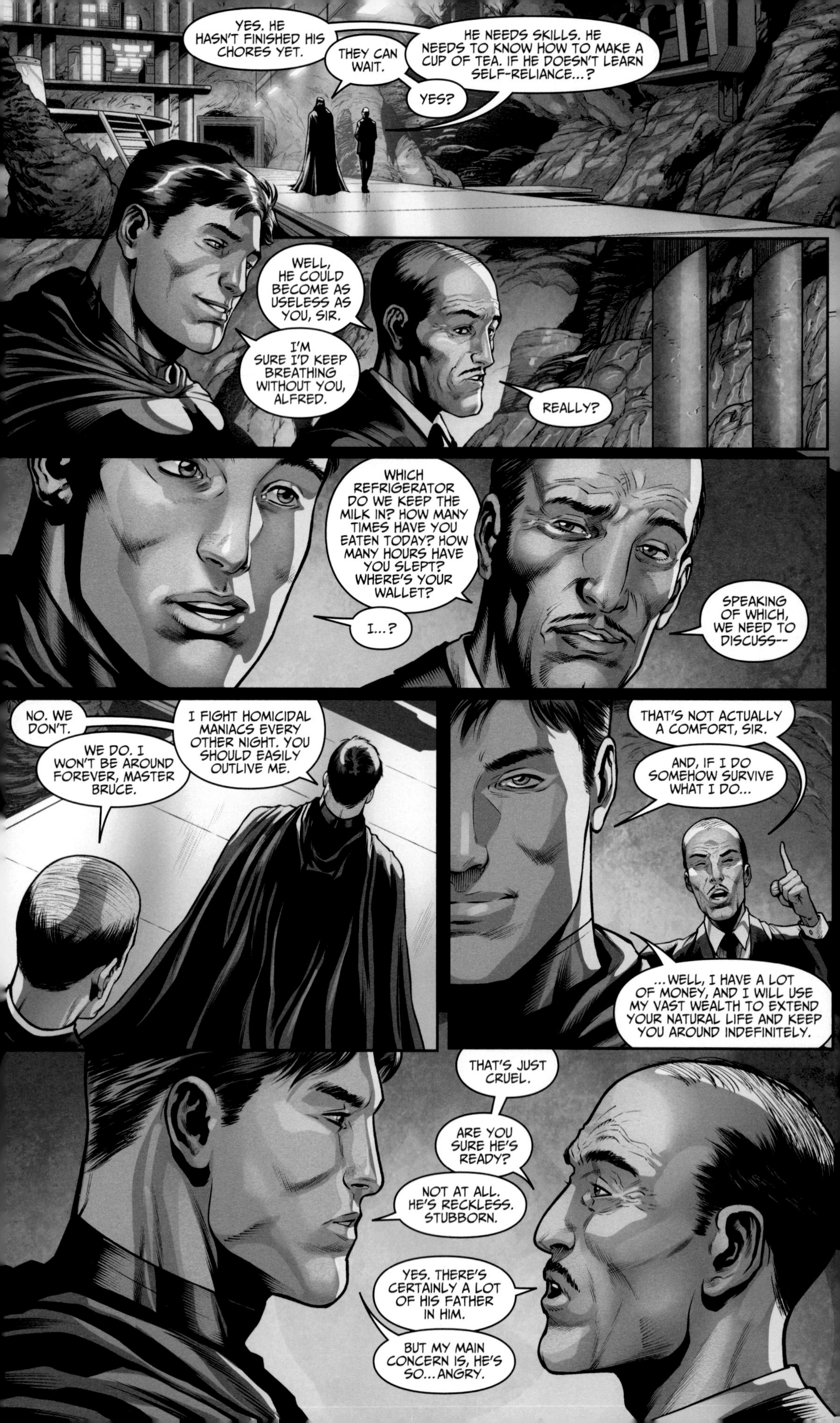
YES. HE HASN'T FINISHED HIS CHORES YET.
THEY CAN WAIT.
HE NEEDS SKILLS. HE NEEDS TO KNOW HOW TO MAKE A CUP OF TEA. IF HE DOESN'T LEARN SELF-RELIANCE...?
YES?
WELL, HE COULD BECOME AS USELESS AS YOU, SIR.
I'M SURE I'D KEEP BREATHING WITHOUT YOU, ALFRED.
REALLY?
WHICH REFRIGERATOR DO WE KEEP THE MILK IN? HOW MANY TIMES HAVE YOU EATEN TODAY? HOW MANY HOURS HAVE YOU SLEPT? WHERE'S YOUR WALLET?
I...?
SPEAKING OF WHICH, WE NEED TO DISCUSS--
NO. WE DON'T.
WE DO. I WON'T BE AROUND FOREVER, MASTER BRUCE.
I FIGHT HOMICIDAL MANIACS EVERY OTHER NIGHT. YOU SHOULD EASILY OUTLIVE ME.
THAT'S NOT ACTUALLY A COMFORT, SIR.
AND, IF I DO SOMEHOW SURVIVE WHAT I DO...
...WELL, I HAVE A LOT OF MONEY, AND I WILL USE MY VAST WEALTH TO EXTEND YOUR NATURAL LIFE AND KEEP YOU AROUND INDEFINITELY.
THAT'S JUST CRUEL.
ARE YOU SURE HE'S READY?
NOT AT ALL. HE'S RECKLESS. STUBBORN.
YES. THERE'S CERTAINLY A LOT OF HIS FATHER IN HIM.
BUT MY MAIN CONCERN IS, HE'S SO...ANGRY.

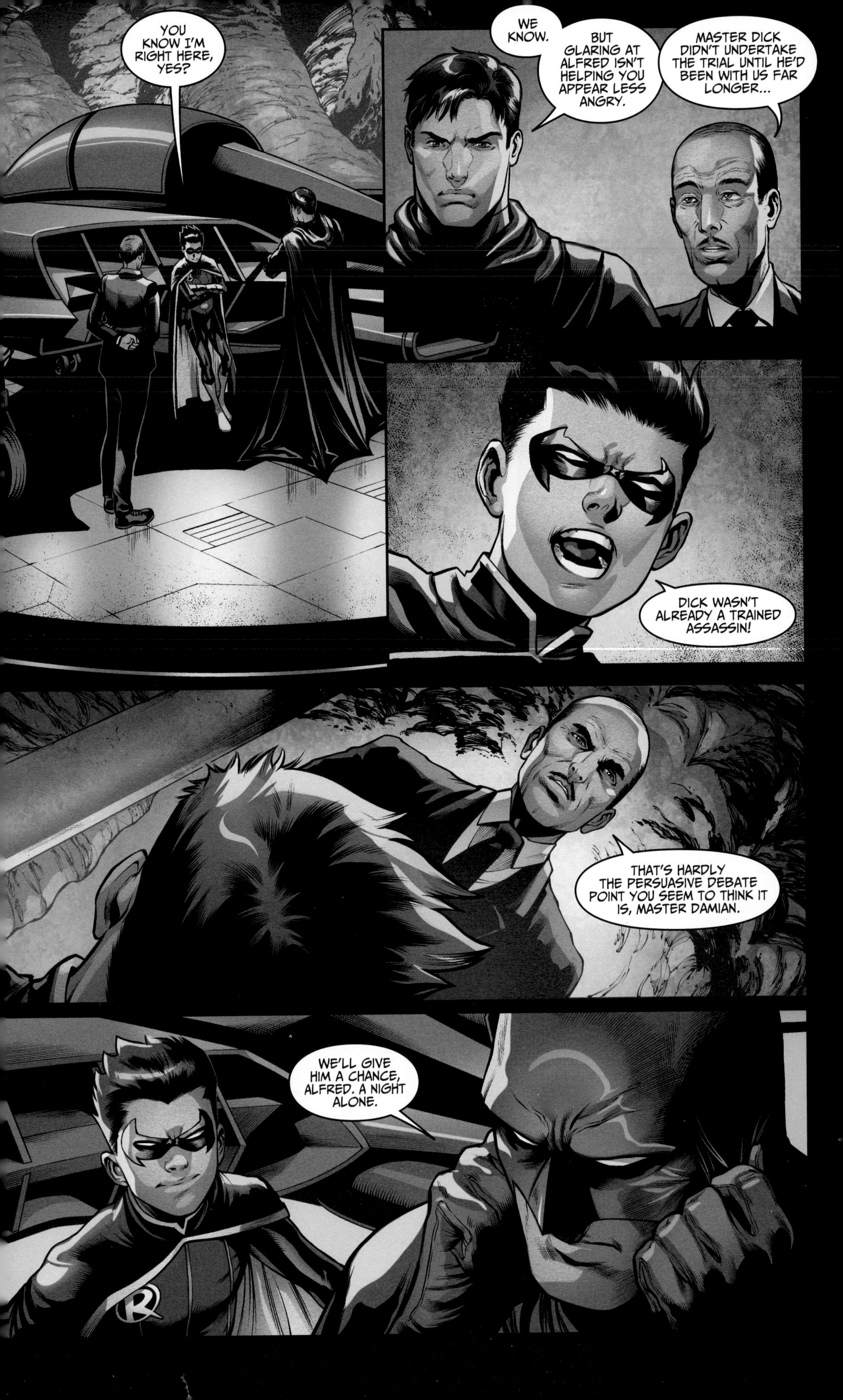
YOU KNOW I'M RIGHT HERE, YES?
WE KNOW.
BUT GLARING AT ALFRED ISN'T HELPING YOU APPEAR LESS ANGRY.
MASTER DICK DIDN'T UNDERTAKE THE TRIAL UNTIL HE'D BEEN WITH US FAR LONGER...
DICK WASN'T ALREADY A TRAINED ASSASSIN!
THAT'S HARDLY THE PERSUASIVE DEBATE POINT YOU SEEM TO THINK IT IS, MASTER DAMIAN.
WE'LL GIVE HIM A CHANCE, ALFRED. A NIGHT ALONE.

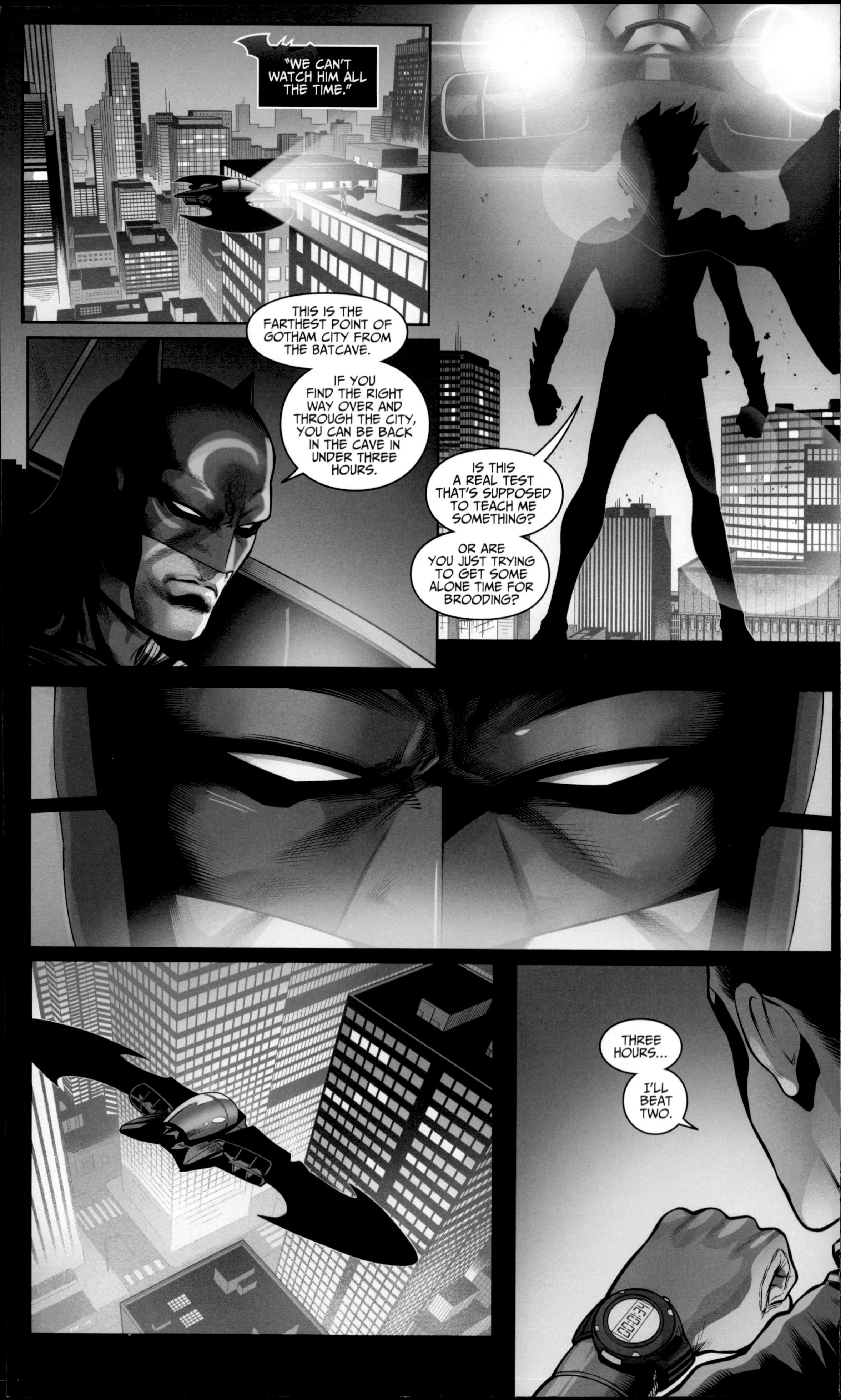
"WE CAN'T WATCH HIM ALL THE TIME."
THIS IS THE FARTHEST POINT OF GOTHAM CITY FROM THE BATCAVE.
IF YOU FIND THE RIGHT WAY OVER AND THROUGH THE CITY, YOU CAN BE BACK IN THE CAVE IN UNDER THREE HOURS.
IS THIS A REAL TEST THAT'S SUPPOSED TO TEACH ME SOMETHING?
OR ARE YOU JUST TRYING TO GET SOME ALONE TIME FOR BROODING?
THREE HOURS...
I'LL BEAT TWO.

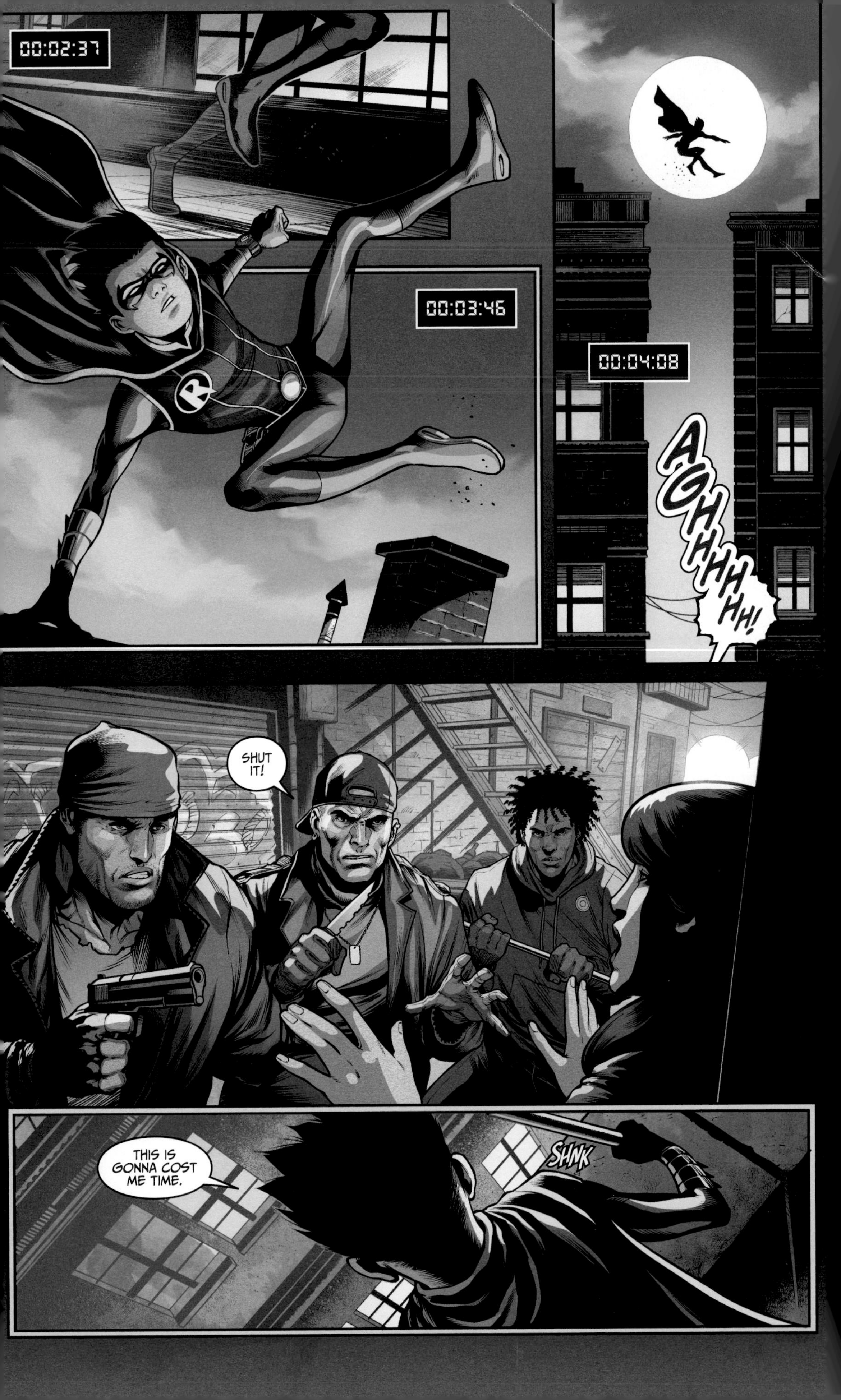
00:02:37
00:03:46
00:04:08
AGHHHHHH!
SHUT IT!
THIS IS GONNA COST ME TIME.
SHNK

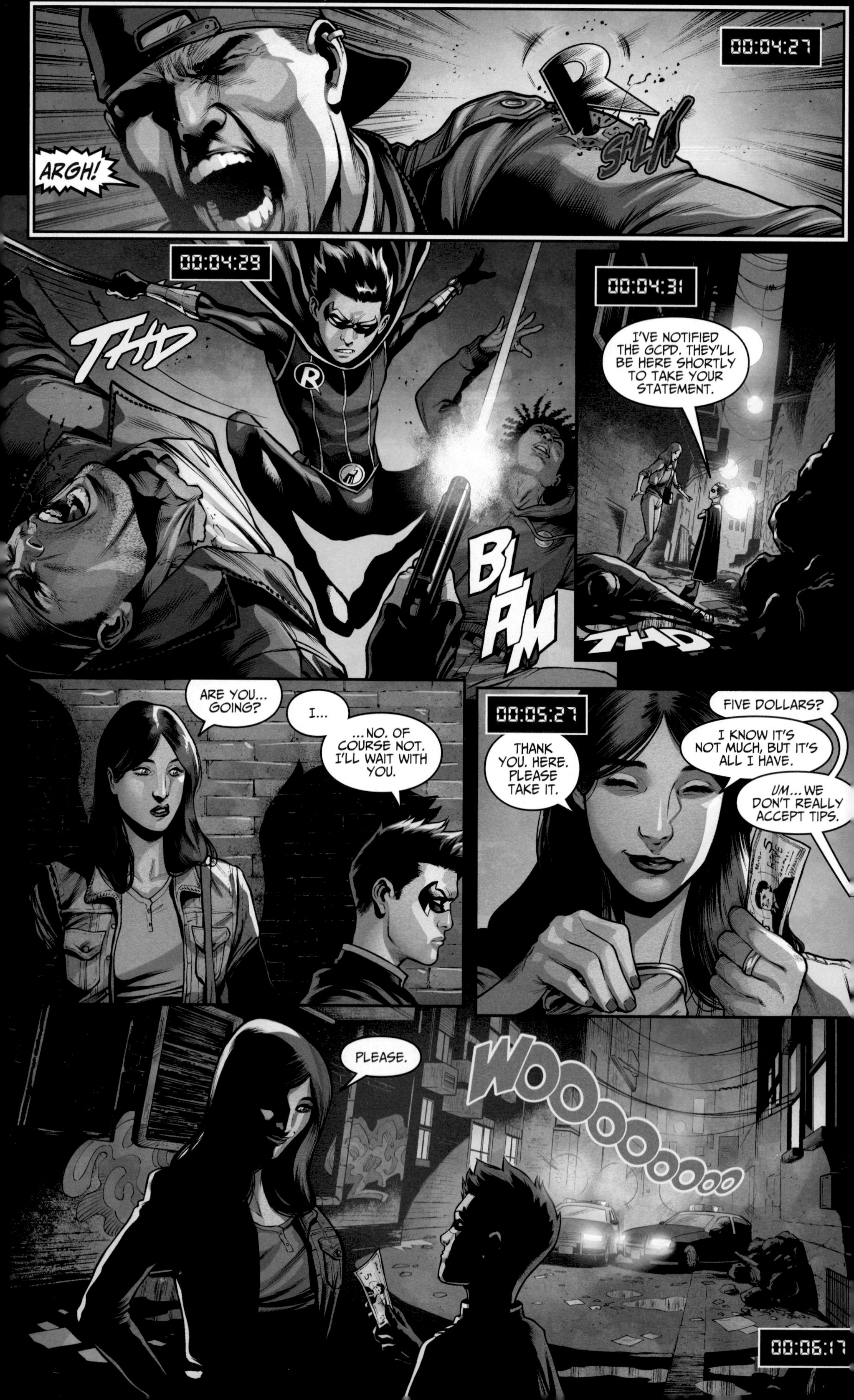
00:04:27
ARGH!
SHLK
00:04:29
THD
BLAM
00:04:31
I'VE NOTIFIED THE GCPD. THEY'LL BE HERE SHORTLY TO TAKE YOUR STATEMENT.
THD
ARE YOU... GOING?
I...
...NO. OF COURSE NOT. I'LL WAIT WITH YOU.
00:05:27
THANK YOU. HERE. PLEASE TAKE IT.
FIVE DOLLARS?
I KNOW IT'S NOT MUCH, BUT IT'S ALL I HAVE.
UM...WE DON'T REALLY ACCEPT TIPS.
PLEASE.
WOOOOOOOOO
00:06:17

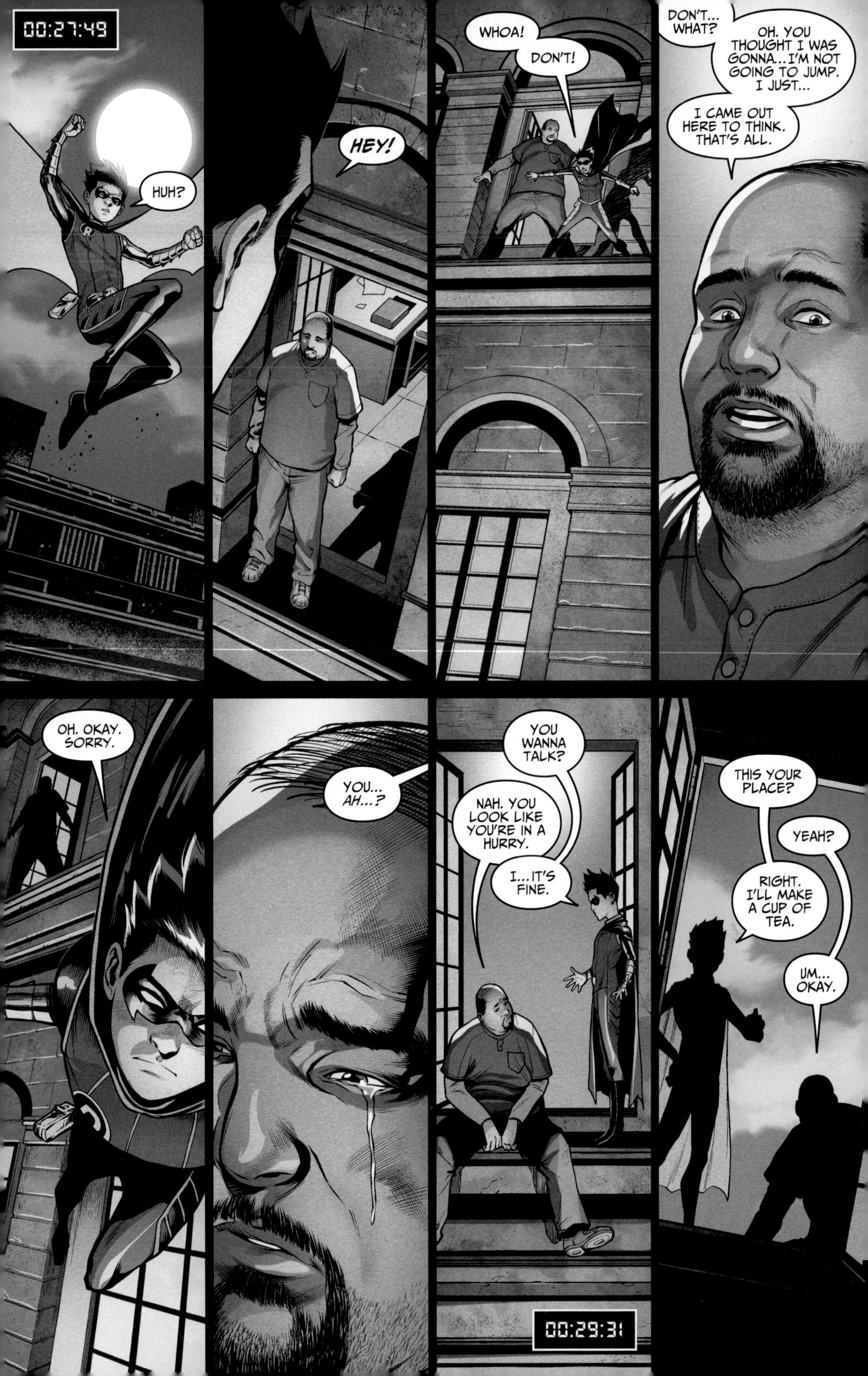
00:27:49
HUH?
HEY!
WHOA!
DON'T!
DON'T... WHAT?
OH. YOU THOUGHT I WAS GONNA...I'M NOT GOING TO JUMP. I JUST...
I CAME OUT HERE TO THINK. THAT'S ALL.
OH. OKAY. SORRY.
YOU... AH...?
YOU WANNA TALK?
NAH. YOU LOOK LIKE YOU'RE IN A HURRY.
I...IT'S FINE.
00:29:31
THIS YOUR PLACE?
YEAH?
RIGHT. I'LL MAKE A CUP OF TEA.
UM... OKAY.

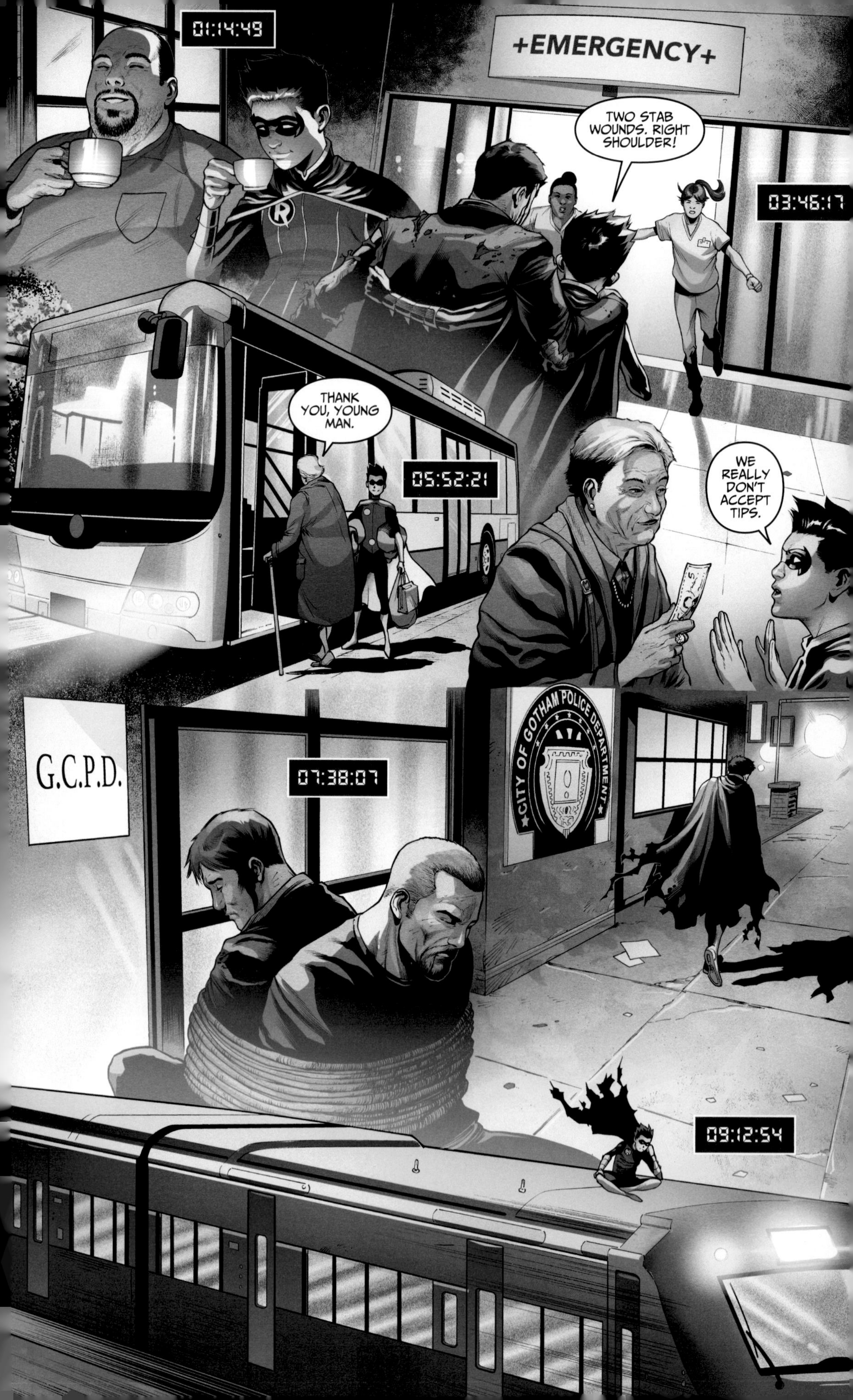
01:14:49
+EMERGENCY+
TWO STAB WOUNDS. RIGHT SHOULDER!
03:46:17
THANK YOU, YOUNG MAN.
05:52:21
WE REALLY DON'T ACCEPT TIPS.
G.C.P.D.
07:38:07
CITY OF GOTHAM POLICE DEPARTMENT
09:12:54

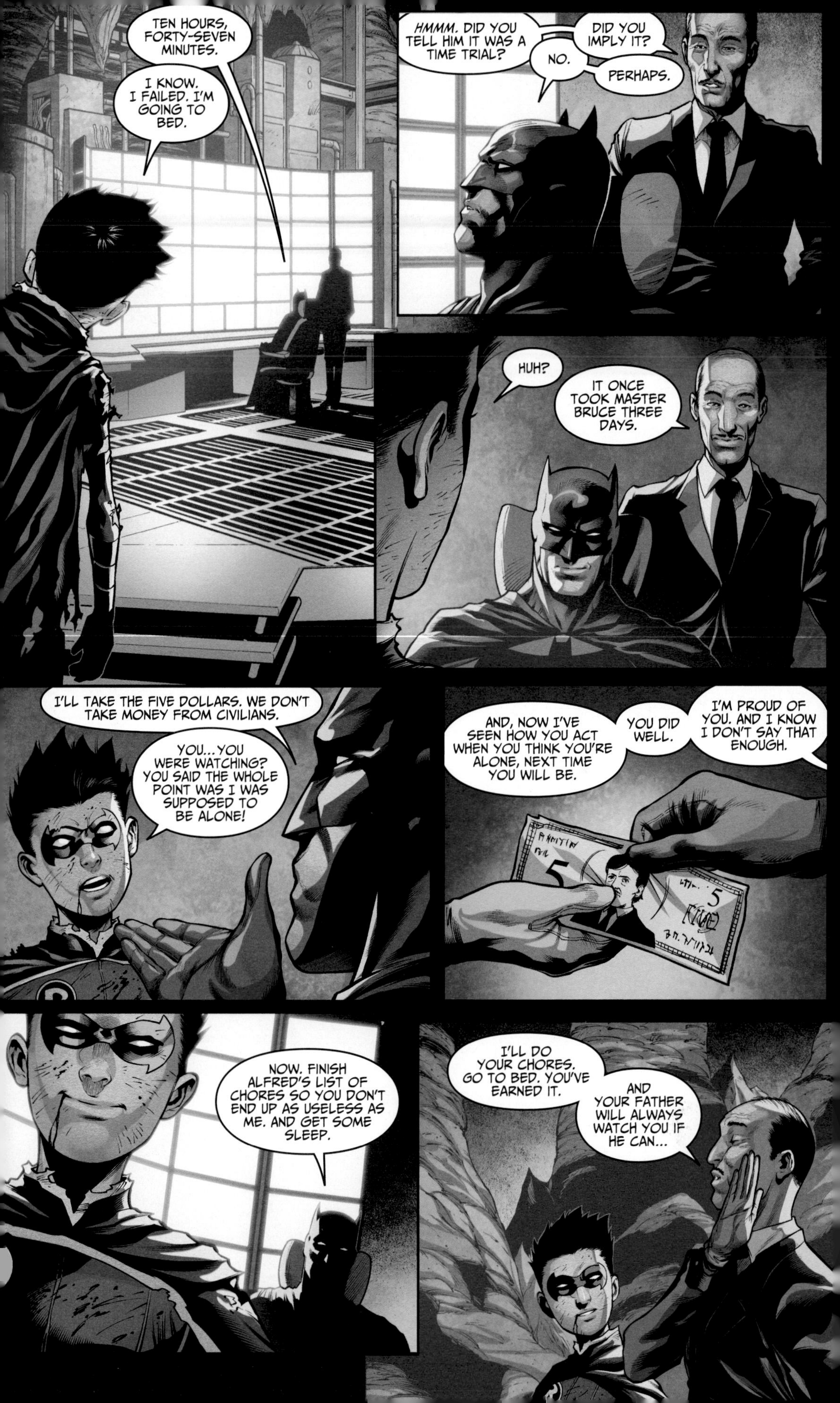
TEN HOURS, FORTY-SEVEN MINUTES.
I KNOW. I FAILED. I'M GOING TO BED.
HMMM. DID YOU TELL HIM IT WAS A TIME TRIAL?
DID YOU IMPLY IT?
NO.
PERHAPS.
HUH?
IT ONCE TOOK MASTER BRUCE THREE DAYS.
I'LL TAKE THE FIVE DOLLARS. WE DON'T TAKE MONEY FROM CIVILIANS.
YOU...YOU WERE WATCHING? YOU SAID THE WHOLE POINT WAS I WAS SUPPOSED TO BE ALONE!
AND, NOW I'VE SEEN HOW YOU ACT WHEN YOU THINK YOU'RE ALONE, NEXT TIME YOU WILL BE.
YOU DID WELL.
I'M PROUD OF YOU. AND I KNOW I DON'T SAY THAT ENOUGH.
NOW. FINISH ALFRED'S LIST OF CHORES SO YOU DON'T END UP AS USELESS AS ME. AND GET SOME SLEEP.
I'LL DO YOUR CHORES. GO TO BED. YOU'VE EARNED IT.
AND YOUR FATHER WILL ALWAYS WATCH YOU IF HE CAN...

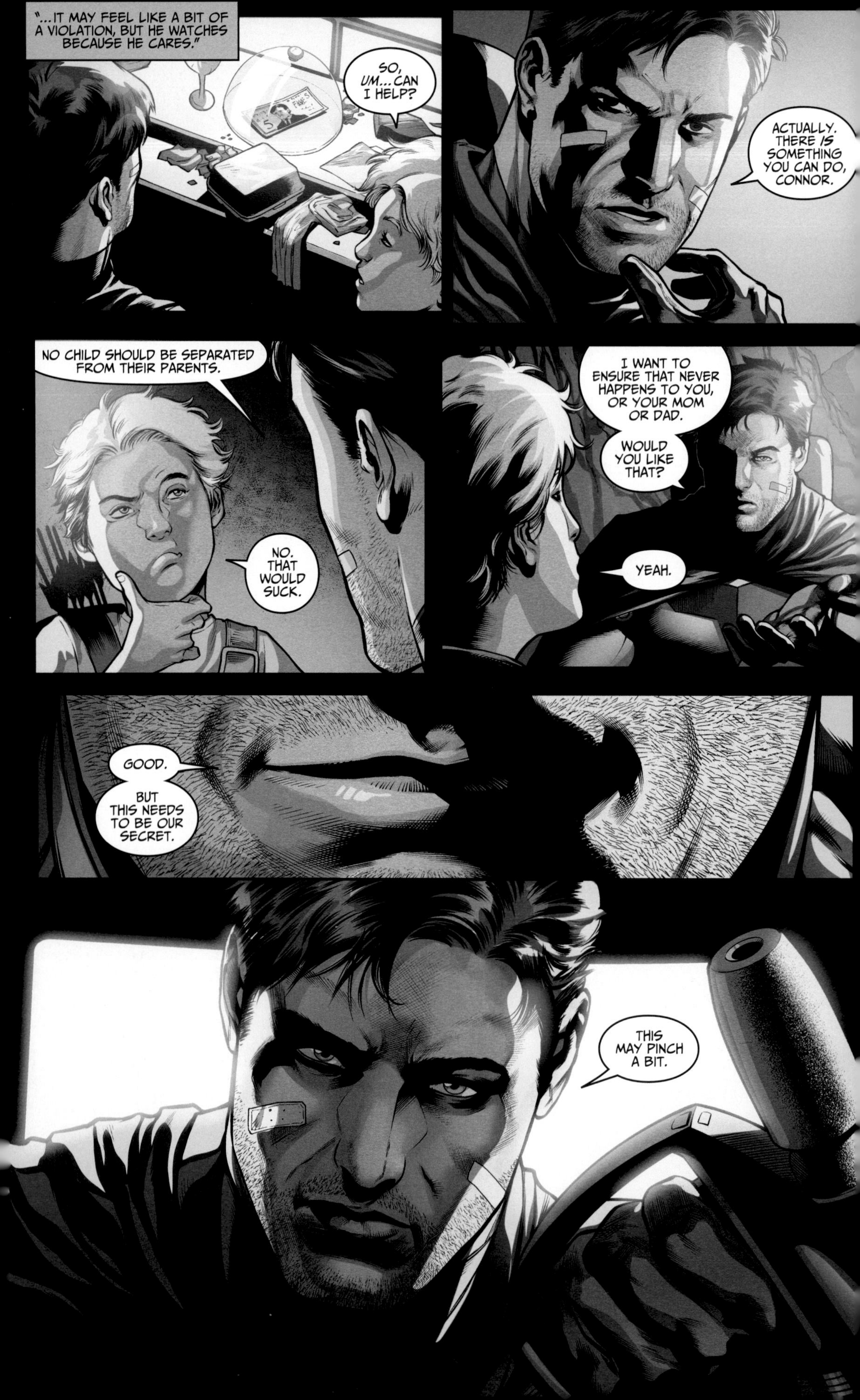
"...IT MAY FEEL LIKE A BIT OF A VIOLATION, BUT HE WATCHES BECAUSE HE CARES."
SO, UM... CAN I HELP?
ACTUALLY. THERE *IS* SOMETHING YOU CAN DO, CONNOR.
NO CHILD SHOULD BE SEPARATED FROM THEIR PARENTS.
NO. THAT WOULD SUCK.
I WANT TO ENSURE THAT NEVER HAPPENS TO YOU, OR YOUR MOM OR DAD.
WOULD YOU LIKE THAT?
YEAH.
GOOD.
BUT THIS NEEDS TO BE OUR SECRET.
THIS MAY PINCH A BIT.

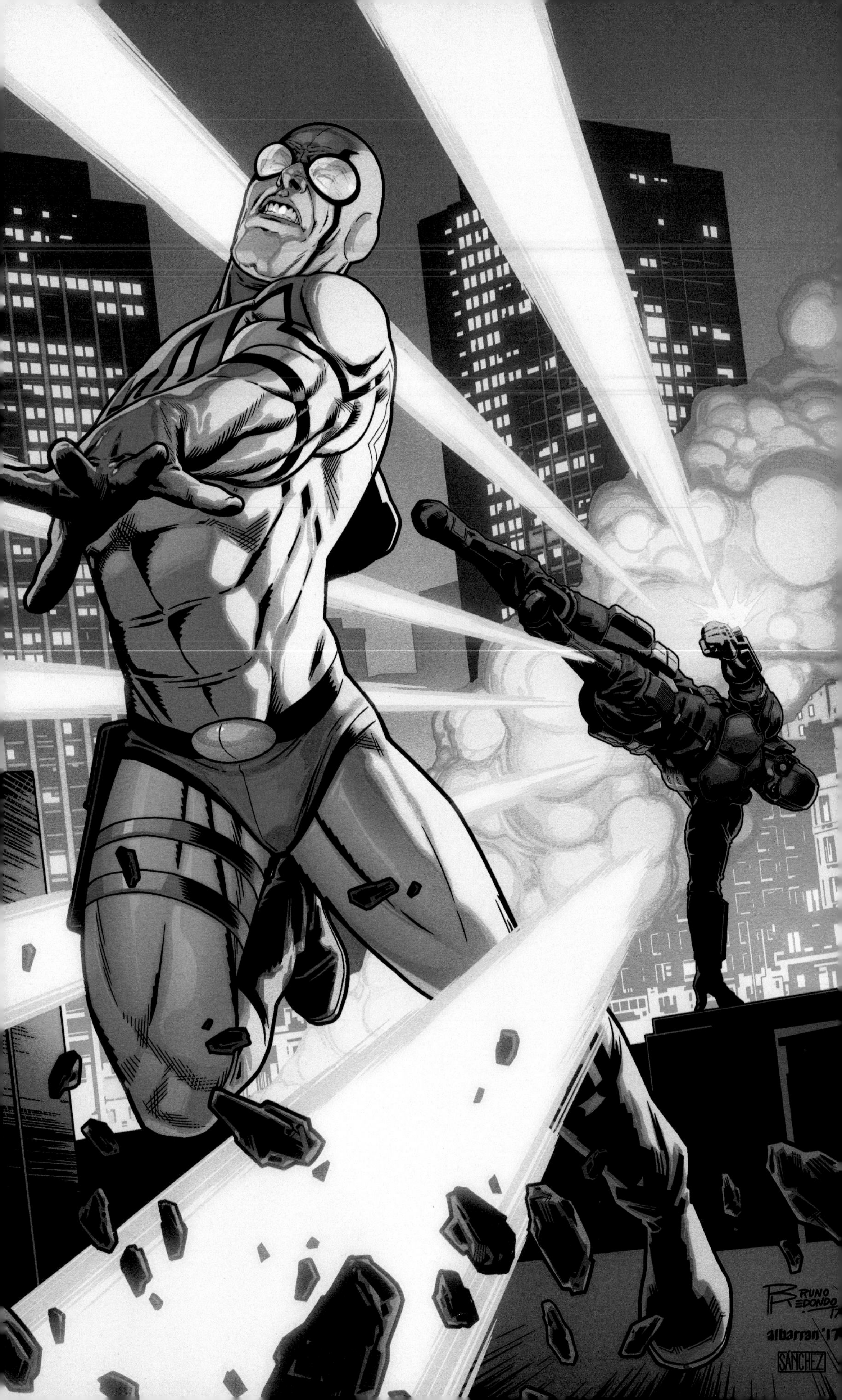
BRUNO REDONDO
albarran'17
SANCHEZ

"Hostile Takeover"

Bruno Redondo Layouts **Vicente Cifuentes** Finishes

Rex Lokus Colorist Cover art by **Bruno Redondo, Juan Albarran** and **Alejandro Sanchez**

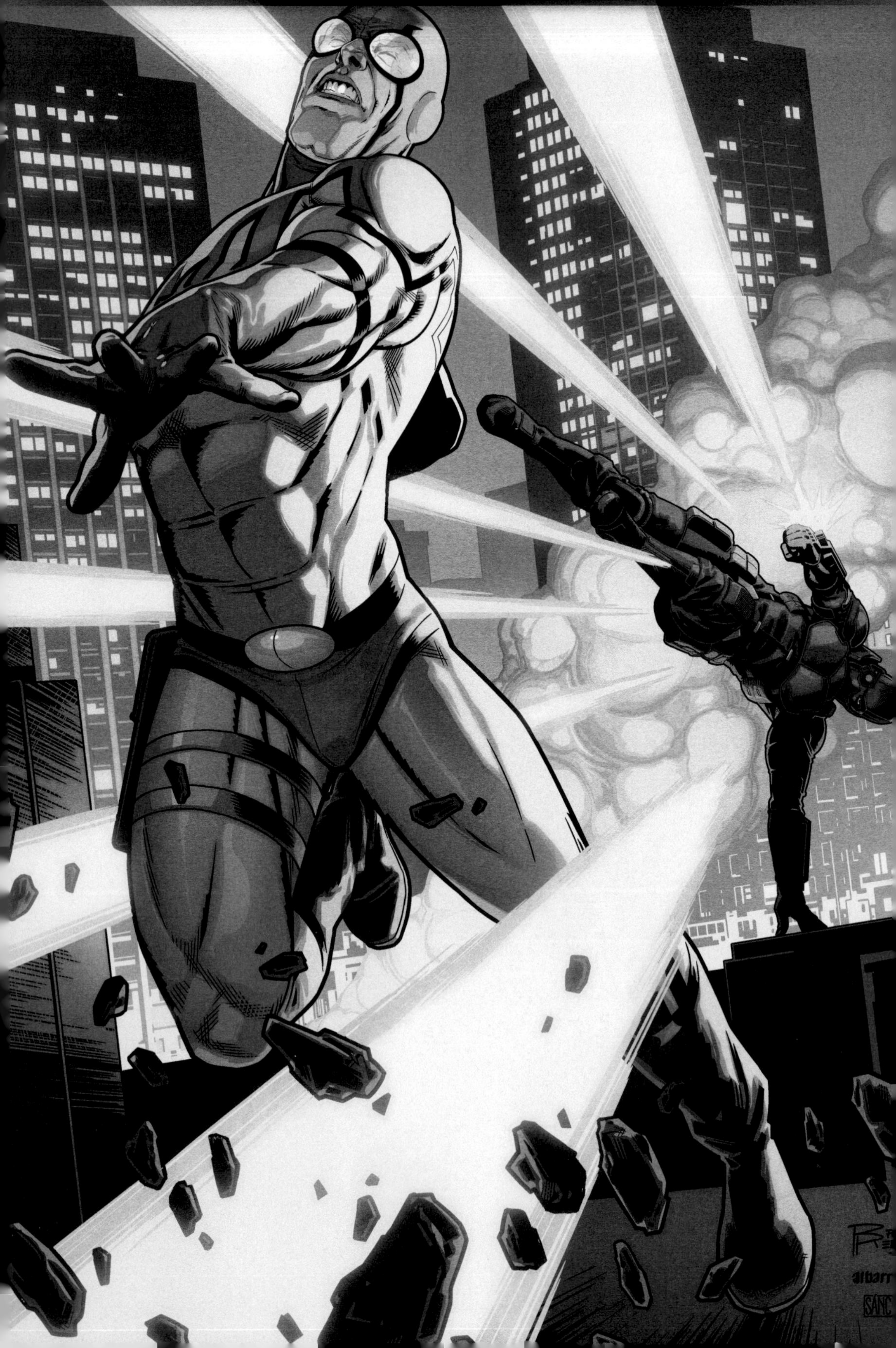

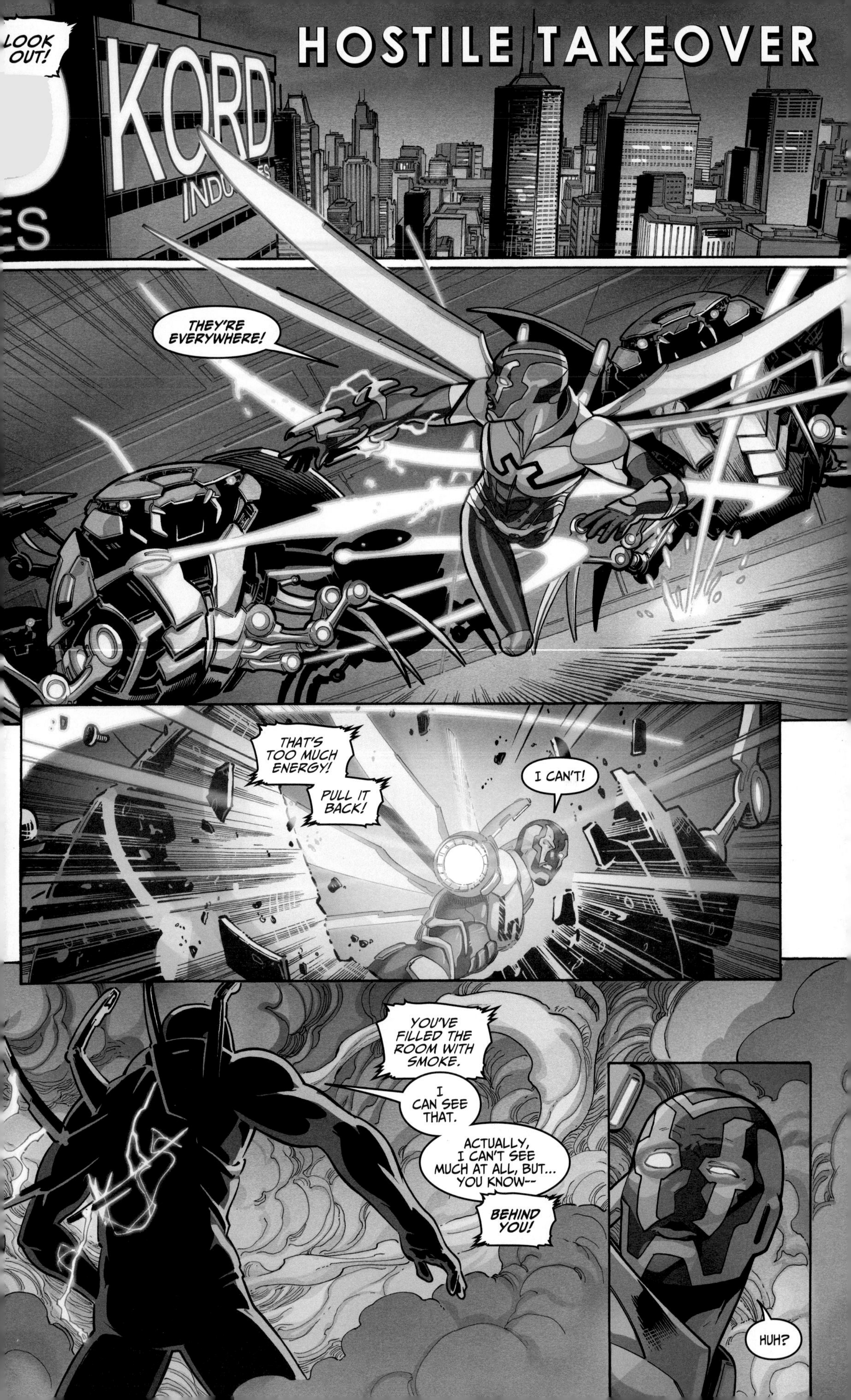

LOOK OUT!
HOSTILE TAKEOVER
KORD
INDU
ES
THEY'RE EVERYWHERE!
THAT'S TOO MUCH ENERGY!
PULL IT BACK!
I CAN'T!
YOU'VE FILLED THE ROOM WITH SMOKE.
I CAN SEE THAT.
ACTUALLY, I CAN'T SEE MUCH AT ALL, BUT... YOU KNOW--
BEHIND YOU!
HUH?

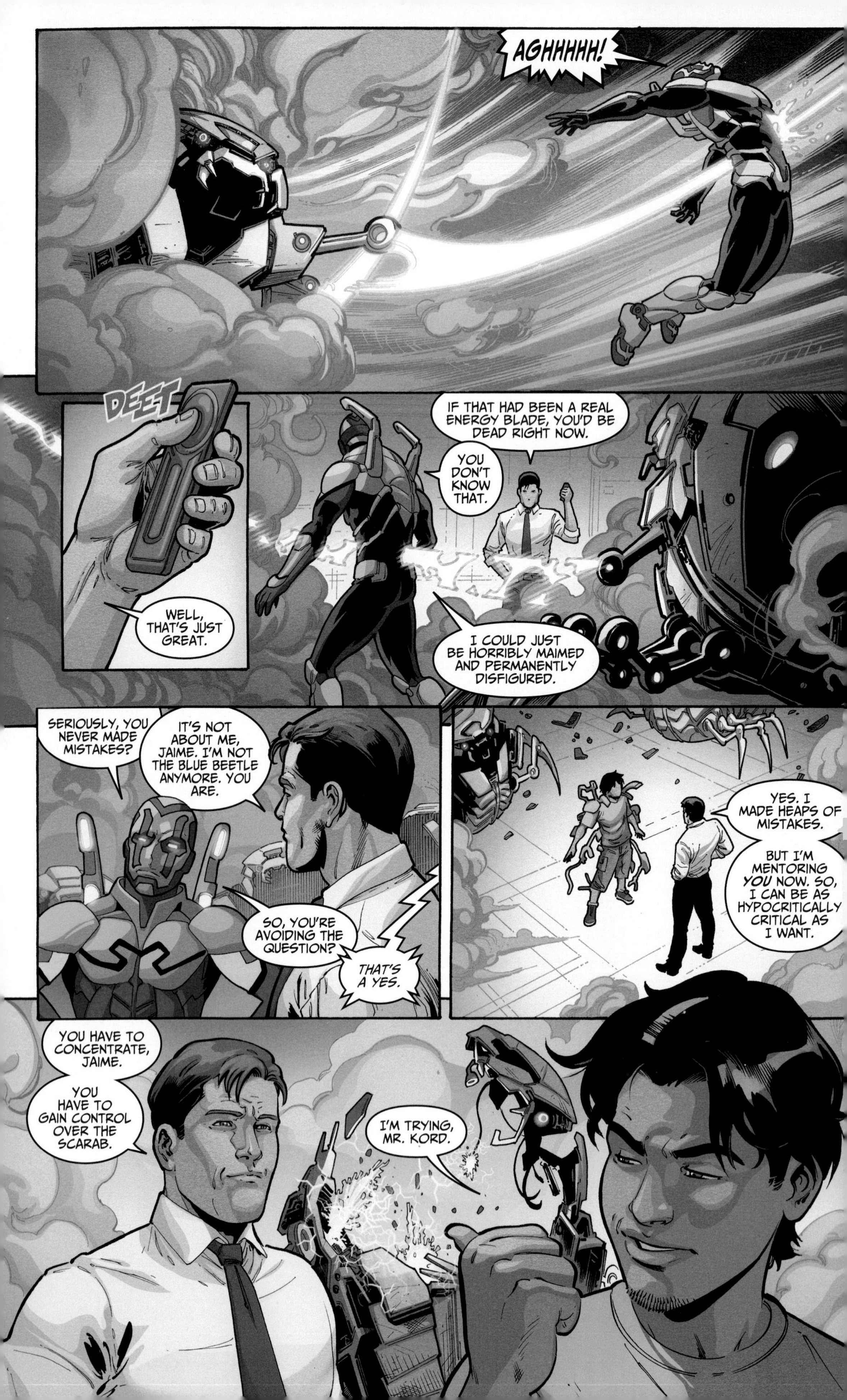
AGHHHHH!
DEET
IF THAT HAD BEEN A REAL ENERGY BLADE, YOU'D BE DEAD RIGHT NOW.
YOU DON'T KNOW THAT.
WELL, THAT'S JUST GREAT.
I COULD JUST BE HORRIBLY MAIMED AND PERMANENTLY DISFIGURED.
SERIOUSLY, YOU NEVER MADE MISTAKES?
IT'S NOT ABOUT ME, JAIME. I'M NOT THE BLUE BEETLE ANYMORE. YOU ARE.
SO, YOU'RE AVOIDING THE QUESTION?
THAT'S A YES.
YES. I MADE HEAPS OF MISTAKES.
BUT I'M MENTORING *YOU* NOW. SO, I CAN BE AS HYPOCRITICALLY CRITICAL AS I WANT.
YOU HAVE TO CONCENTRATE, JAIME.
YOU HAVE TO GAIN CONTROL OVER THE SCARAB.
I'M TRYING, MR. KORD.

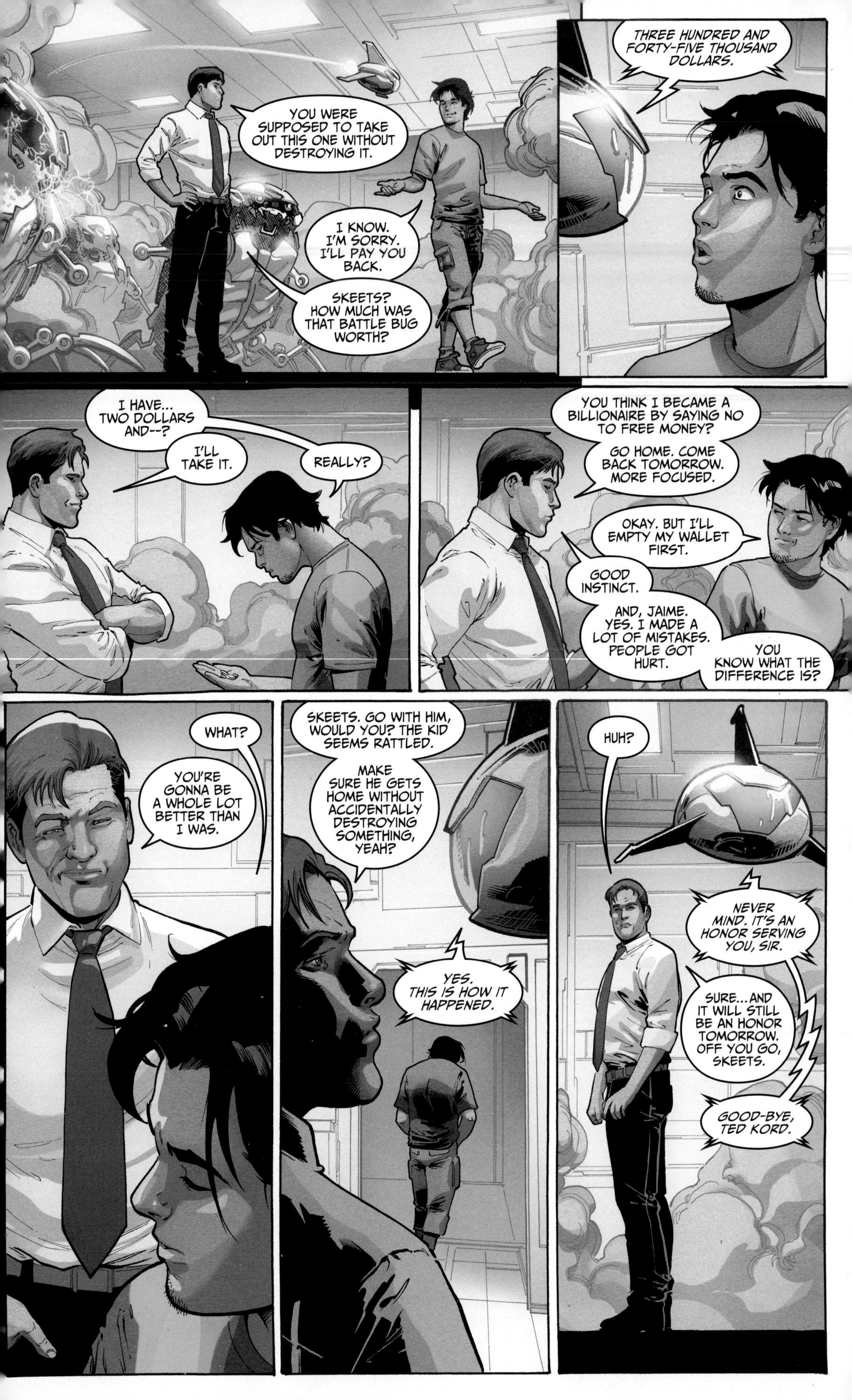
YOU WERE SUPPOSED TO TAKE OUT THIS ONE WITHOUT DESTROYING IT.
I KNOW. I'M SORRY. I'LL PAY YOU BACK.
SKEETS? HOW MUCH WAS THAT BATTLE BUG WORTH?
THREE HUNDRED AND FORTY-FIVE THOUSAND DOLLARS.
I HAVE... TWO DOLLARS AND--?
I'LL TAKE IT.
REALLY?
YOU THINK I BECAME A BILLIONAIRE BY SAYING NO TO FREE MONEY?
GO HOME. COME BACK TOMORROW. MORE FOCUSED.
OKAY. BUT I'LL EMPTY MY WALLET FIRST.
GOOD INSTINCT.
AND, JAIME. YES. I MADE A LOT OF MISTAKES. PEOPLE GOT HURT.
YOU KNOW WHAT THE DIFFERENCE IS?
WHAT?
YOU'RE GONNA BE A WHOLE LOT BETTER THAN I WAS.
SKEETS. GO WITH HIM, WOULD YOU? THE KID SEEMS RATTLED.
MAKE SURE HE GETS HOME WITHOUT ACCIDENTALLY DESTROYING SOMETHING, YEAH?
YES. THIS IS HOW IT HAPPENED.
HUH?
NEVER MIND. IT'S AN HONOR SERVING YOU, SIR.
SURE...AND IT WILL STILL BE AN HONOR TOMORROW. OFF YOU GO, SKEETS.
GOOD-BYE, TED KORD.

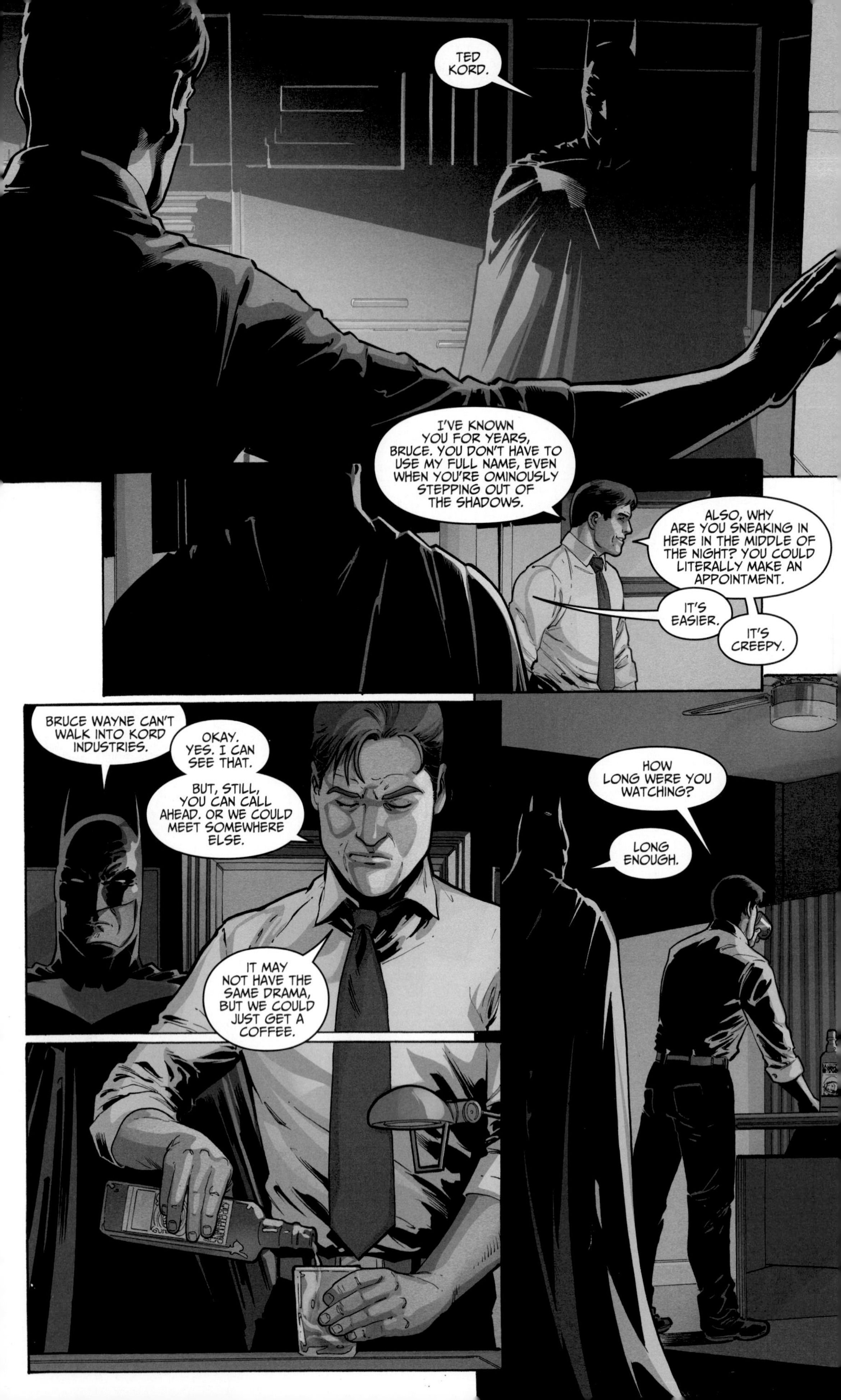
TED KORD.
I'VE KNOWN YOU FOR YEARS, BRUCE. YOU DON'T HAVE TO USE MY FULL NAME, EVEN WHEN YOU'RE OMINOUSLY STEPPING OUT OF THE SHADOWS.
ALSO, WHY ARE YOU SNEAKING IN HERE IN THE MIDDLE OF THE NIGHT? YOU COULD LITERALLY MAKE AN APPOINTMENT.
IT'S EASIER.
IT'S CREEPY.
BRUCE WAYNE CAN'T WALK INTO KORD INDUSTRIES.
OKAY. YES. I CAN SEE THAT.
BUT, STILL, YOU CAN CALL AHEAD. OR WE COULD MEET SOMEWHERE ELSE.
IT MAY NOT HAVE THE SAME DRAMA, BUT WE COULD JUST GET A COFFEE.
HOW LONG WERE YOU WATCHING?
LONG ENOUGH.

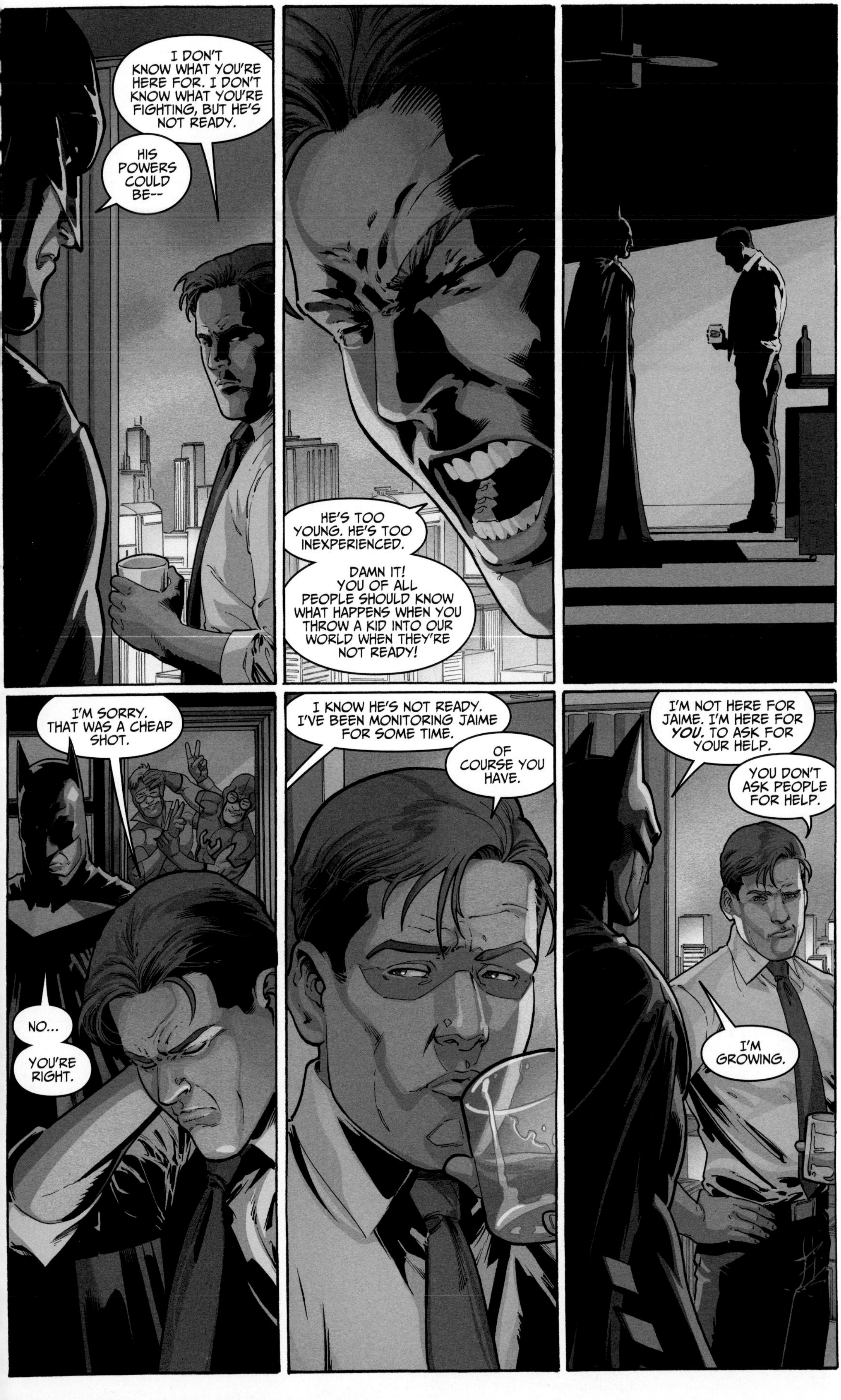

I DON'T KNOW WHAT YOU'RE HERE FOR. I DON'T KNOW WHAT YOU'RE FIGHTING, BUT HE'S NOT READY.
HIS POWERS COULD BE--
HE'S TOO YOUNG. HE'S TOO INEXPERIENCED.
DAMN IT! YOU OF ALL PEOPLE SHOULD KNOW WHAT HAPPENS WHEN YOU THROW A KID INTO OUR WORLD WHEN THEY'RE NOT READY!
I'M SORRY. THAT WAS A CHEAP SHOT.
NO...
YOU'RE RIGHT.
I KNOW HE'S NOT READY. I'VE BEEN MONITORING JAIME FOR SOME TIME.
OF COURSE YOU HAVE.
I'M NOT HERE FOR JAIME. I'M HERE FOR *YOU.* TO ASK FOR YOUR HELP.
YOU DON'T ASK PEOPLE FOR HELP.
I'M GROWING.

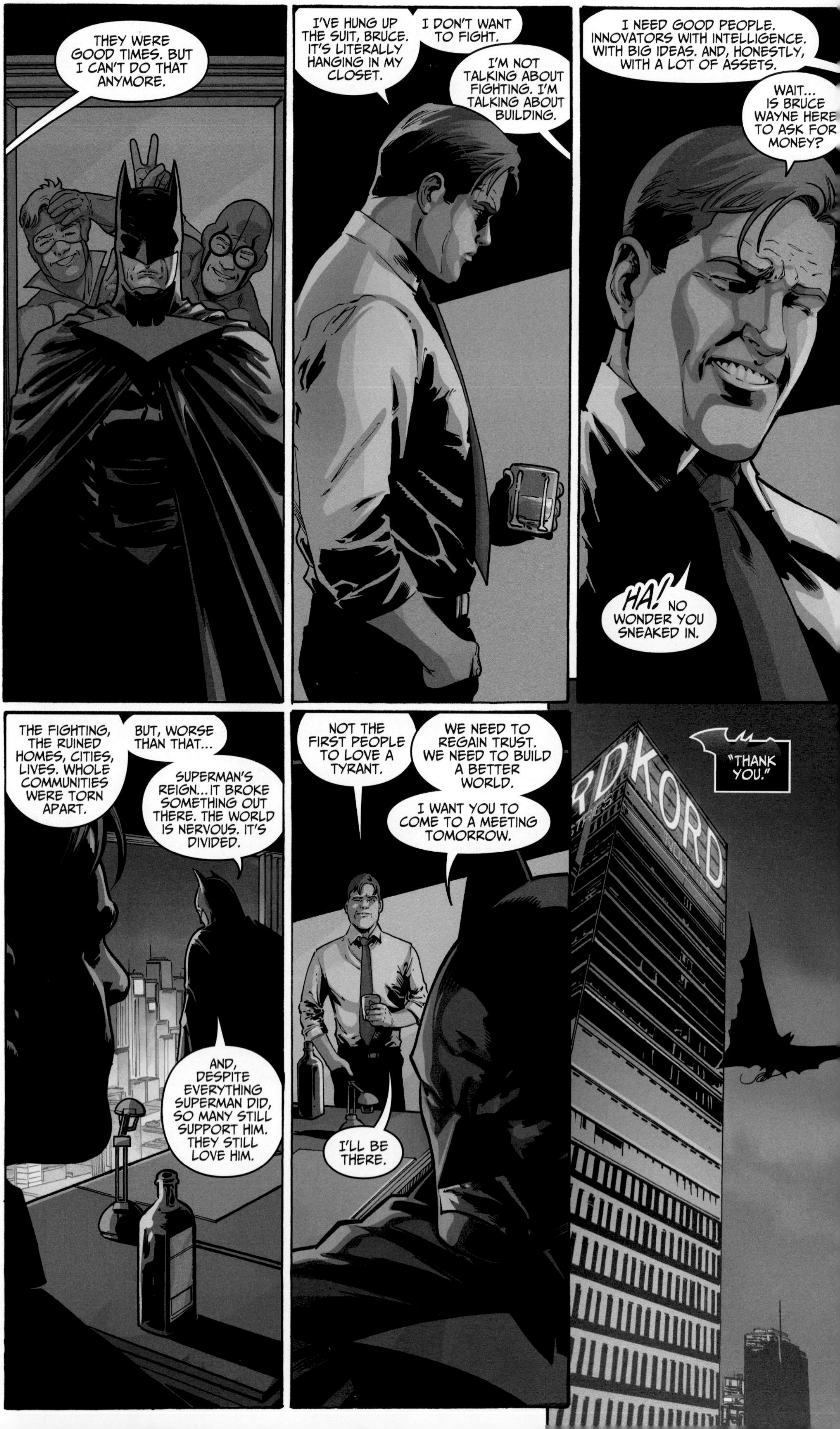
THEY WERE GOOD TIMES. BUT I CAN'T DO THAT ANYMORE.
I'VE HUNG UP THE SUIT, BRUCE. IT'S LITERALLY HANGING IN MY CLOSET.
I DON'T WANT TO FIGHT.
I'M NOT TALKING ABOUT FIGHTING. I'M TALKING ABOUT BUILDING.
I NEED GOOD PEOPLE. INNOVATORS WITH INTELLIGENCE. WITH BIG IDEAS. AND, HONESTLY, WITH A LOT OF ASSETS.
WAIT... IS BRUCE WAYNE HERE TO ASK FOR MONEY?
HA! NO WONDER YOU SNEAKED IN.
THE FIGHTING, THE RUINED HOMES, CITIES, LIVES. WHOLE COMMUNITIES WERE TORN APART.
BUT, WORSE THAN THAT...
SUPERMAN'S REIGN...IT BROKE SOMETHING OUT THERE. THE WORLD IS NERVOUS. IT'S DIVIDED.
AND, DESPITE EVERYTHING SUPERMAN DID, SO MANY STILL SUPPORT HIM. THEY STILL LOVE HIM.
NOT THE FIRST PEOPLE TO LOVE A TYRANT.
WE NEED TO REGAIN TRUST. WE NEED TO BUILD A BETTER WORLD.
I WANT YOU TO COME TO A MEETING TOMORROW.
I'LL BE THERE.
RDKORD
"THANK YOU."

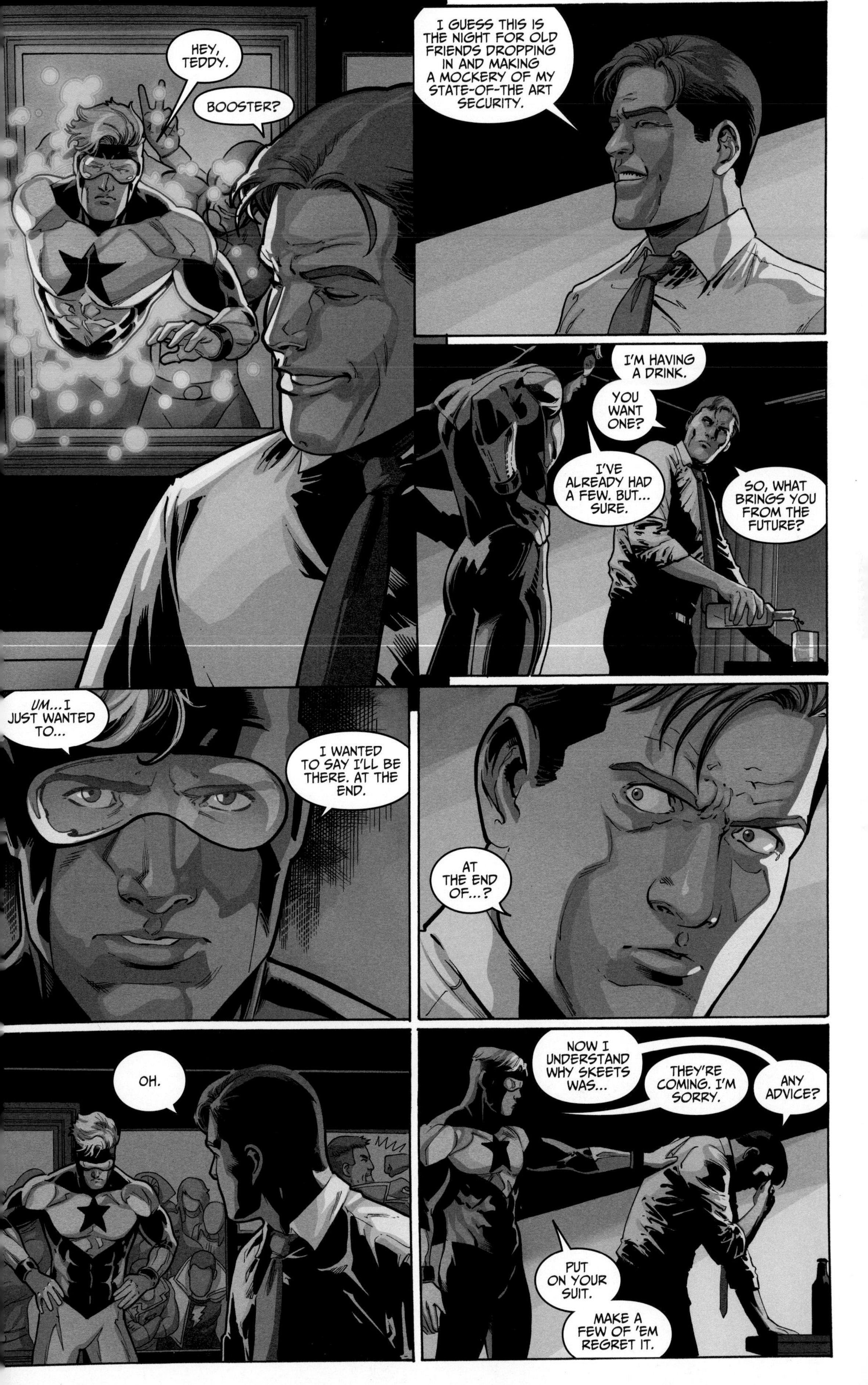
HEY, TEDDY.
BOOSTER?
I GUESS THIS IS THE NIGHT FOR OLD FRIENDS DROPPING IN AND MAKING A MOCKERY OF MY STATE-OF-THE ART SECURITY.
I'M HAVING A DRINK.
YOU WANT ONE?
I'VE ALREADY HAD A FEW. BUT... SURE.
SO, WHAT BRINGS YOU FROM THE FUTURE?
UM...I JUST WANTED TO...
I WANTED TO SAY I'LL BE THERE. AT THE END.
AT THE END OF...?
OH.
NOW I UNDERSTAND WHY SKEETS WAS...
THEY'RE COMING. I'M SORRY.
ANY ADVICE?
PUT ON YOUR SUIT.
MAKE A FEW OF 'EM REGRET IT.

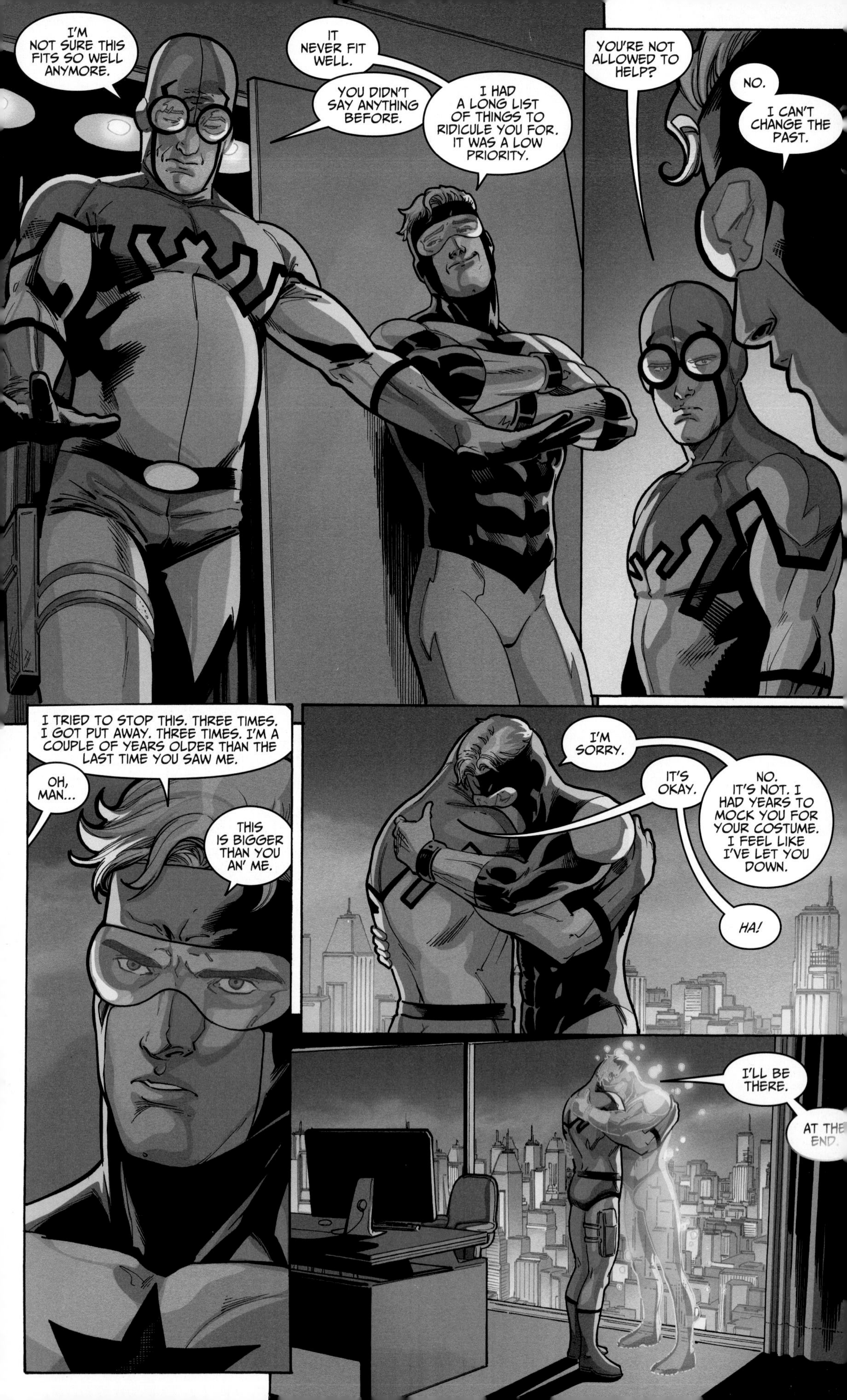
I'M NOT SURE THIS FITS SO WELL ANYMORE.
IT NEVER FIT WELL.
YOU DIDN'T SAY ANYTHING BEFORE.
I HAD A LONG LIST OF THINGS TO RIDICULE YOU FOR. IT WAS A LOW PRIORITY.
YOU'RE NOT ALLOWED TO HELP?
NO.
I CAN'T CHANGE THE PAST.
I TRIED TO STOP THIS. THREE TIMES. I GOT PUT AWAY. THREE TIMES. I'M A COUPLE OF YEARS OLDER THAN THE LAST TIME YOU SAW ME.
OH, MAN...
THIS IS BIGGER THAN YOU AN' ME.
I'M SORRY.
IT'S OKAY.
NO. IT'S NOT. I HAD YEARS TO MOCK YOU FOR YOUR COSTUME. I FEEL LIKE I'VE LET YOU DOWN.
HA!
I'LL BE THERE.
AT THE END.

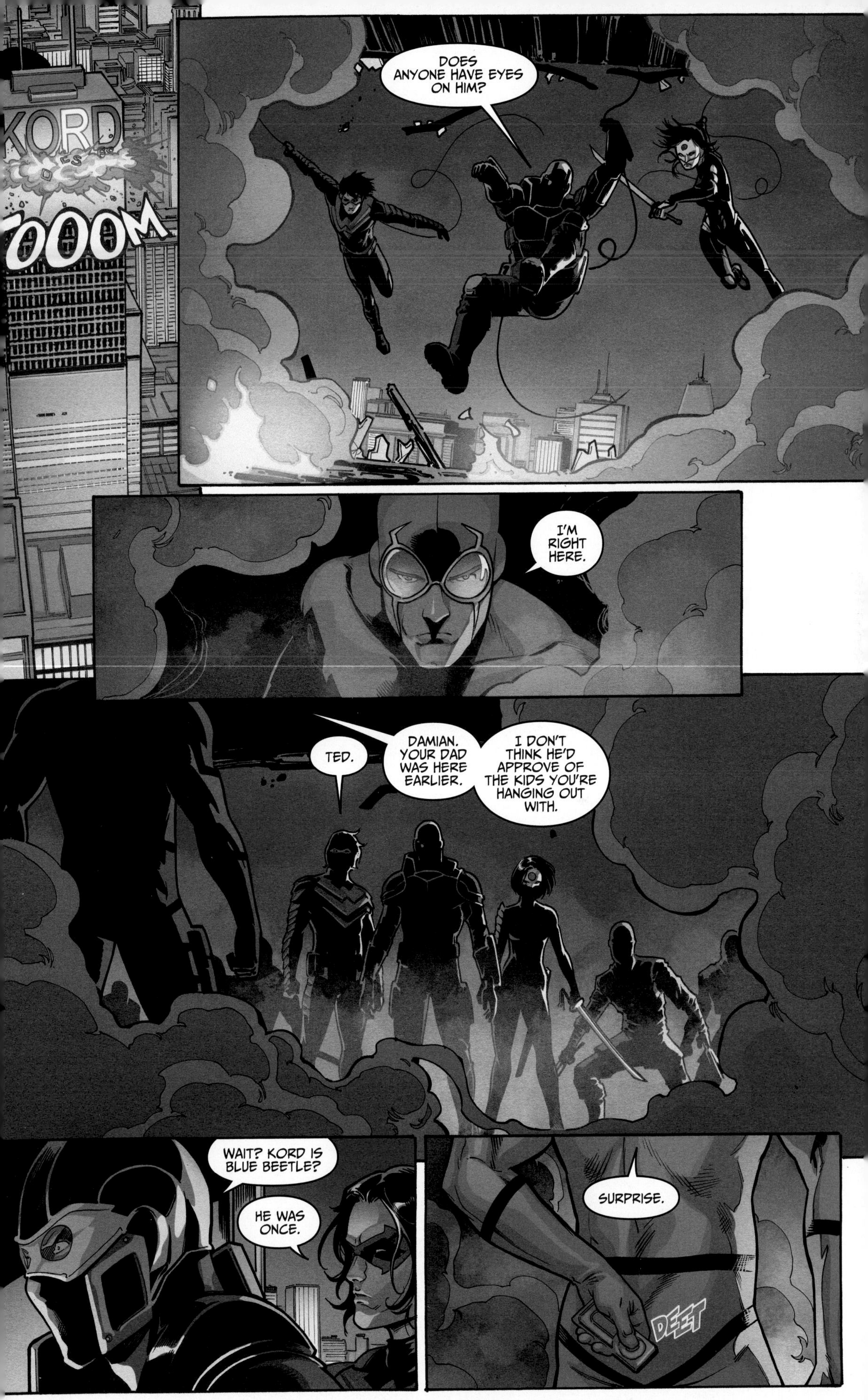
KORD
OOOM
DOES ANYONE HAVE EYES ON HIM?
I'M RIGHT HERE.
TED.
DAMIAN. YOUR DAD WAS HERE EARLIER.
I DON'T THINK HE'D APPROVE OF THE KIDS YOU'RE HANGING OUT WITH.
WAIT? KORD IS BLUE BEETLE?
HE WAS ONCE.
SURPRISE.
DEET

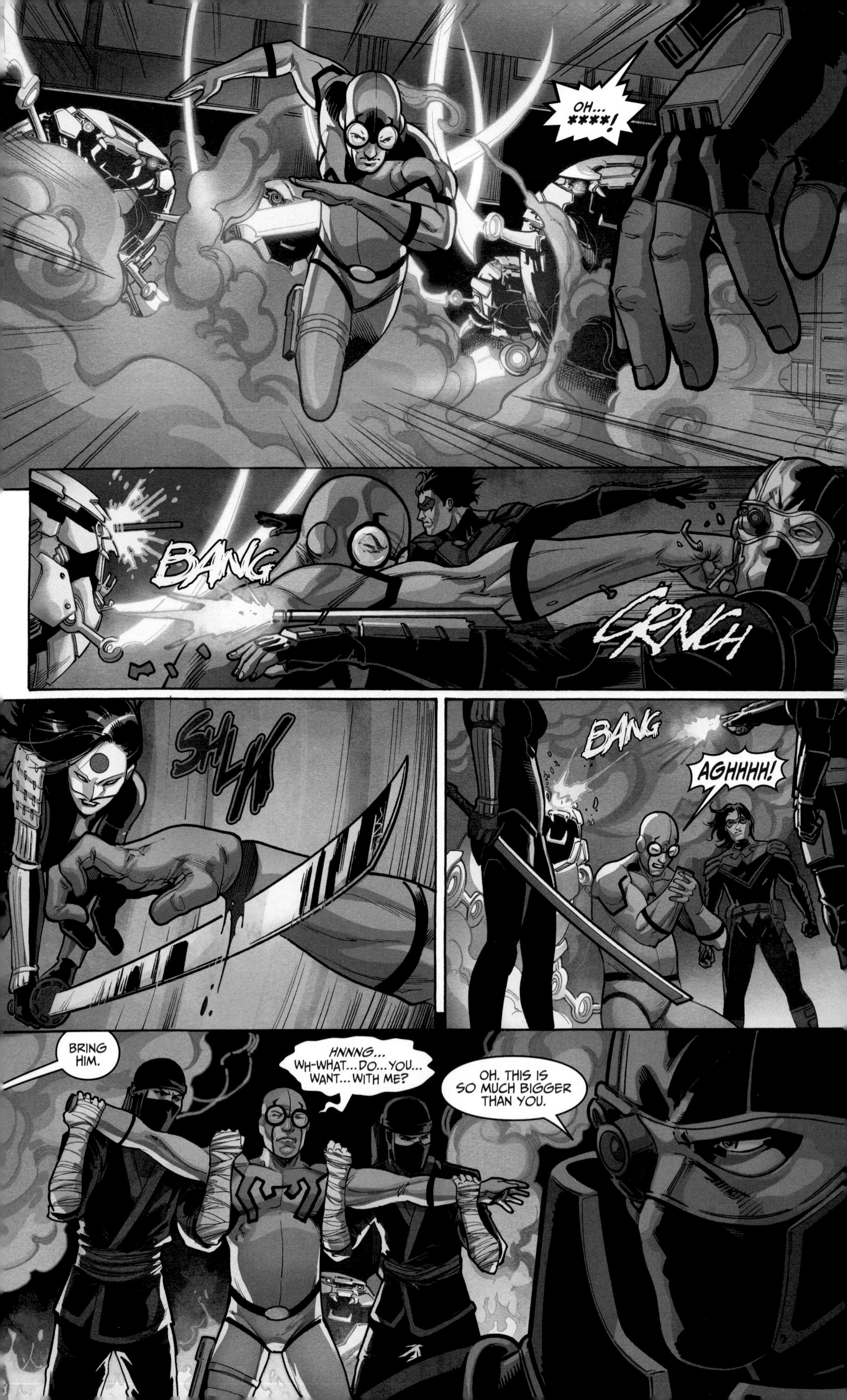
OH... ****!
BANG
CRNCH
SHLK
BANG
AGHHHH!
BRING HIM.
HNNNG... WH-WHAT...DO...YOU... WANT...WITH ME?
OH. THIS IS SO MUCH BIGGER THAN YOU.

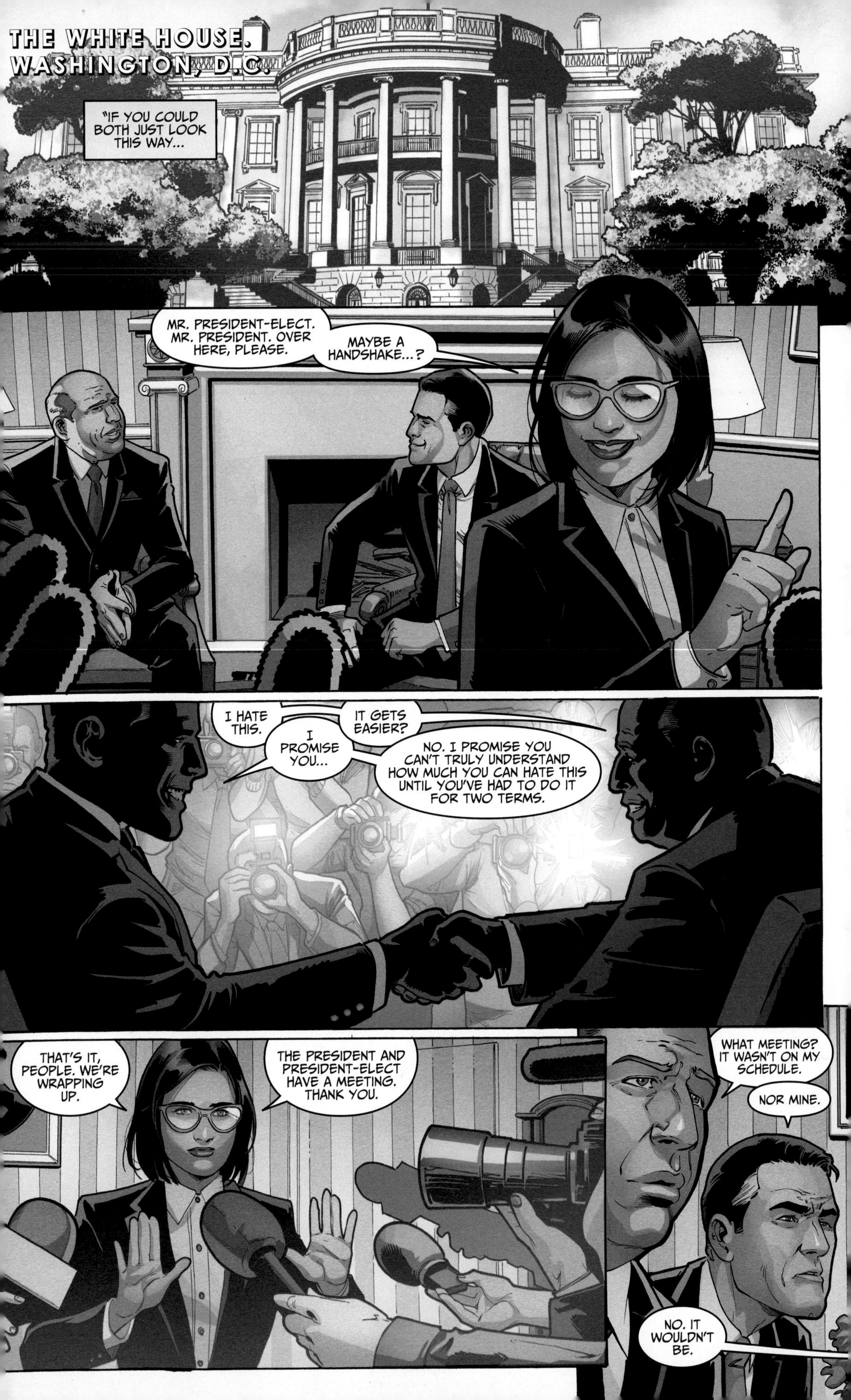
THE WHITE HOUSE. WASHINGTON, D.C.
"IF YOU COULD BOTH JUST LOOK THIS WAY...
MR. PRESIDENT-ELECT. MR. PRESIDENT. OVER HERE, PLEASE.
MAYBE A HANDSHAKE...?
I HATE THIS.
IT GETS EASIER?
I PROMISE YOU...
NO. I PROMISE YOU CAN'T TRULY UNDERSTAND HOW MUCH YOU CAN HATE THIS UNTIL YOU'VE HAD TO DO IT FOR TWO TERMS.
THAT'S IT, PEOPLE. WE'RE WRAPPING UP.
THE PRESIDENT AND PRESIDENT-ELECT HAVE A MEETING. THANK YOU.
WHAT MEETING? IT WASN'T ON MY SCHEDULE.
NOR MINE.
NO. IT WOULDN'T BE.

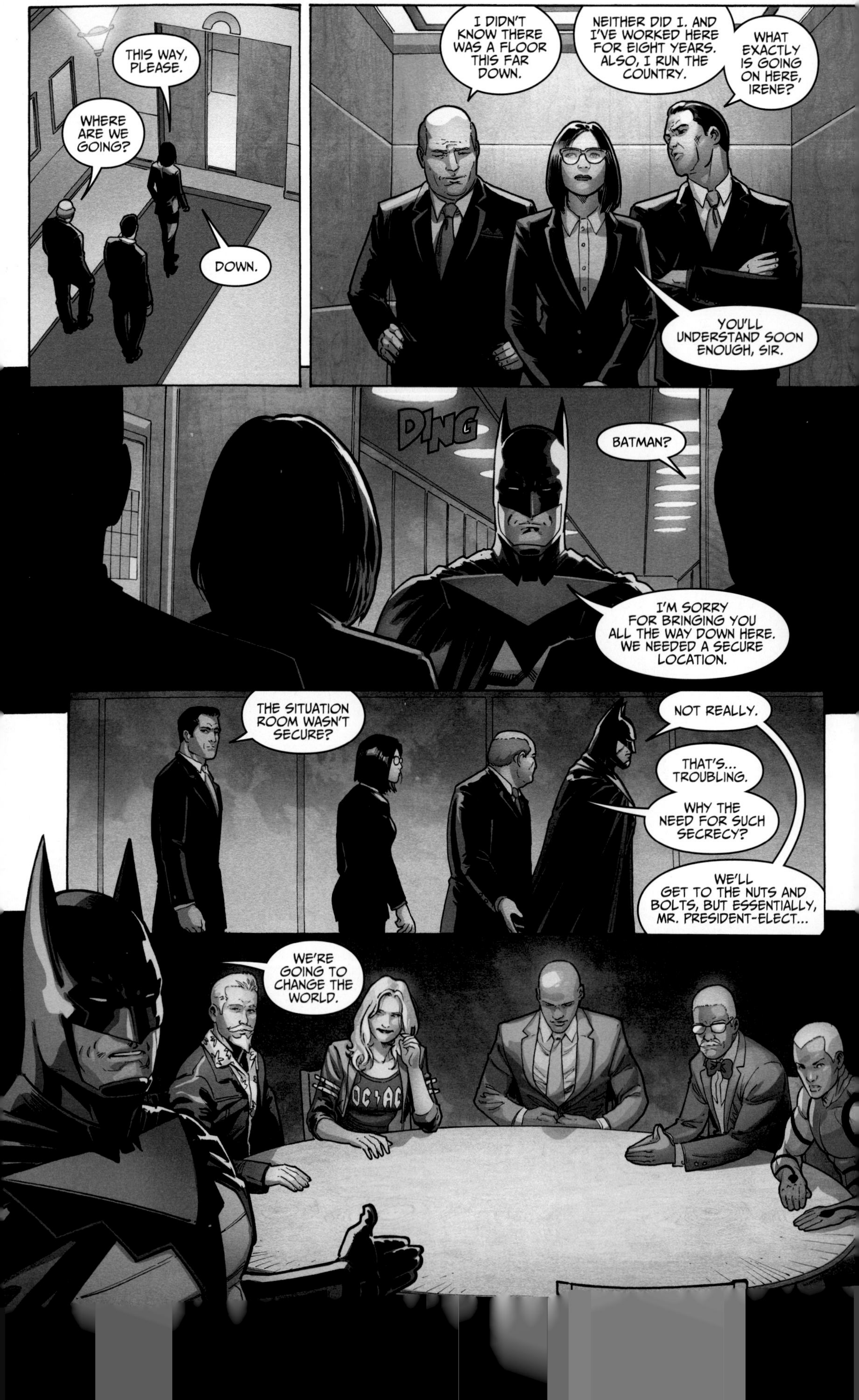
THIS WAY, PLEASE.
WHERE ARE WE GOING?
DOWN.
I DIDN'T KNOW THERE WAS A FLOOR THIS FAR DOWN.
NEITHER DID I. AND I'VE WORKED HERE FOR EIGHT YEARS. ALSO, I RUN THE COUNTRY.
WHAT EXACTLY IS GOING ON HERE, IRENE?
YOU'LL UNDERSTAND SOON ENOUGH, SIR.
DING
BATMAN?
I'M SORRY FOR BRINGING YOU ALL THE WAY DOWN HERE. WE NEEDED A SECURE LOCATION.
THE SITUATION ROOM WASN'T SECURE?
NOT REALLY.
THAT'S... TROUBLING.
WHY THE NEED FOR SUCH SECRECY?
WE'LL GET TO THE NUTS AND BOLTS, BUT ESSENTIALLY, MR. PRESIDENT-ELECT...
WE'RE GOING TO CHANGE THE WORLD.

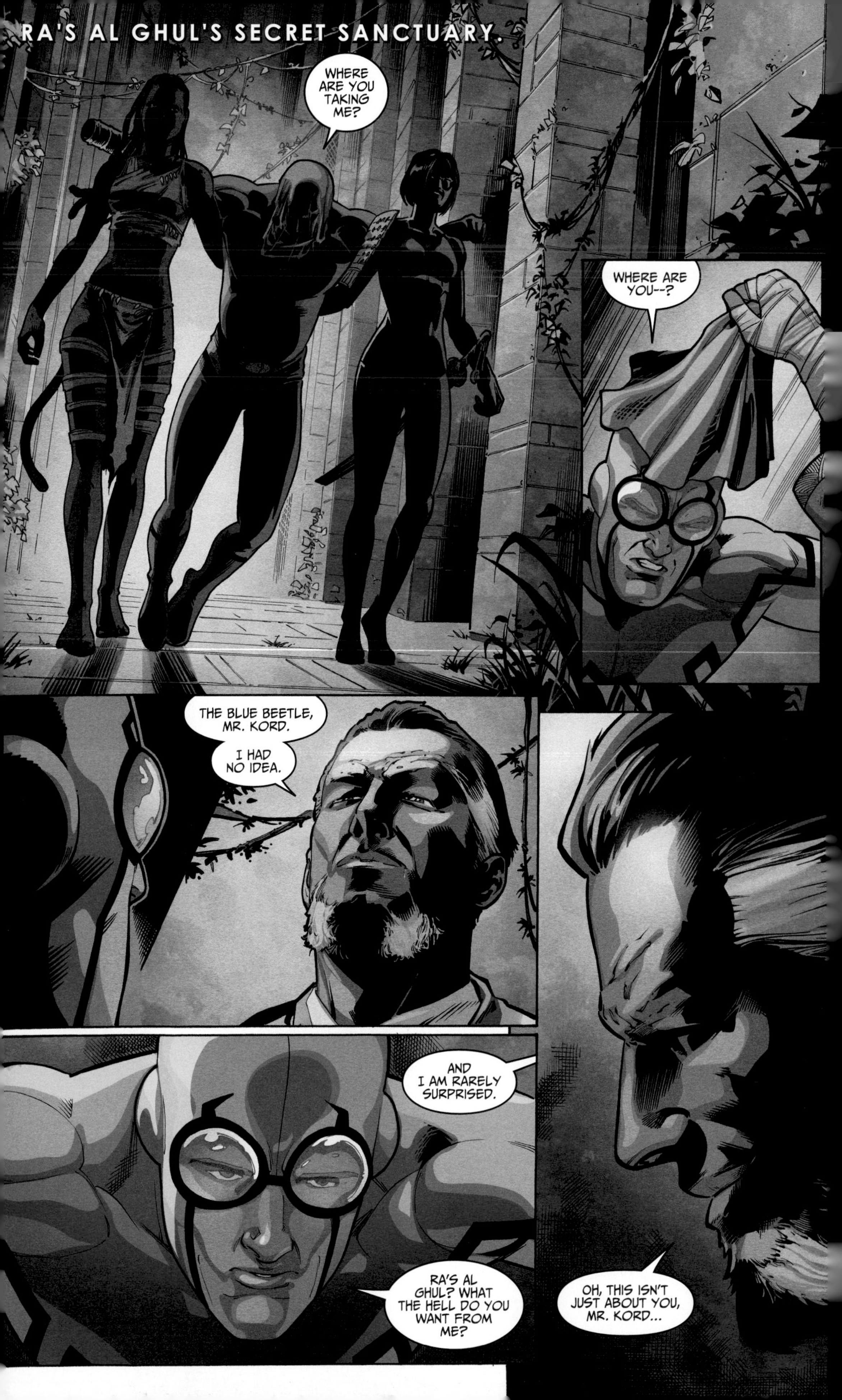
RA'S AL GHUL'S SECRET SANCTUARY.
WHERE ARE YOU TAKING ME?
WHERE ARE YOU--?
THE BLUE BEETLE, MR. KORD.
I HAD NO IDEA.
AND I AM RARELY SURPRISED.
RA'S AL GHUL? WHAT THE HELL DO YOU WANT FROM ME?
OH, THIS ISN'T JUST ABOUT YOU, MR. KORD...

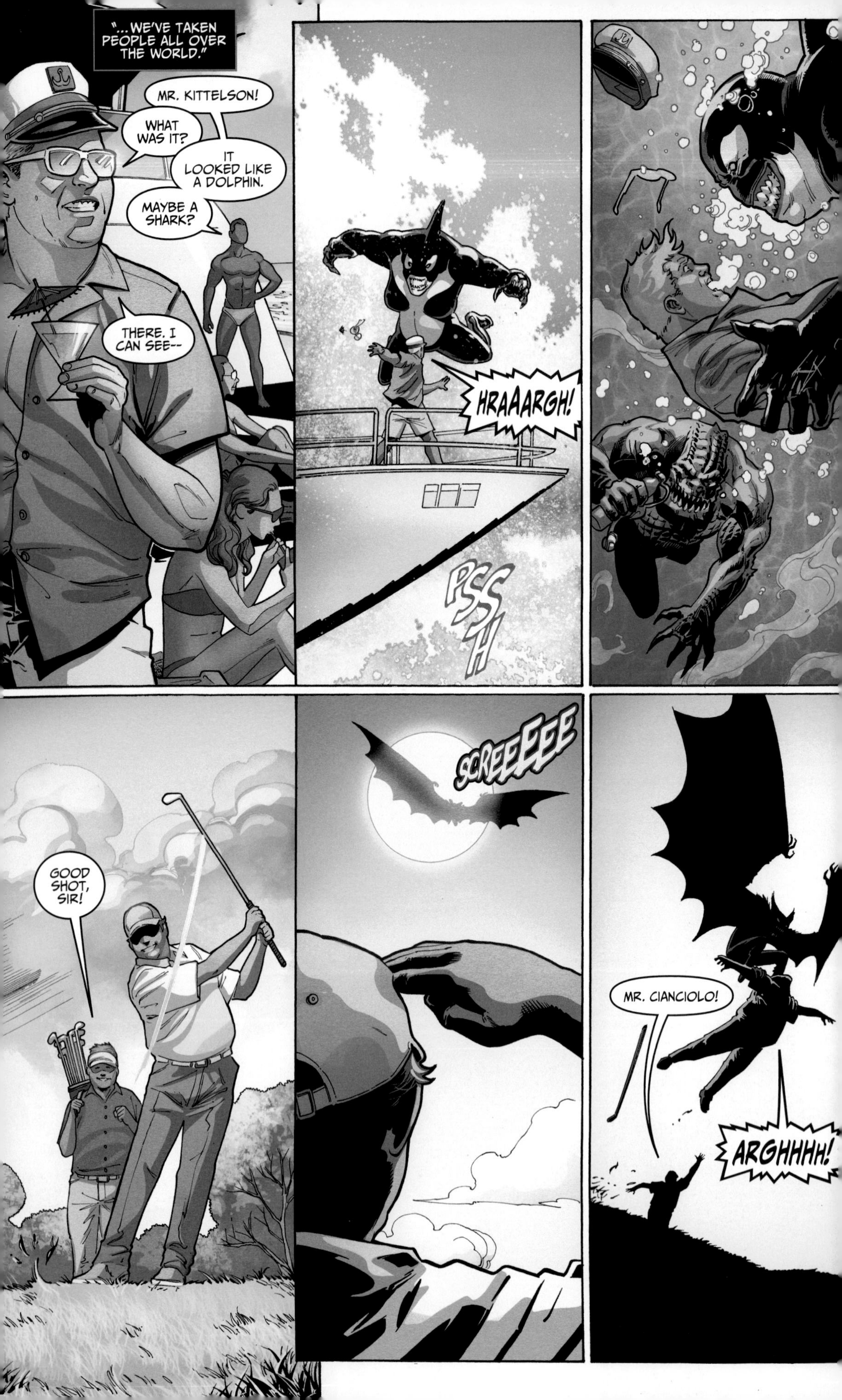
"...WE'VE TAKEN PEOPLE ALL OVER THE WORLD."
MR. KITTELSON!
WHAT WAS IT?
IT LOOKED LIKE A DOLPHIN.
MAYBE A SHARK?
THERE. I CAN SEE--
HRAAARGH!
PSSSH
GOOD SHOT, SIR!
SCREEEEE
MR. CIANCIOLO!
ARGHHHH!

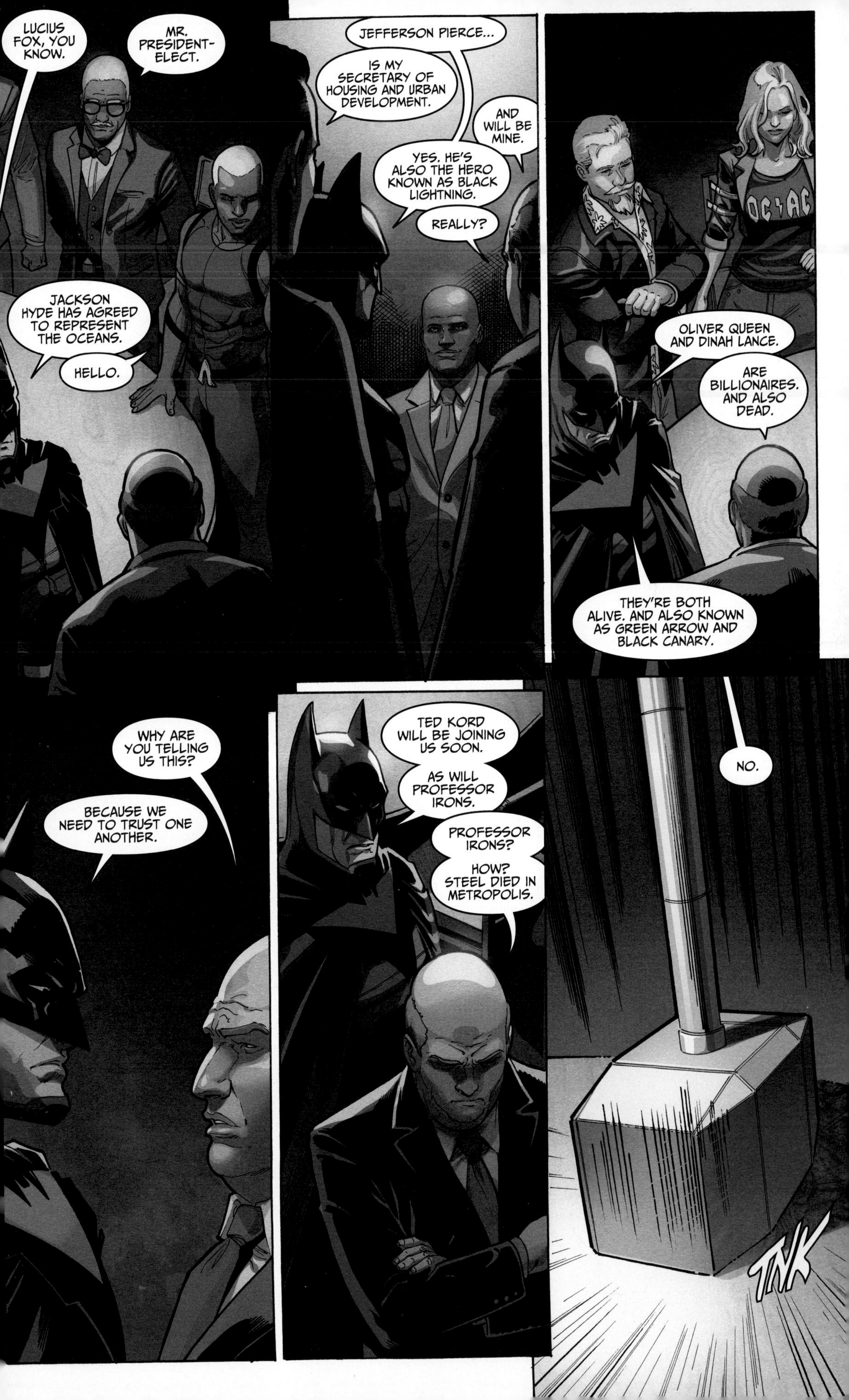
LUCIUS FOX, YOU KNOW.
MR. PRESIDENT-ELECT.
JACKSON HYDE HAS AGREED TO REPRESENT THE OCEANS.
HELLO.
JEFFERSON PIERCE...
IS MY SECRETARY OF HOUSING AND URBAN DEVELOPMENT.
AND WILL BE MINE.
YES. HE'S ALSO THE HERO KNOWN AS BLACK LIGHTNING.
REALLY?
OLIVER QUEEN AND DINAH LANCE.
ARE BILLIONAIRES. AND ALSO DEAD.
THEY'RE BOTH ALIVE. AND ALSO KNOWN AS GREEN ARROW AND BLACK CANARY.
WHY ARE YOU TELLING US THIS?
BECAUSE WE NEED TO TRUST ONE ANOTHER.
TED KORD WILL BE JOINING US SOON.
AS WILL PROFESSOR IRONS.
PROFESSOR IRONS?
HOW? STEEL DIED IN METROPOLIS.
NO.
TNK

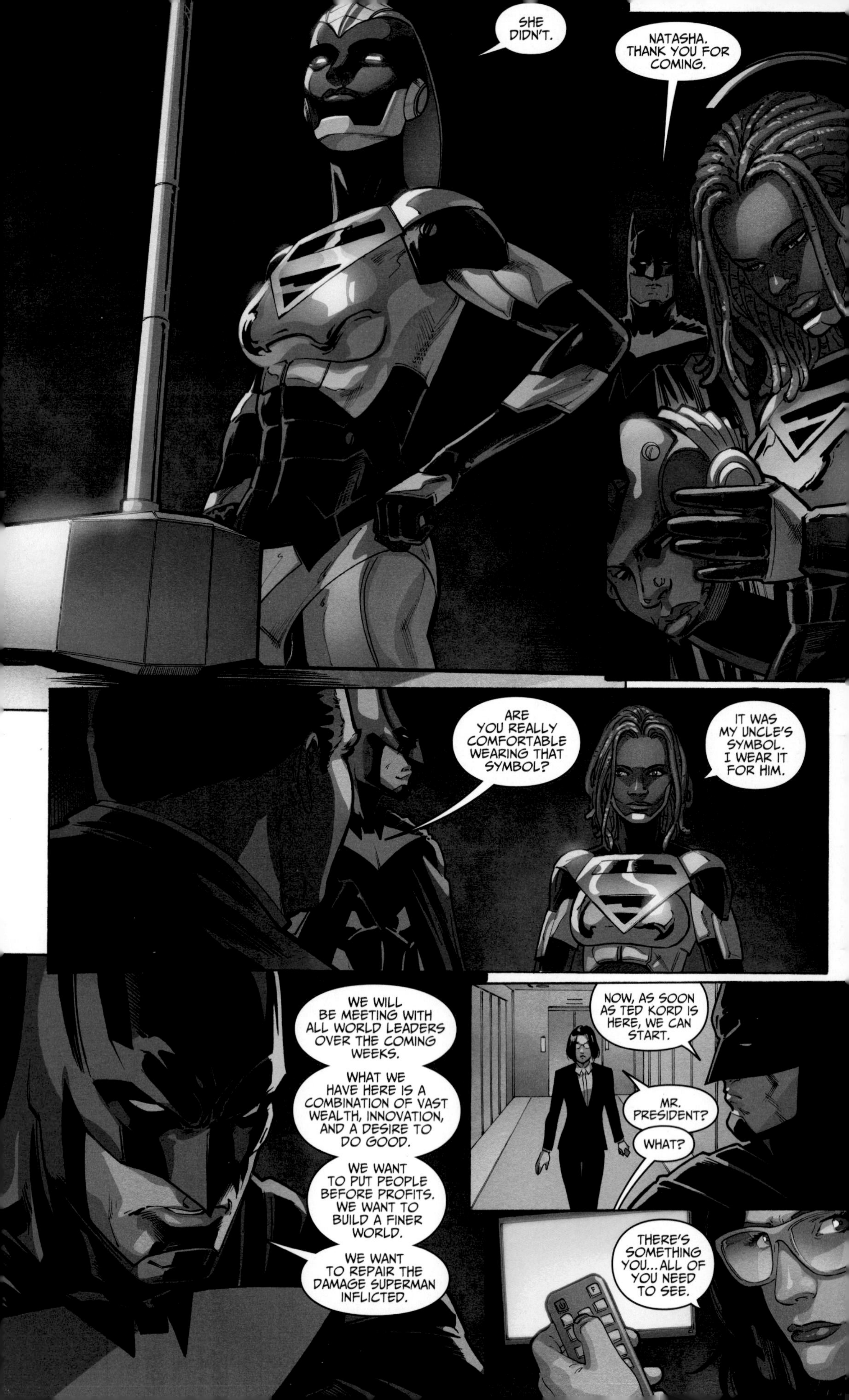
SHE DIDN'T.
NATASHA. THANK YOU FOR COMING.
ARE YOU REALLY COMFORTABLE WEARING THAT SYMBOL?
IT WAS MY UNCLE'S SYMBOL. I WEAR IT FOR HIM.
WE WILL BE MEETING WITH ALL WORLD LEADERS OVER THE COMING WEEKS.
WHAT WE HAVE HERE IS A COMBINATION OF VAST WEALTH, INNOVATION, AND A DESIRE TO DO GOOD.
WE WANT TO PUT PEOPLE BEFORE PROFITS. WE WANT TO BUILD A FINER WORLD.
WE WANT TO REPAIR THE DAMAGE SUPERMAN INFLICTED.
NOW, AS SOON AS TED KORD IS HERE, WE CAN START.
MR. PRESIDENT?
WHAT?
THERE'S SOMETHING YOU...ALL OF YOU NEED TO SEE.

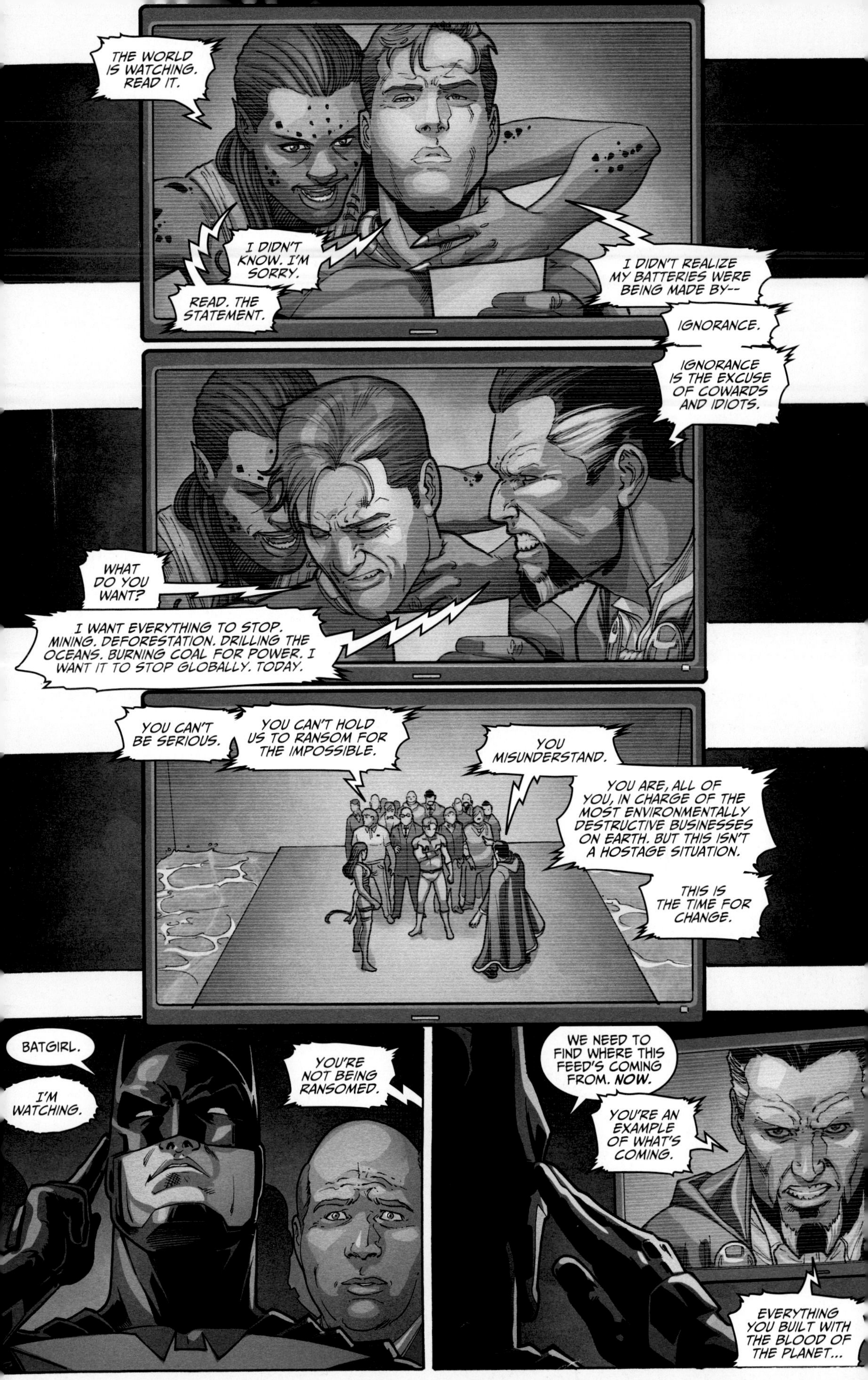
THE WORLD IS WATCHING. READ IT.
I DIDN'T KNOW. I'M SORRY.
READ. THE STATEMENT.
I DIDN'T REALIZE MY BATTERIES WERE BEING MADE BY--
IGNORANCE.
IGNORANCE IS THE EXCUSE OF COWARDS AND IDIOTS.
WHAT DO YOU WANT?
I WANT EVERYTHING TO STOP. MINING. DEFORESTATION. DRILLING THE OCEANS. BURNING COAL FOR POWER. I WANT IT TO STOP GLOBALLY. TODAY.
YOU CAN'T BE SERIOUS.
YOU CAN'T HOLD US TO RANSOM FOR THE IMPOSSIBLE.
YOU MISUNDERSTAND.
YOU ARE, ALL OF YOU, IN CHARGE OF THE MOST ENVIRONMENTALLY DESTRUCTIVE BUSINESSES ON EARTH. BUT THIS ISN'T A HOSTAGE SITUATION.
THIS IS THE TIME FOR CHANGE.
BATGIRL.
I'M WATCHING.
YOU'RE NOT BEING RANSOMED.
WE NEED TO FIND WHERE THIS FEED'S COMING FROM. NOW.
YOU'RE AN EXAMPLE OF WHAT'S COMING.
EVERYTHING YOU BUILT WITH THE BLOOD OF THE PLANET...

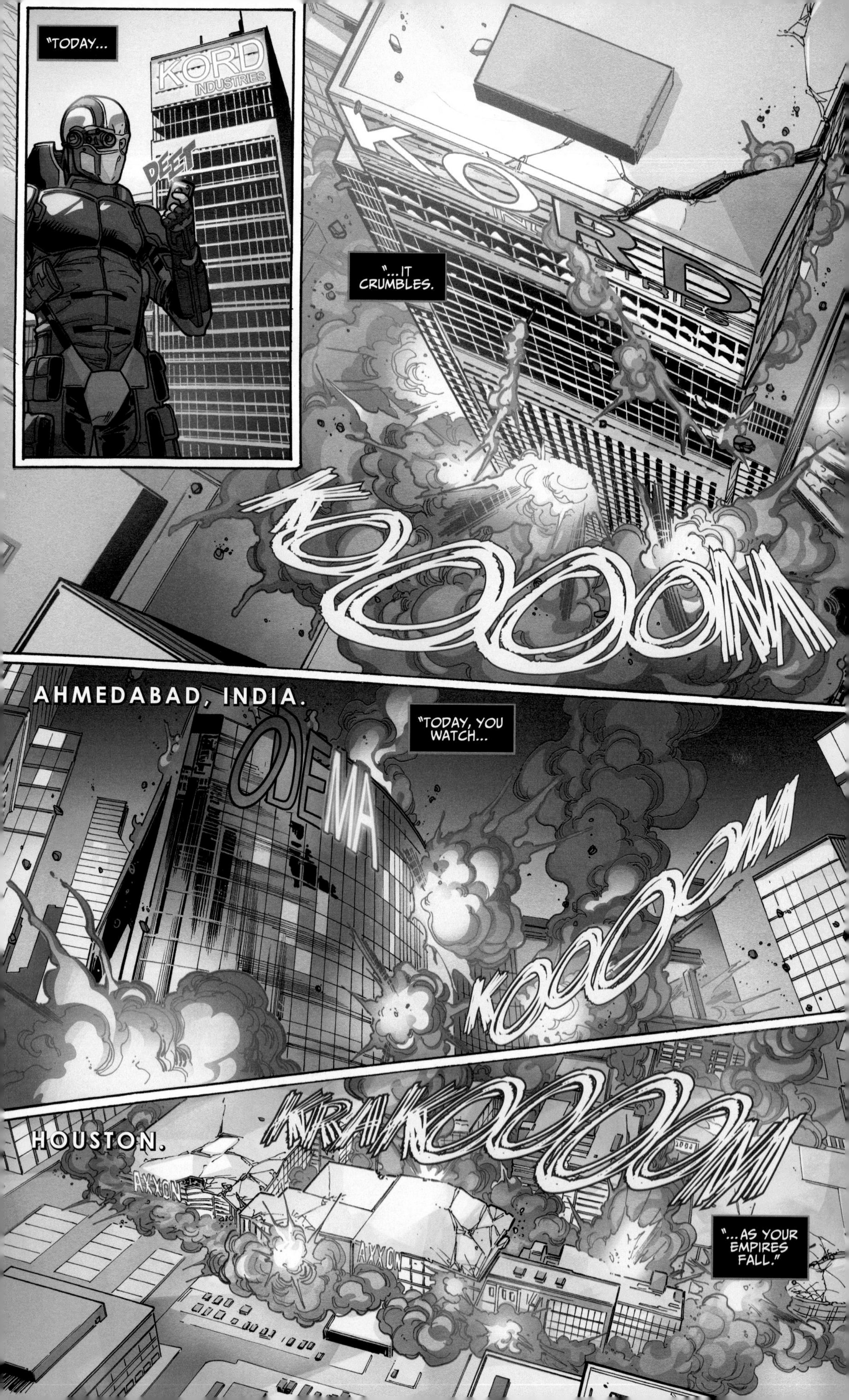
"TODAY...
KORD INDUSTRIES
DEET
"...IT CRUMBLES.
KOOOOOM
AHMEDABAD, INDIA.
"TODAY, YOU WATCH...
ODEMA
KOOOOOM
HOUSTON.
KRAKOOOOOM
AXXON
AXXON
"...AS YOUR EMPIRES FALL."

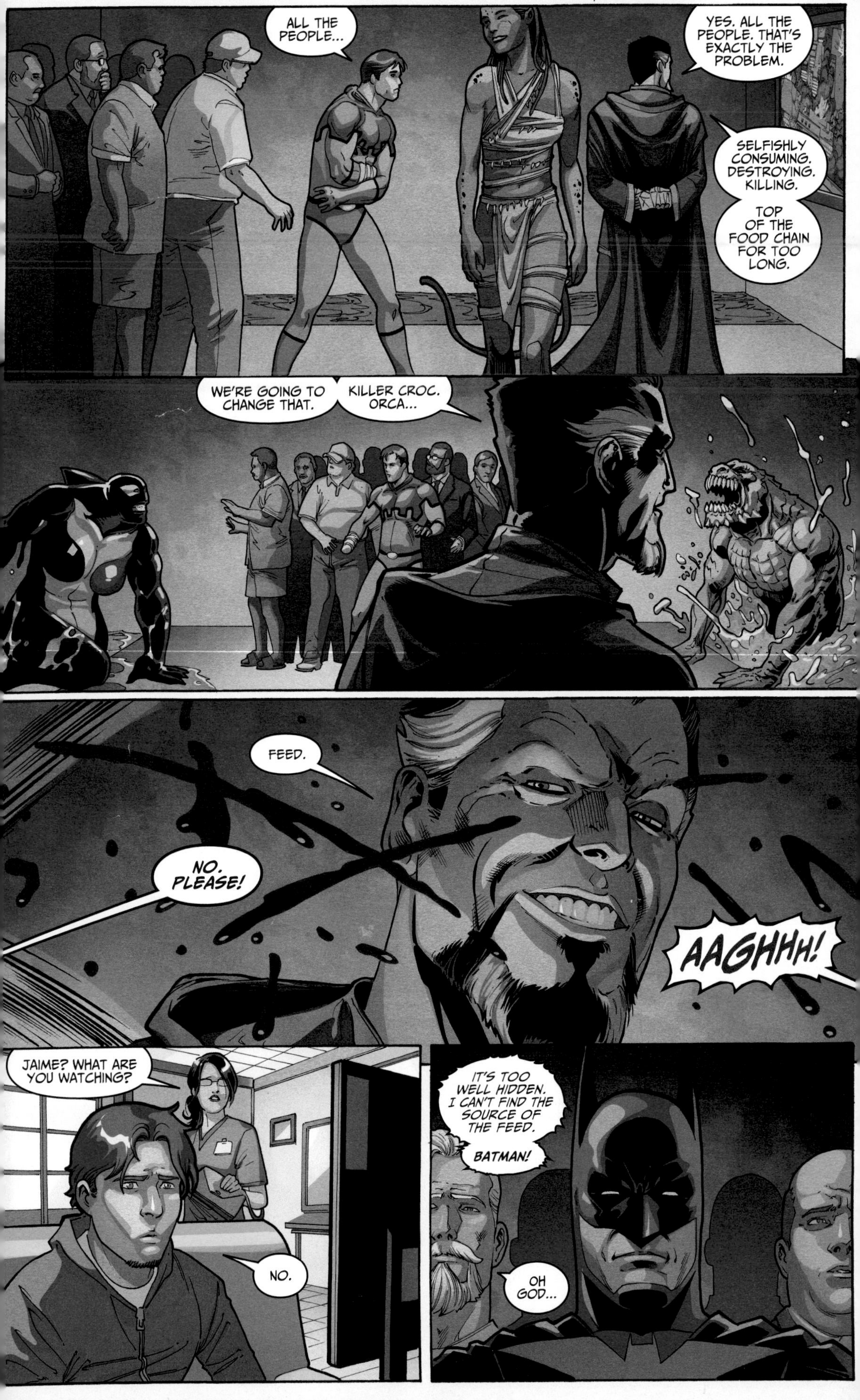
ALL THE PEOPLE...
YES. ALL THE PEOPLE. THAT'S EXACTLY THE PROBLEM.
SELFISHLY CONSUMING. DESTROYING. KILLING.
TOP OF THE FOOD CHAIN FOR TOO LONG.
WE'RE GOING TO CHANGE THAT.
KILLER CROC. ORCA...
FEED.
NO. PLEASE!
AAGHHH!
JAIME? WHAT ARE YOU WATCHING?
NO.
IT'S TOO WELL HIDDEN. I CAN'T FIND THE SOURCE OF THE FEED.
BATMAN!
OH GOD...

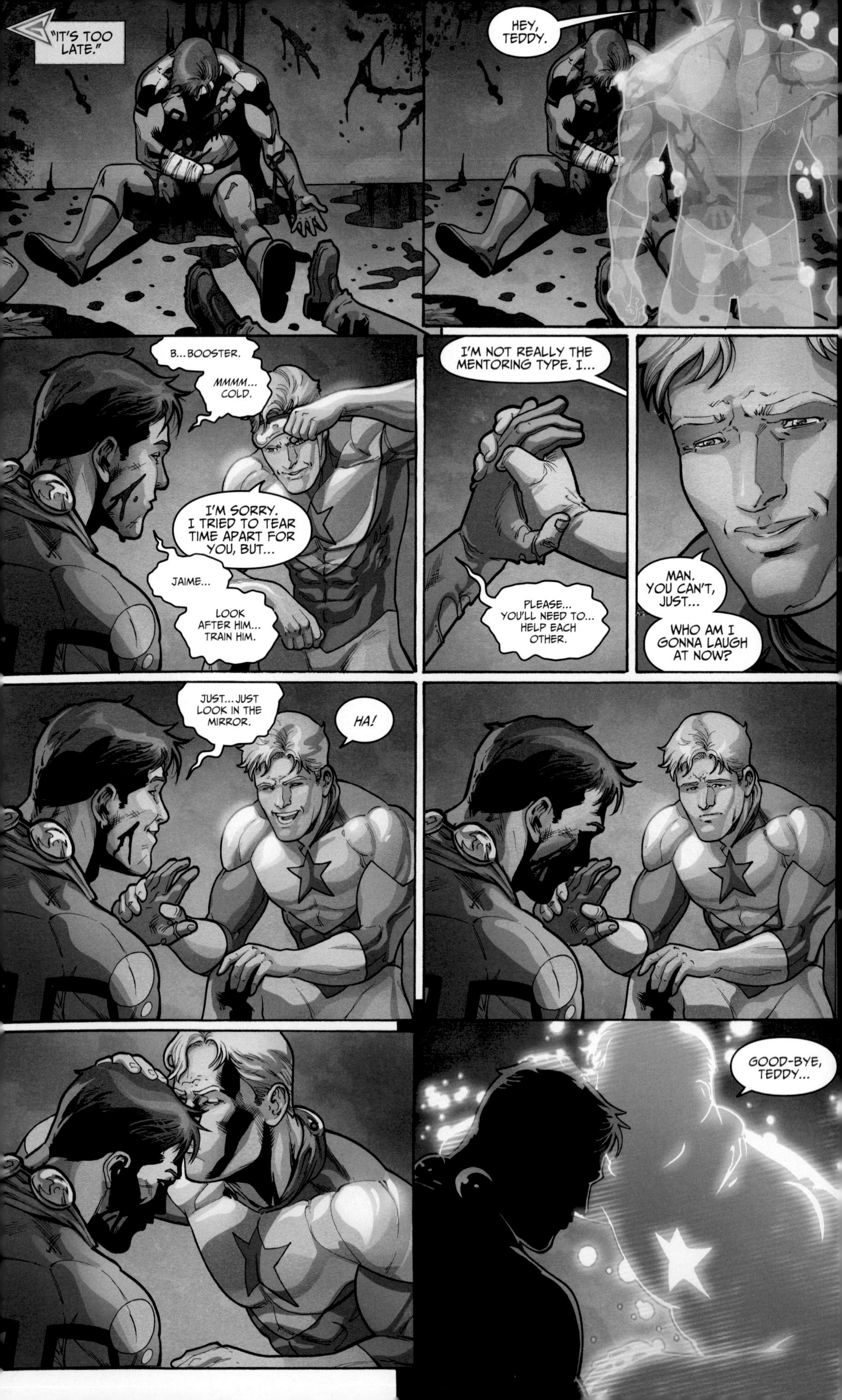
"IT'S TOO LATE."
HEY, TEDDY.
B...BOOSTER.
MMMM... COLD.
I'M SORRY. I TRIED TO TEAR TIME APART FOR YOU, BUT...
JAIME...
LOOK AFTER HIM... TRAIN HIM.
I'M NOT REALLY THE MENTORING TYPE. I...
PLEASE... YOU'LL NEED TO... HELP EACH OTHER.
MAN. YOU CAN'T, JUST...
WHO AM I GONNA LAUGH AT NOW?
JUST... JUST LOOK IN THE MIRROR.
HA!
GOOD-BYE, TEDDY...

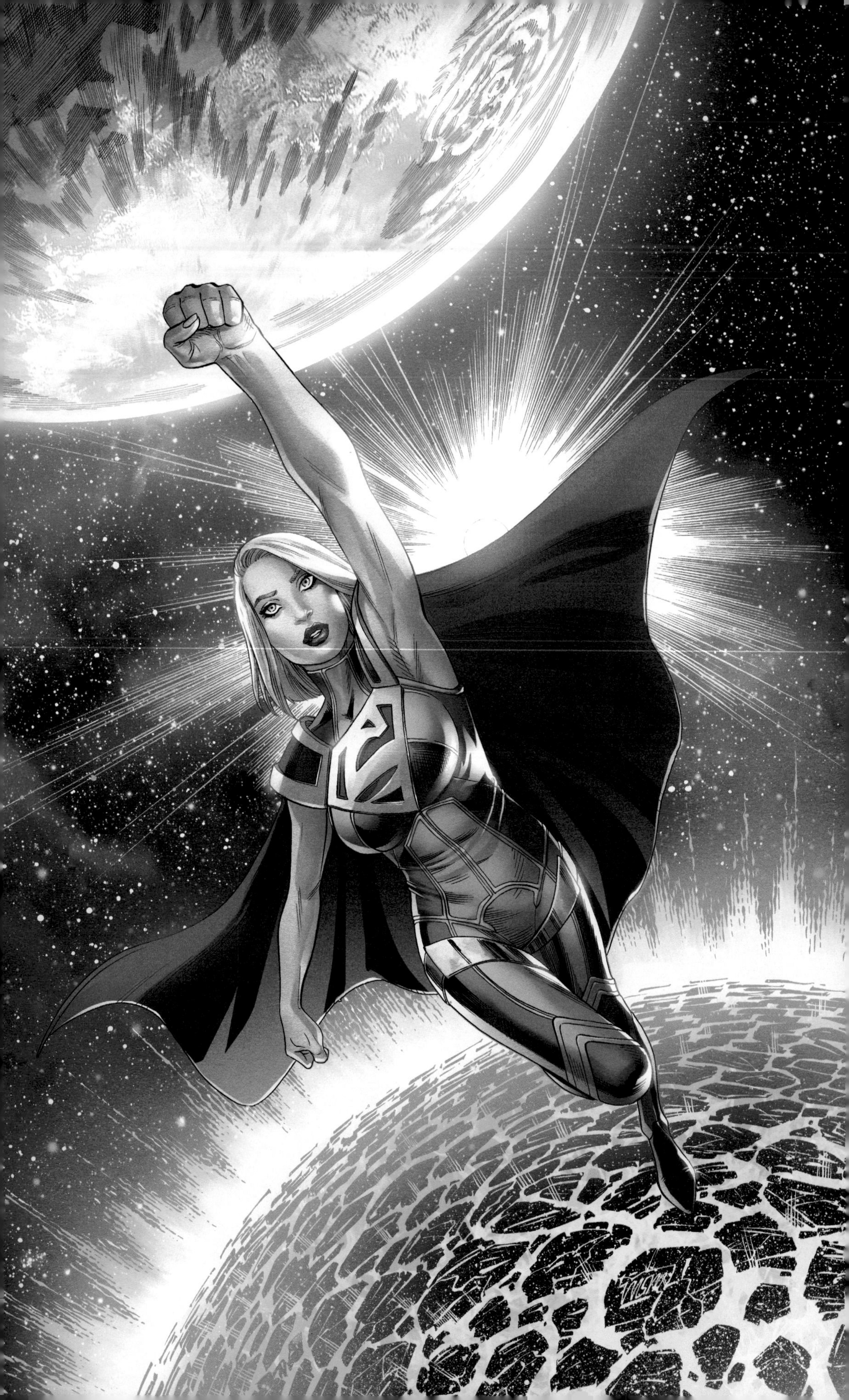

"When You Wake Up"

Mike S. Miller Artist **J. Nanjan** Colorist

Cover Art by **Mike S. Miller** and **J. Nanjan**

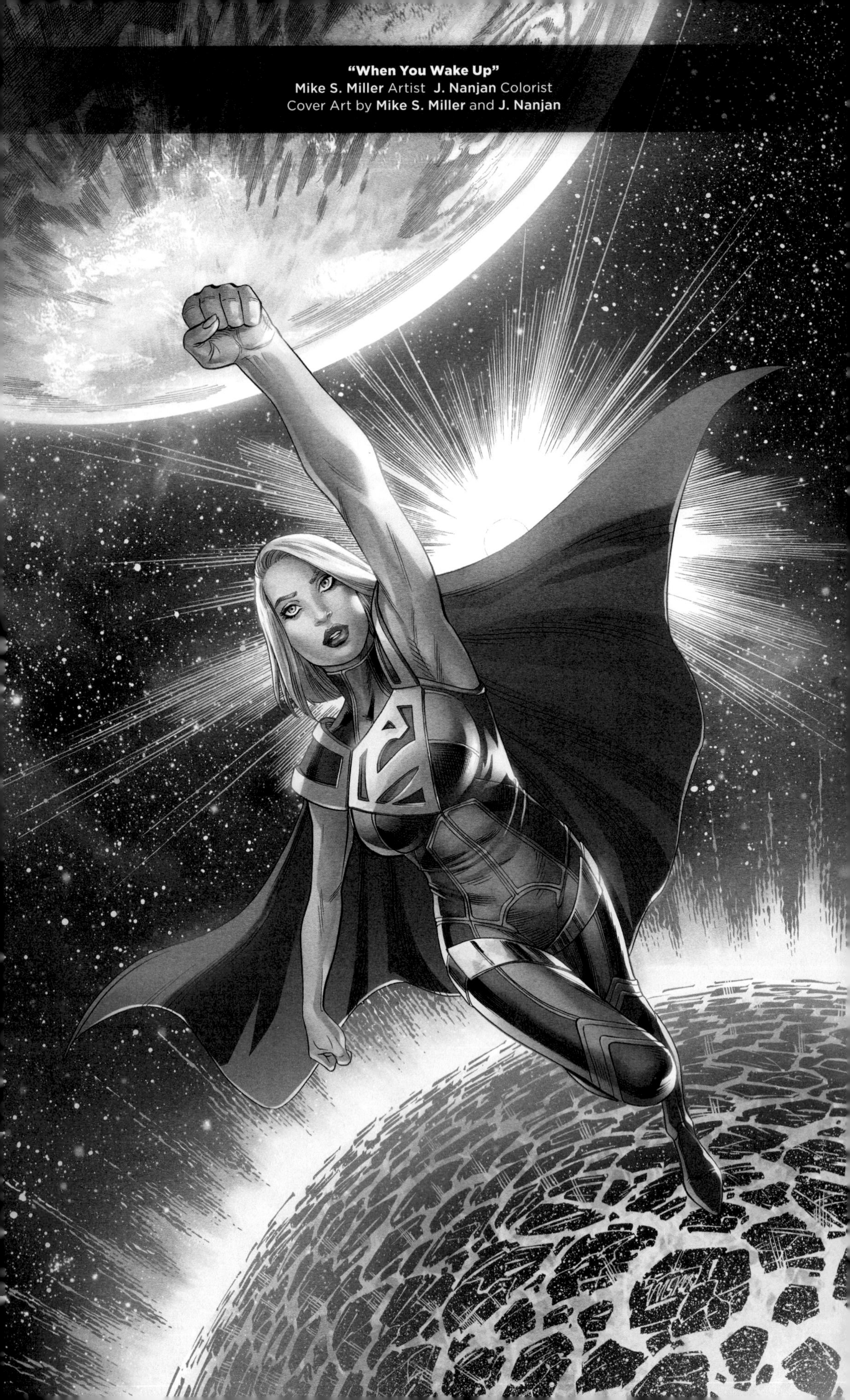

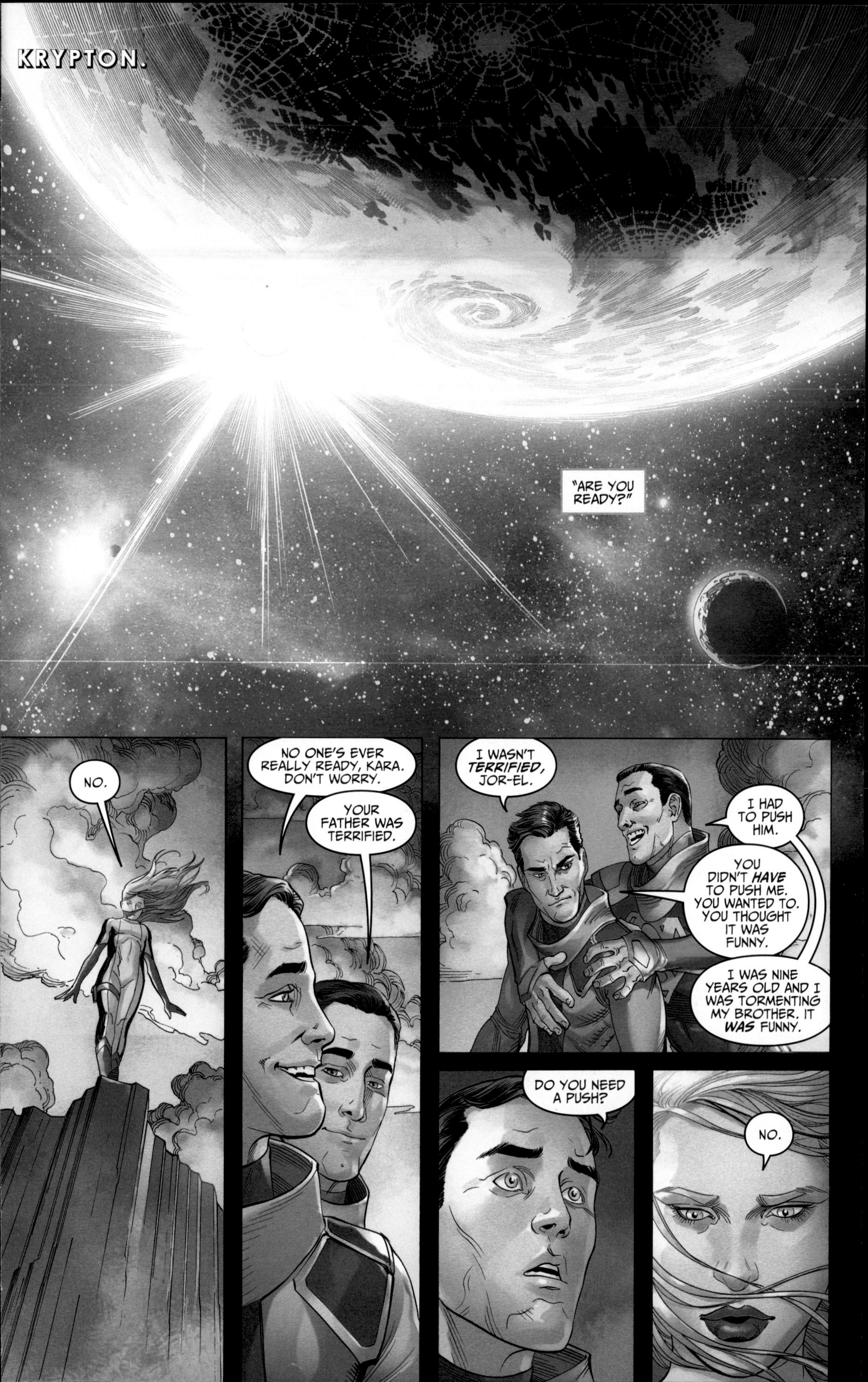
KRYPTON.
"ARE YOU READY?"
NO.
NO ONE'S EVER REALLY READY, KARA. DON'T WORRY.
YOUR FATHER WAS TERRIFIED.
I WASN'T *TERRIFIED,* JOR-EL.
I HAD TO PUSH HIM.
YOU DIDN'T *HAVE* TO PUSH ME. YOU WANTED TO. YOU THOUGHT IT WAS FUNNY.
I WAS NINE YEARS OLD AND I WAS TORMENTING MY BROTHER. IT *WAS* FUNNY.
DO YOU NEED A PUSH?
NO.

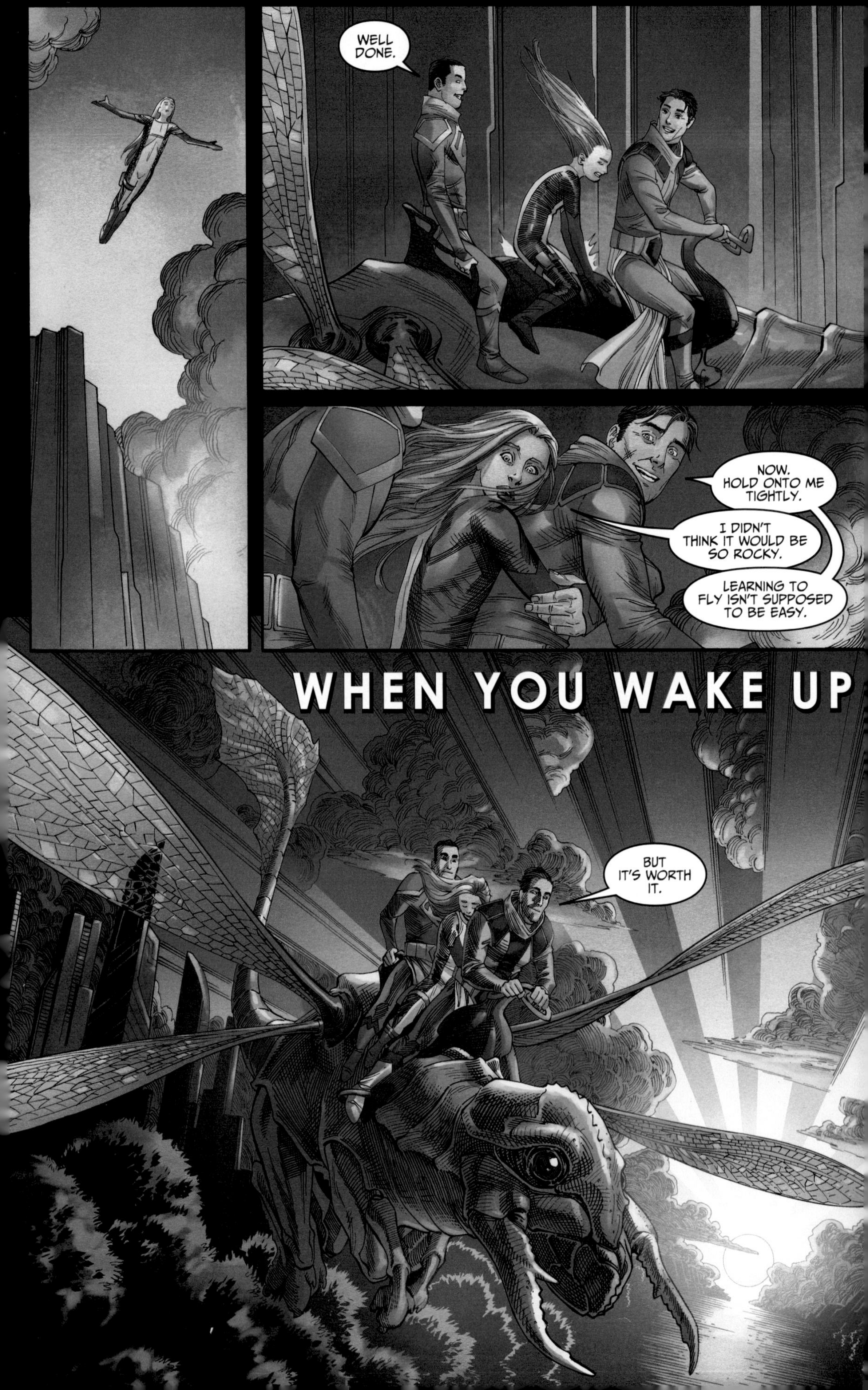
WELL DONE.
NOW. HOLD ONTO ME TIGHTLY.
I DIDN'T THINK IT WOULD BE SO ROCKY.
LEARNING TO FLY ISN'T SUPPOSED TO BE EASY.
WHEN YOU WAKE UP
BUT IT'S WORTH IT.

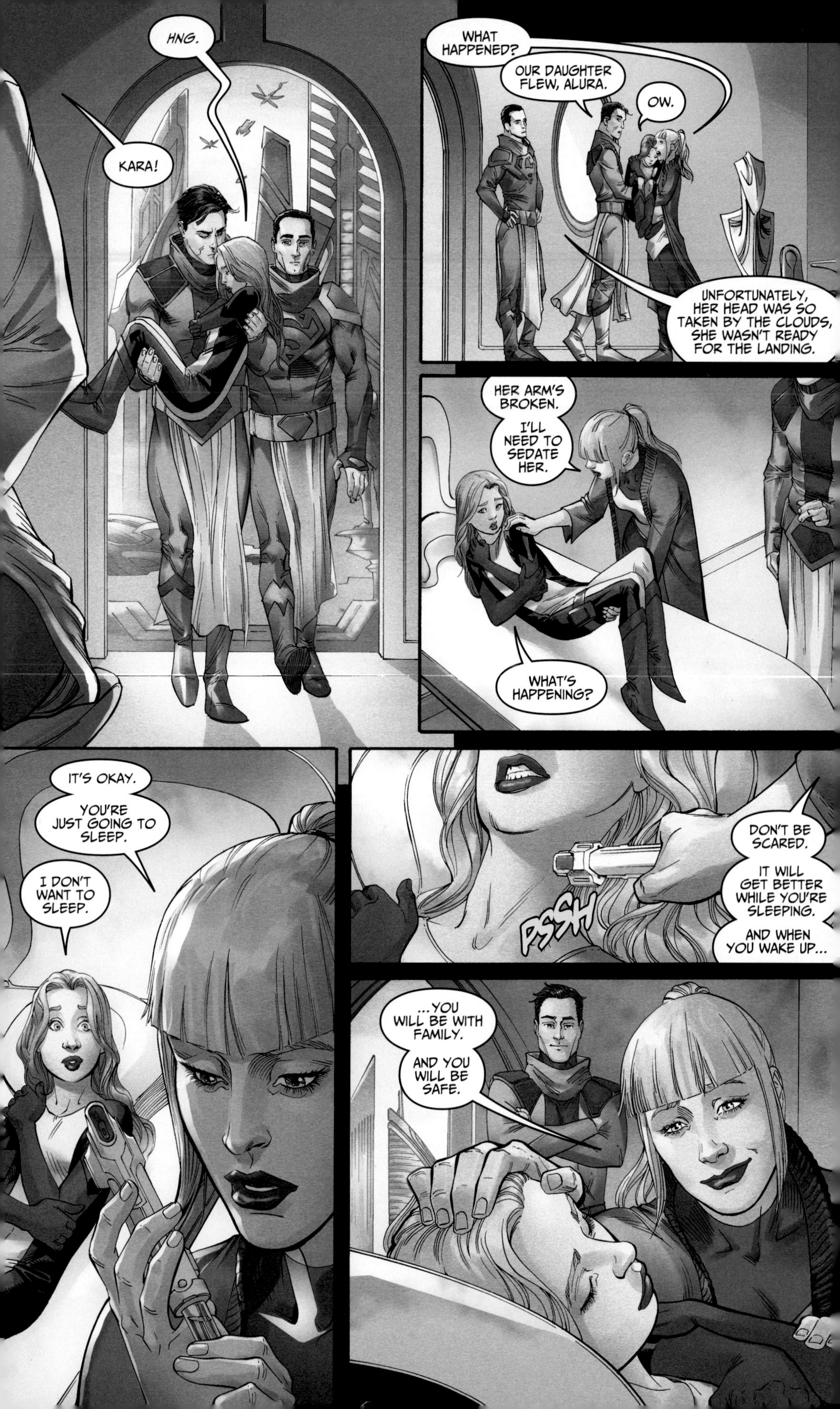
HNG.
KARA!
WHAT HAPPENED?
OUR DAUGHTER FLEW, ALURA.
OW.
UNFORTUNATELY, HER HEAD WAS SO TAKEN BY THE CLOUDS, SHE WASN'T READY FOR THE LANDING.
HER ARM'S BROKEN.
I'LL NEED TO SEDATE HER.
WHAT'S HAPPENING?
IT'S OKAY.
YOU'RE JUST GOING TO SLEEP.
I DON'T WANT TO SLEEP.
DON'T BE SCARED.
IT WILL GET BETTER WHILE YOU'RE SLEEPING.
AND WHEN YOU WAKE UP...
PSSH
...YOU WILL BE WITH FAMILY.
AND YOU WILL BE SAFE.

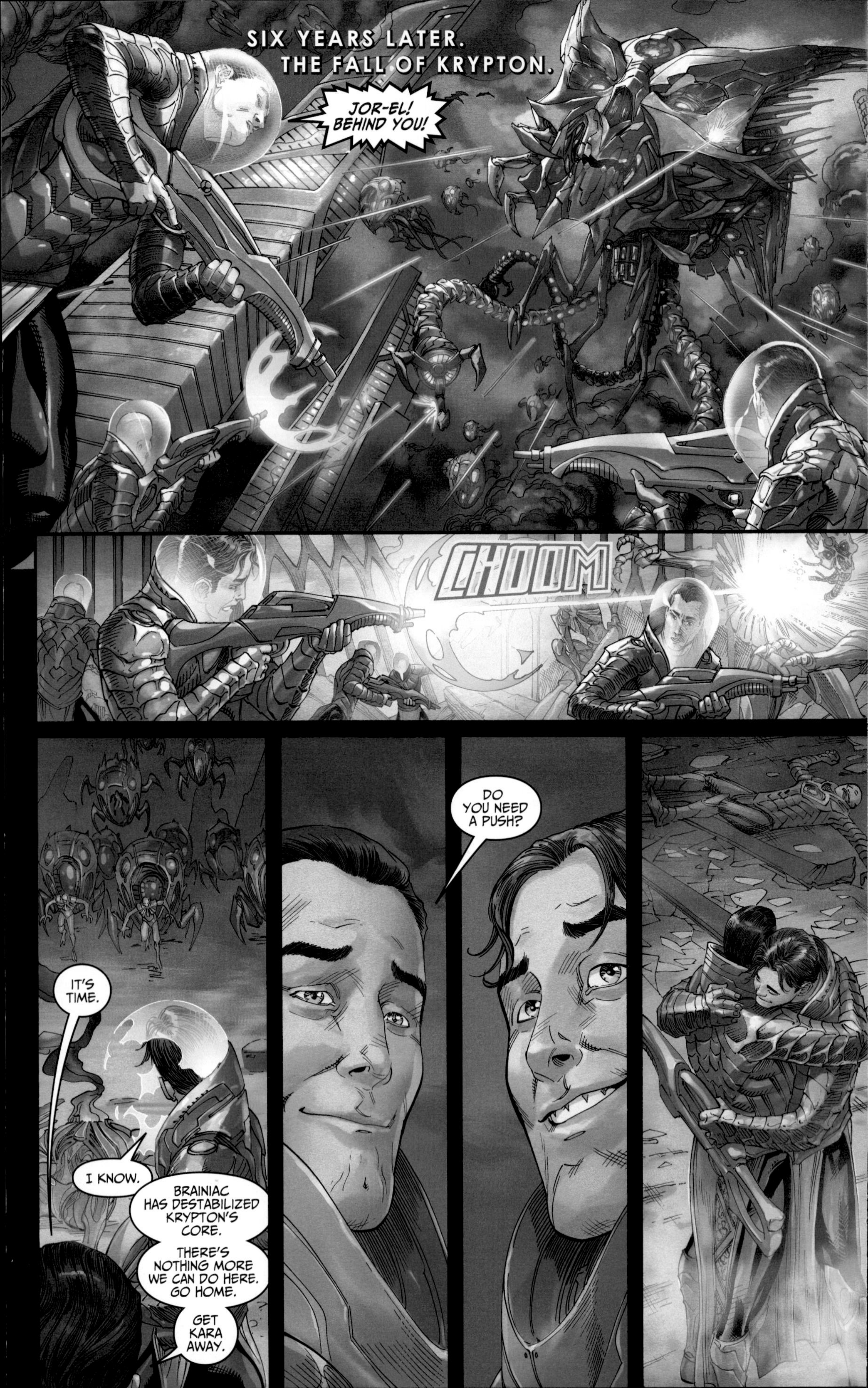
SIX YEARS LATER.
THE FALL OF KRYPTON.
JOR-EL! BEHIND YOU!
CHOOM
IT'S TIME.
I KNOW.
BRAINIAC HAS DESTABILIZED KRYPTON'S CORE.
THERE'S NOTHING MORE WE CAN DO HERE. GO HOME.
GET KARA AWAY.
DO YOU NEED A PUSH?

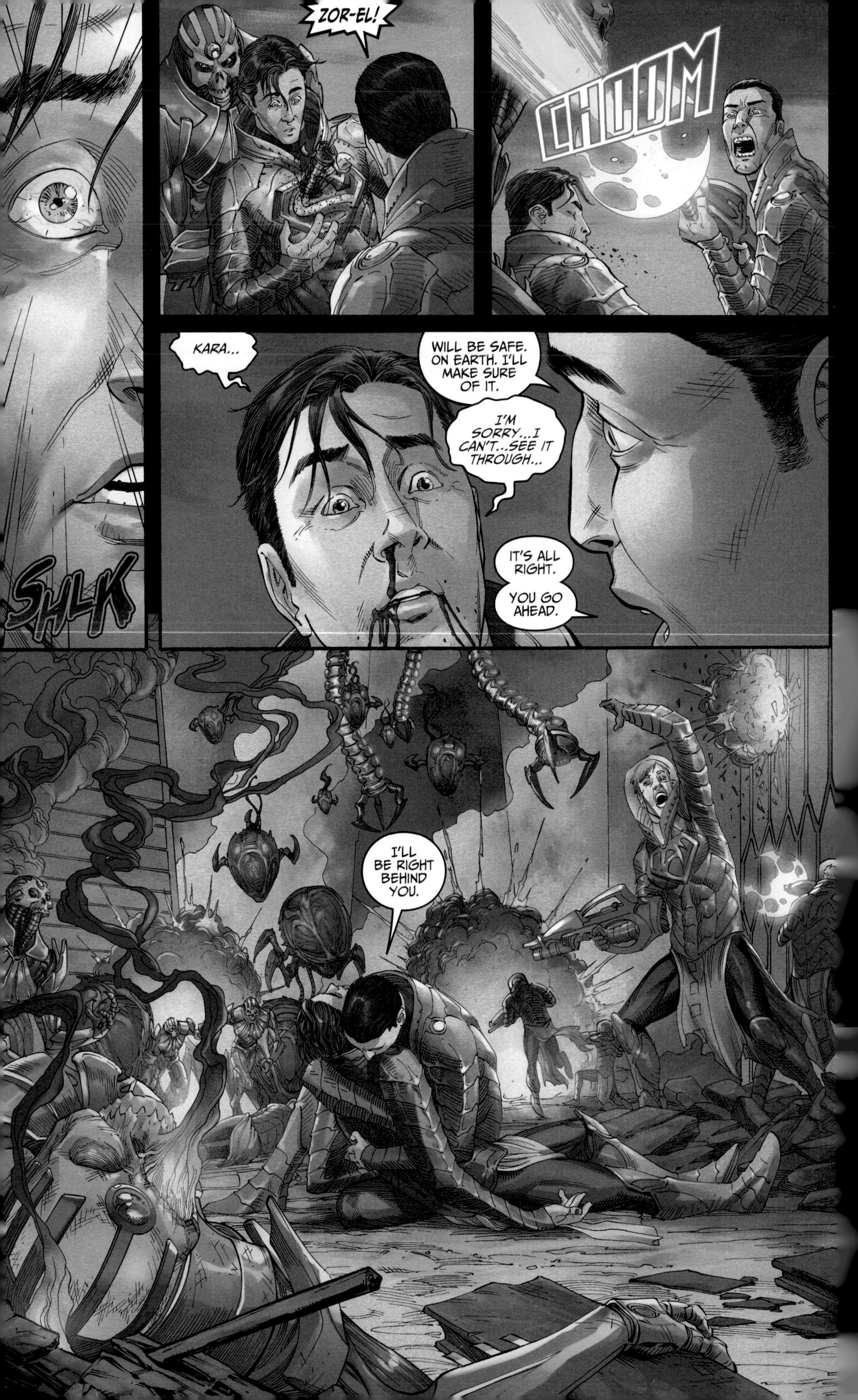
ZOR-EL!
CHOOM
SHLK
KARA...
WILL BE SAFE. ON EARTH. I'LL MAKE SURE OF IT.
I'M SORRY...I CAN'T...SEE IT THROUGH...
IT'S ALL RIGHT.
YOU GO AHEAD.
I'LL BE RIGHT BEHIND YOU.

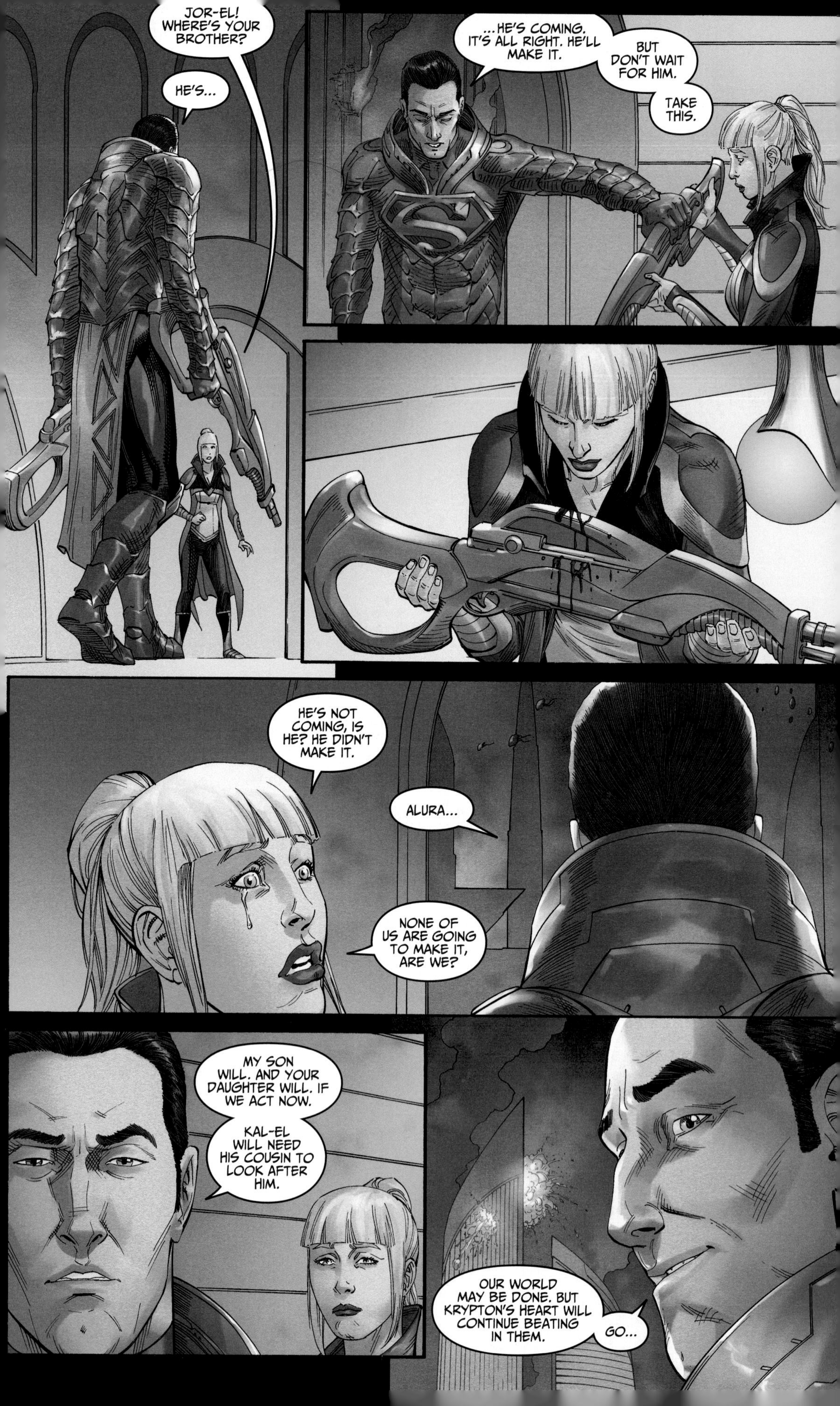
JOR-EL! WHERE'S YOUR BROTHER?
HE'S...
...HE'S COMING. IT'S ALL RIGHT. HE'LL MAKE IT.
BUT DON'T WAIT FOR HIM.
TAKE THIS.
HE'S NOT COMING, IS HE? HE DIDN'T MAKE IT.
ALURA...
NONE OF US ARE GOING TO MAKE IT, ARE WE?
MY SON WILL. AND YOUR DAUGHTER WILL. IF WE ACT NOW.
KAL-EL WILL NEED HIS COUSIN TO LOOK AFTER HIM.
OUR WORLD MAY BE DONE. BUT KRYPTON'S HEART WILL CONTINUE BEATING IN THEM.
GO...

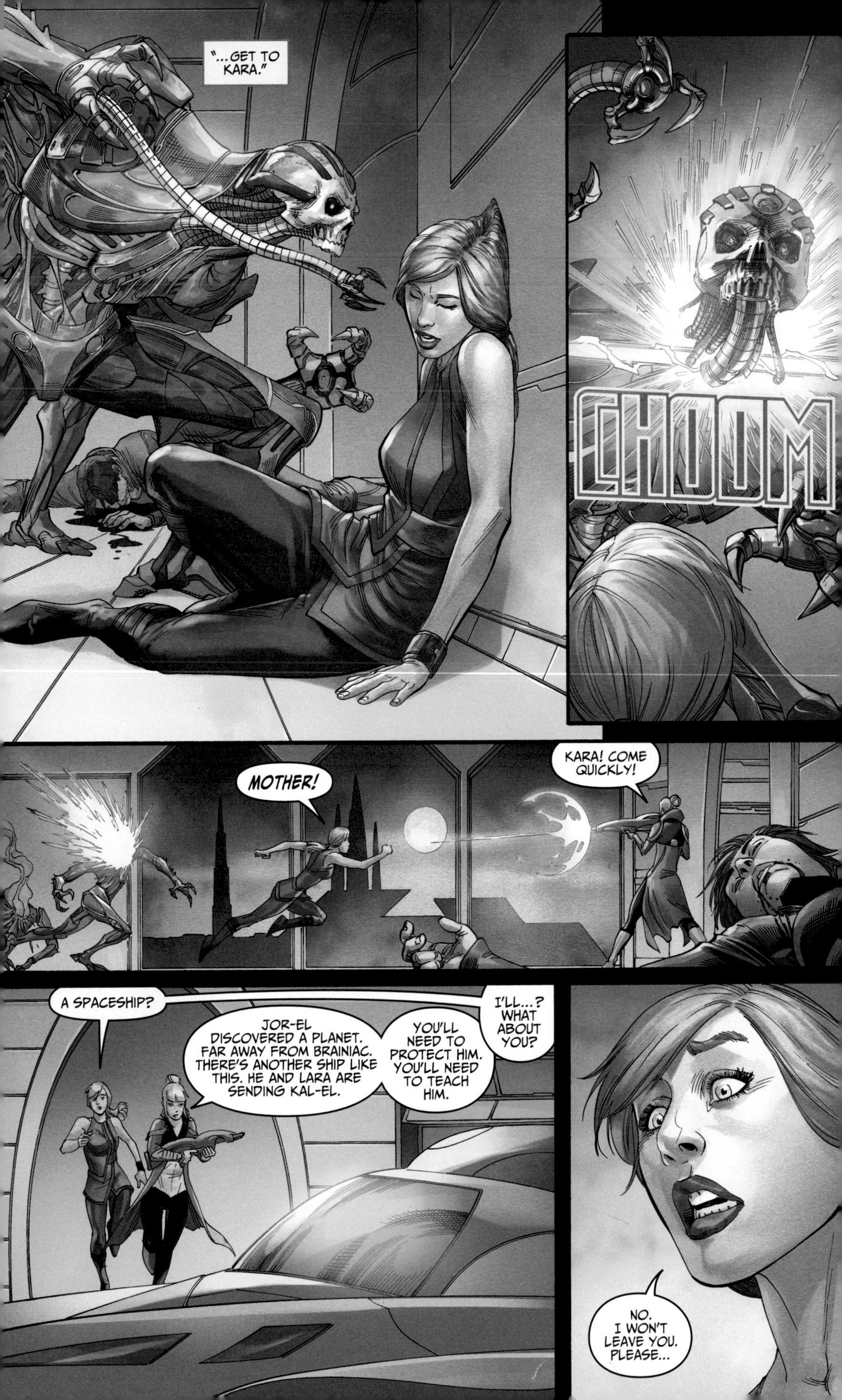

"...GET TO KARA."
CHOOM
MOTHER!
KARA! COME QUICKLY!
A SPACESHIP?
JOR-EL DISCOVERED A PLANET. FAR AWAY FROM BRAINIAC. THERE'S ANOTHER SHIP LIKE THIS. HE AND LARA ARE SENDING KAL-EL.
YOU'LL NEED TO PROTECT HIM. YOU'LL NEED TO TEACH HIM.
I'LL...? WHAT ABOUT YOU?
NO. I WON'T LEAVE YOU. PLEASE...

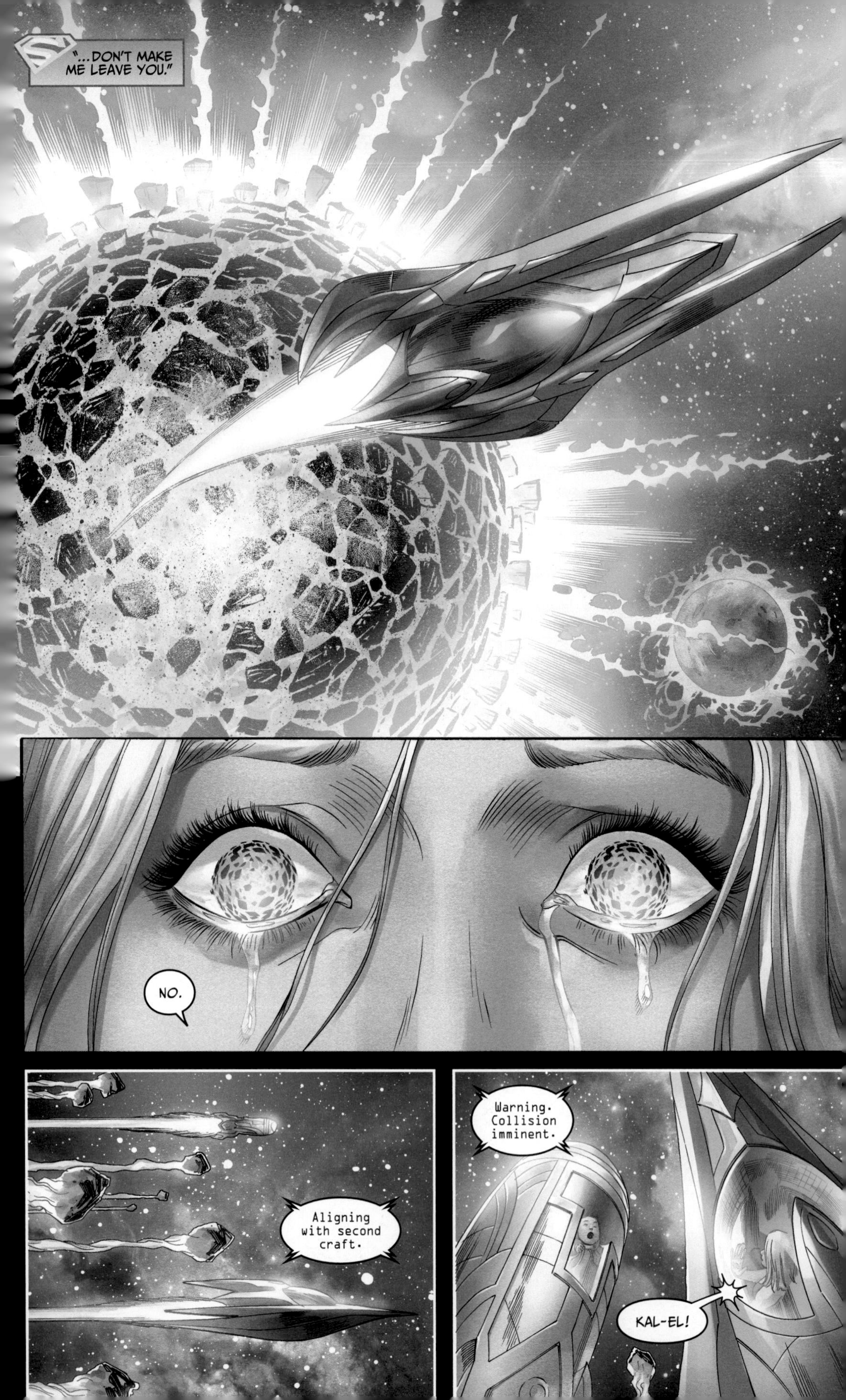
"...DON'T MAKE ME LEAVE YOU."
NO.
Aligning with second craft.
Warning. Collision imminent.
KAL-EL!

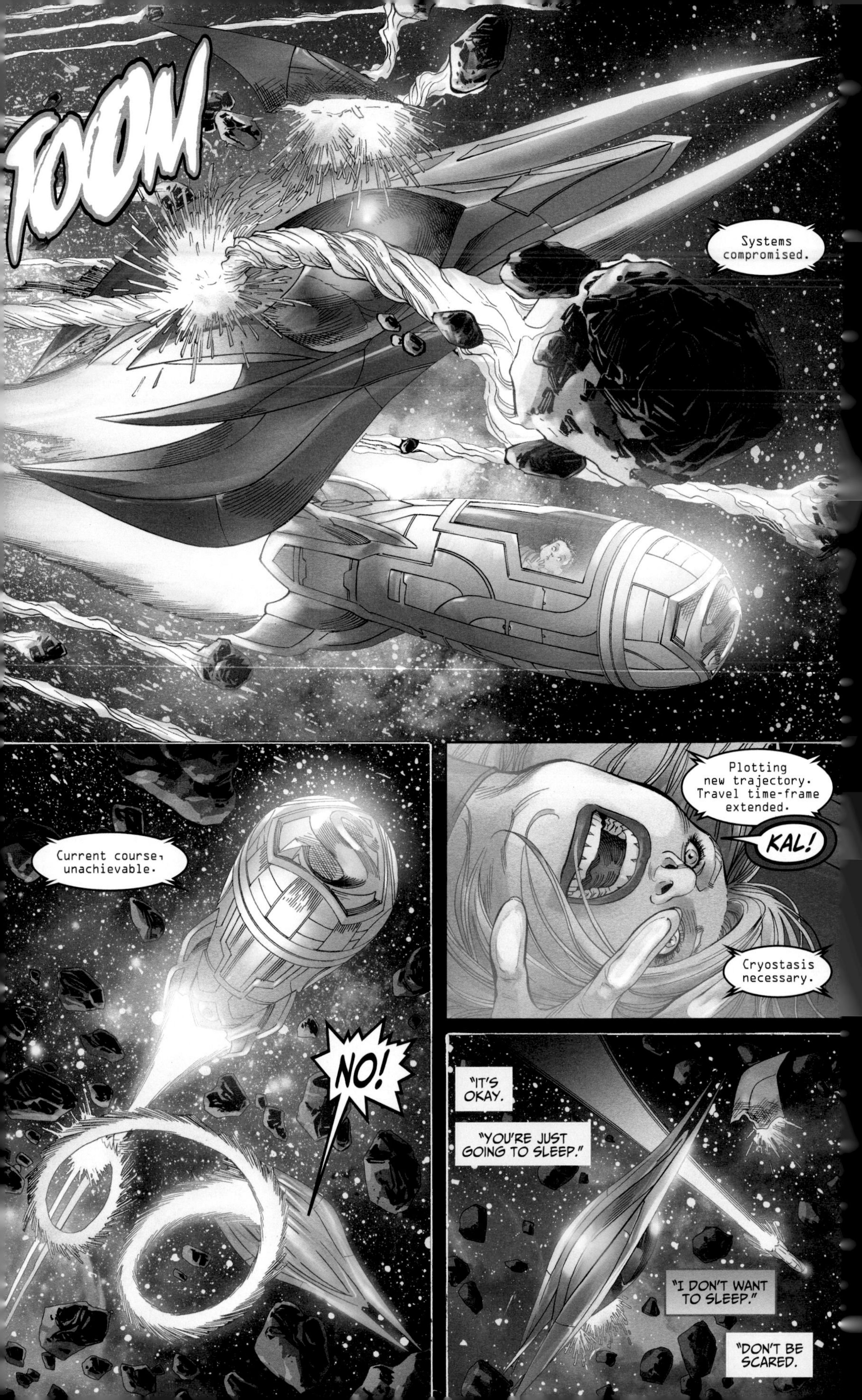
TOOM
Systems compromised.
Current course, unachievable.
NO!
Plotting new trajectory. Travel time-frame extended.
KAL!
Cryostasis necessary.
"IT'S OKAY.
"YOU'RE JUST GOING TO SLEEP."
"I DON'T WANT TO SLEEP."
"DON'T BE SCARED.

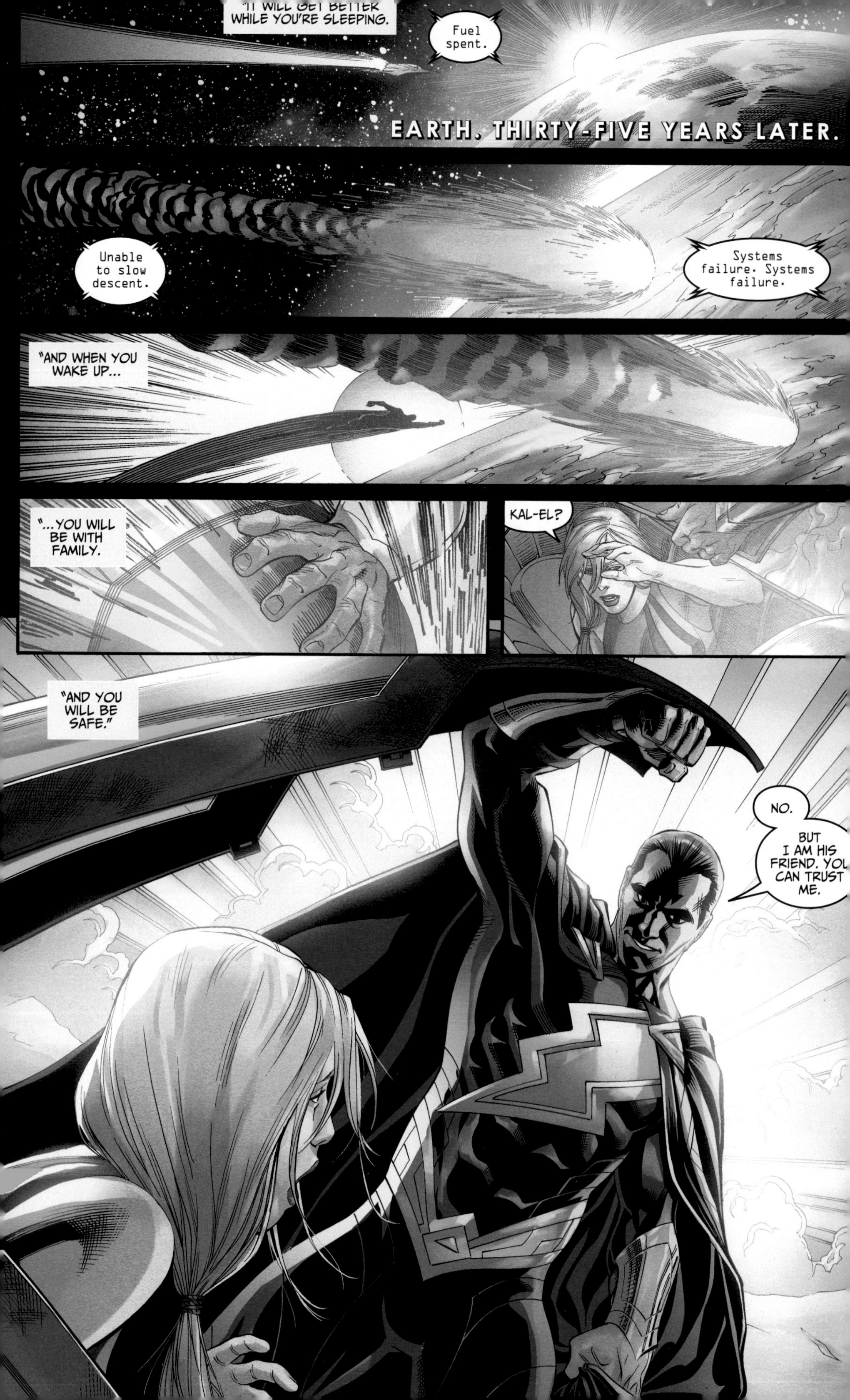
"IT WILL GET BETTER
WHILE YOU'RE SLEEPING.
Fuel spent.
EARTH. THIRTY-FIVE YEARS LATER.
Unable to slow descent.
Systems failure. Systems failure.
"AND WHEN YOU WAKE UP...
"...YOU WILL BE WITH FAMILY.
KAL-EL?
"AND YOU WILL BE SAFE."
NO.
BUT I AM HIS FRIEND. YOU CAN TRUST ME.

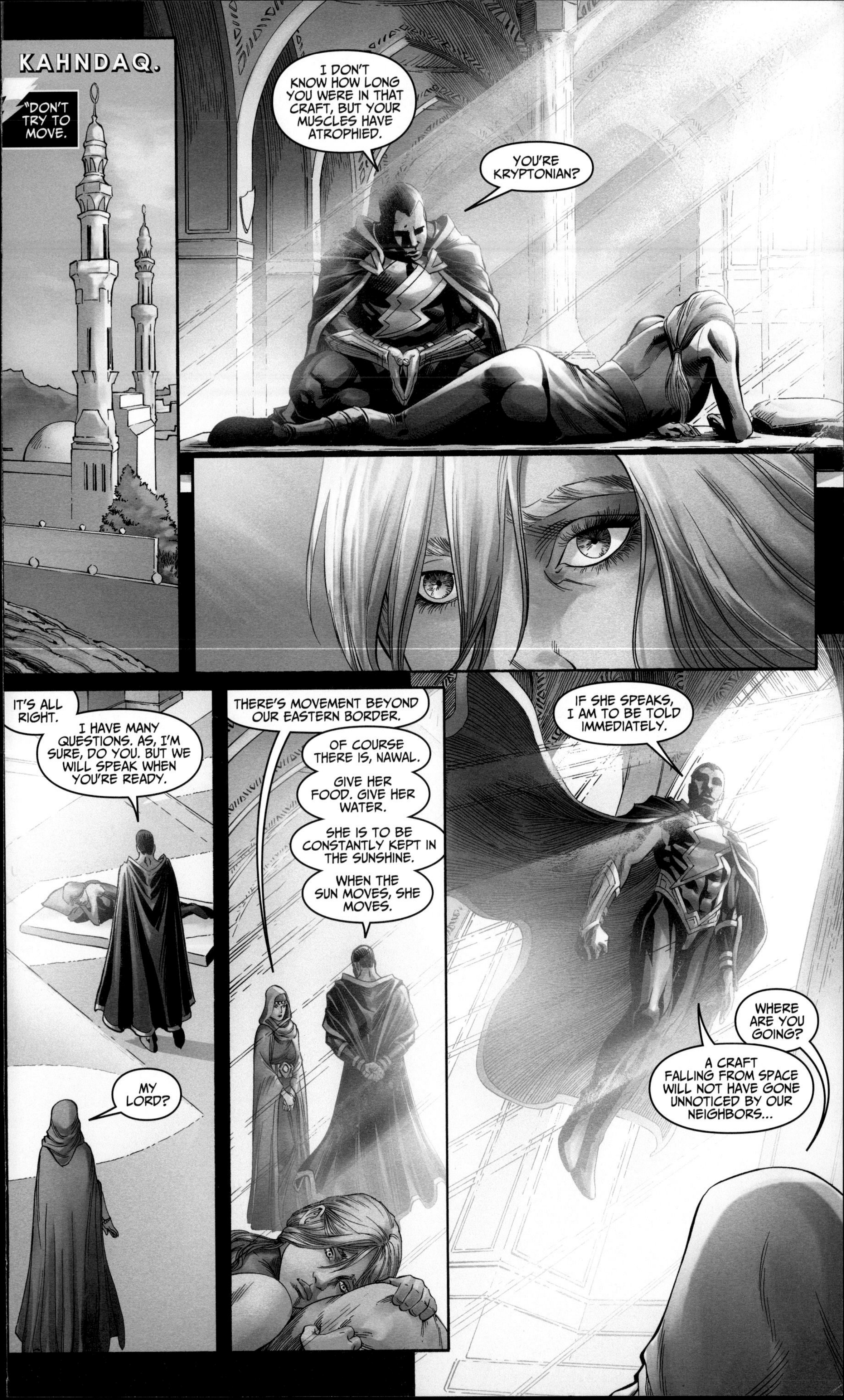

KAHNDAQ.
"DON'T TRY TO MOVE.
I DON'T KNOW HOW LONG YOU WERE IN THAT CRAFT, BUT YOUR MUSCLES HAVE ATROPHIED.
YOU'RE KRYPTONIAN?
IT'S ALL RIGHT.
I HAVE MANY QUESTIONS. AS, I'M SURE, DO YOU. BUT WE WILL SPEAK WHEN YOU'RE READY.
MY LORD?
THERE'S MOVEMENT BEYOND OUR EASTERN BORDER.
OF COURSE THERE IS, NAWAL.
GIVE HER FOOD. GIVE HER WATER.
SHE IS TO BE CONSTANTLY KEPT IN THE SUNSHINE.
WHEN THE SUN MOVES, SHE MOVES.
IF SHE SPEAKS, I AM TO BE TOLD IMMEDIATELY.
WHERE ARE YOU GOING?
A CRAFT FALLING FROM SPACE WILL NOT HAVE GONE UNNOTICED BY OUR NEIGHBORS...

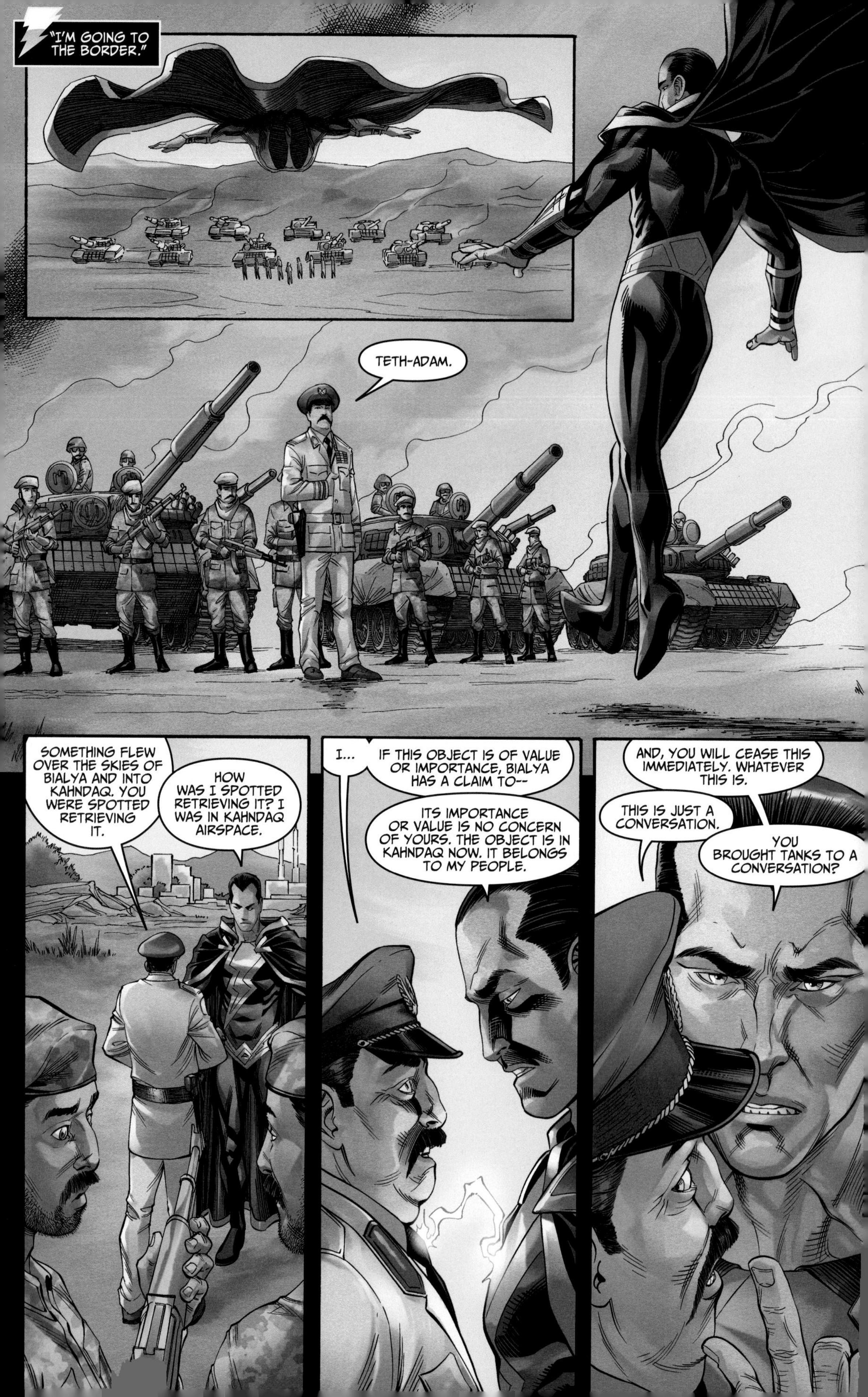
"I'M GOING TO THE BORDER."
TETH-ADAM.
SOMETHING FLEW OVER THE SKIES OF BIALYA AND INTO KAHNDAQ. YOU WERE SPOTTED RETRIEVING IT.
HOW WAS I SPOTTED RETRIEVING IT? I WAS IN KAHNDAQ AIRSPACE.
I...
IF THIS OBJECT IS OF VALUE OR IMPORTANCE, BIALYA HAS A CLAIM TO--
ITS IMPORTANCE OR VALUE IS NO CONCERN OF YOURS. THE OBJECT IS IN KAHNDAQ NOW. IT BELONGS TO MY PEOPLE.
AND, YOU WILL CEASE THIS IMMEDIATELY. WHATEVER THIS IS.
THIS IS JUST A CONVERSATION.
YOU BROUGHT TANKS TO A CONVERSATION?

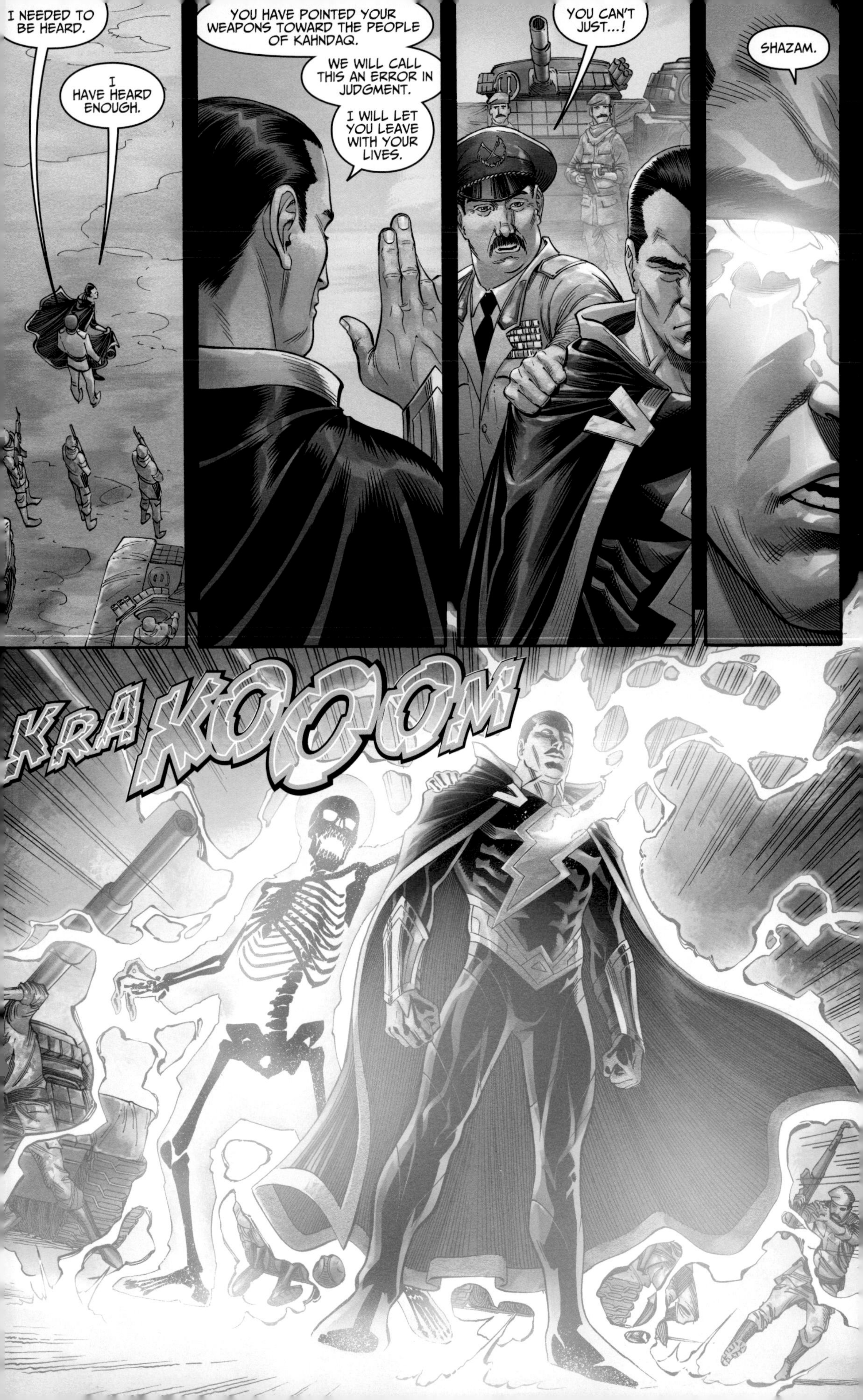
I NEEDED TO BE HEARD.
I HAVE HEARD ENOUGH.
YOU HAVE POINTED YOUR WEAPONS TOWARD THE PEOPLE OF KAHNDAQ.
WE WILL CALL THIS AN ERROR IN JUDGMENT.
I WILL LET YOU LEAVE WITH YOUR LIVES.
YOU CAN'T JUST...!
SHAZAM.
KRAKOOOOM

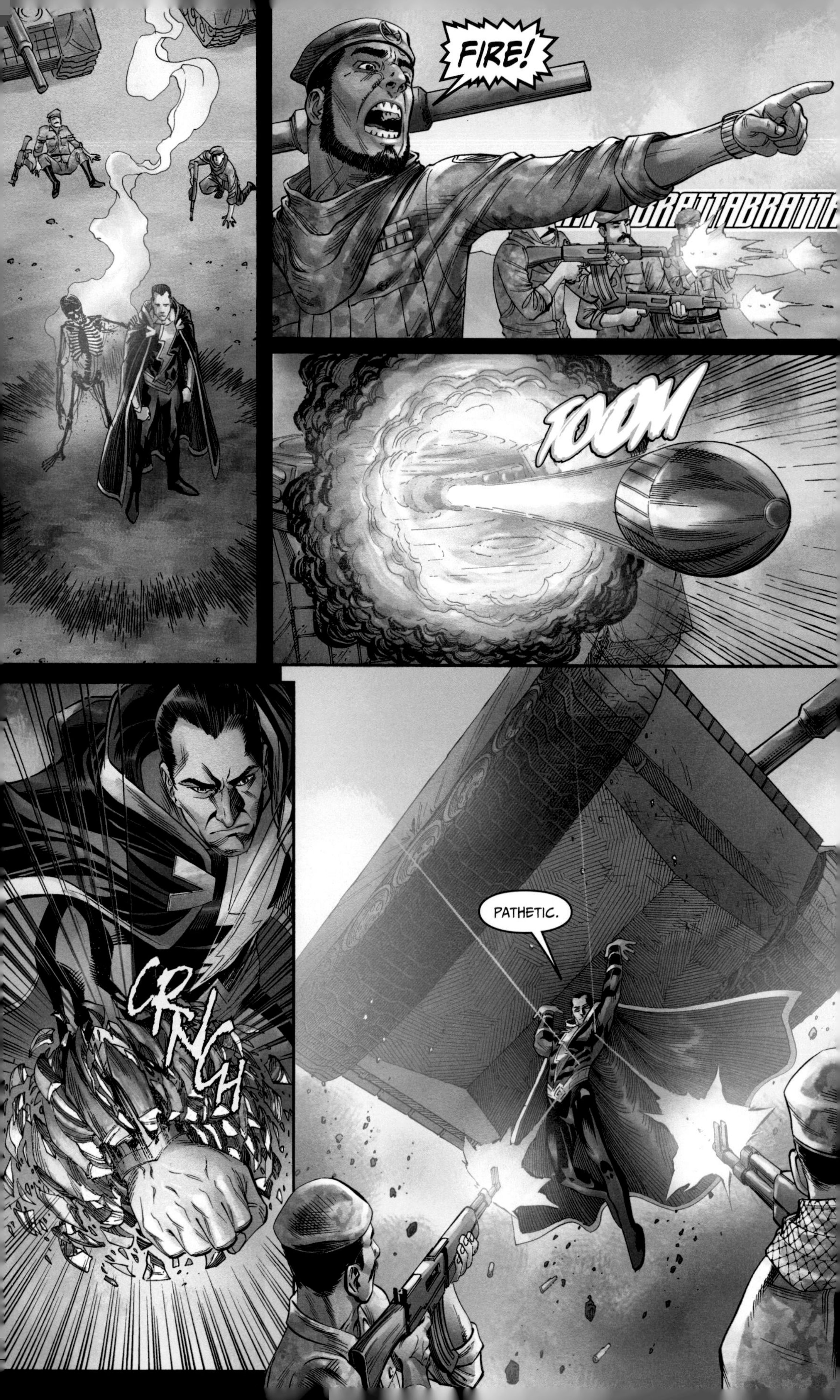
FIRE!
BRATTABRATTA
TOOOM
CRUNCH
PATHETIC.

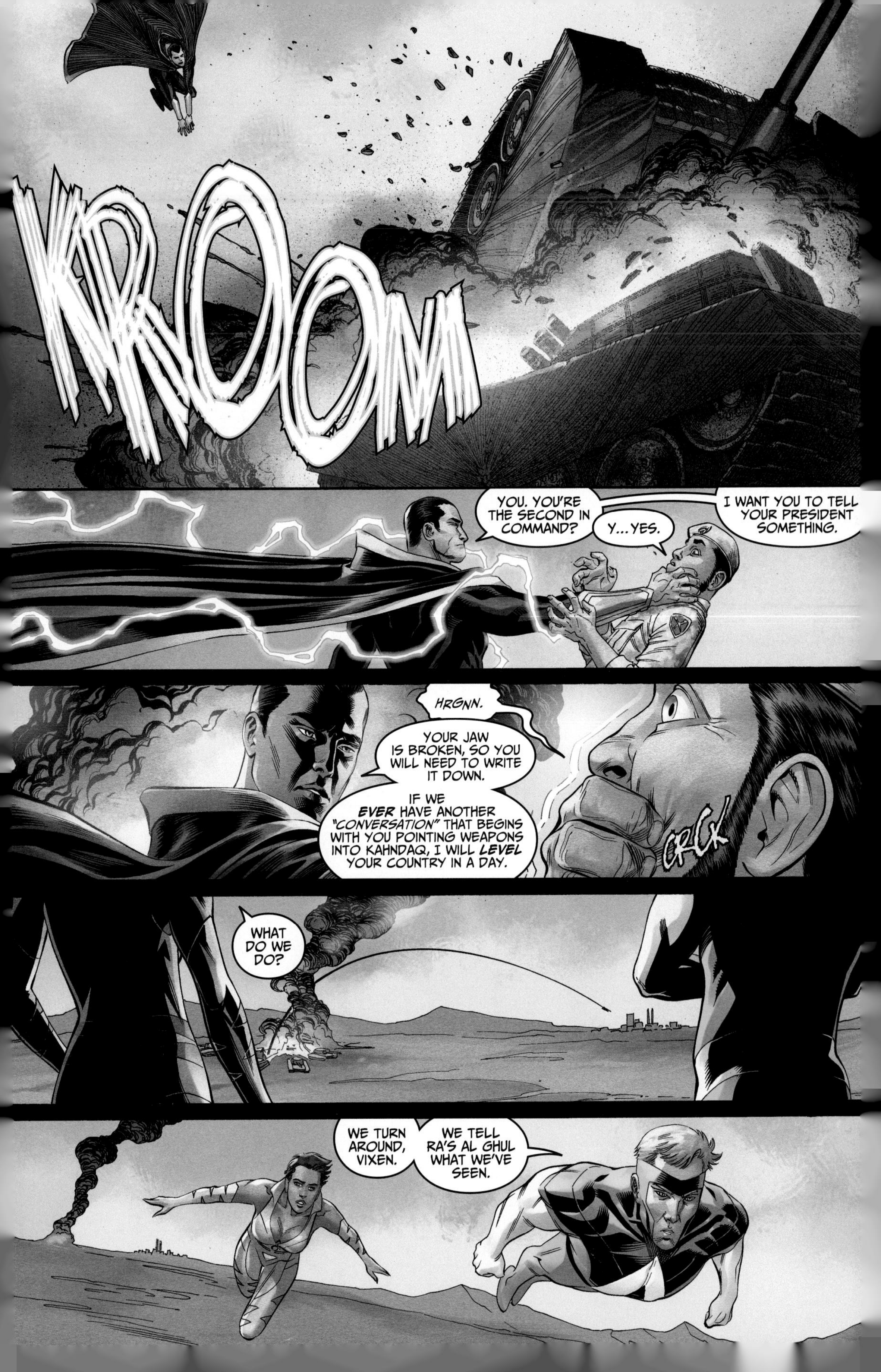
KROOM
YOU. YOU'RE THE SECOND IN COMMAND?
Y...YES.
I WANT YOU TO TELL YOUR PRESIDENT SOMETHING.
HRGNN.
CRCK
YOUR JAW IS BROKEN, SO YOU WILL NEED TO WRITE IT DOWN.
IF WE EVER HAVE ANOTHER "CONVERSATION" THAT BEGINS WITH YOU POINTING WEAPONS INTO KAHNDAQ, I WILL LEVEL YOUR COUNTRY IN A DAY.
WHAT DO WE DO?
WE TURN AROUND, VIXEN.
WE TELL RA'S AL GHUL WHAT WE'VE SEEN.

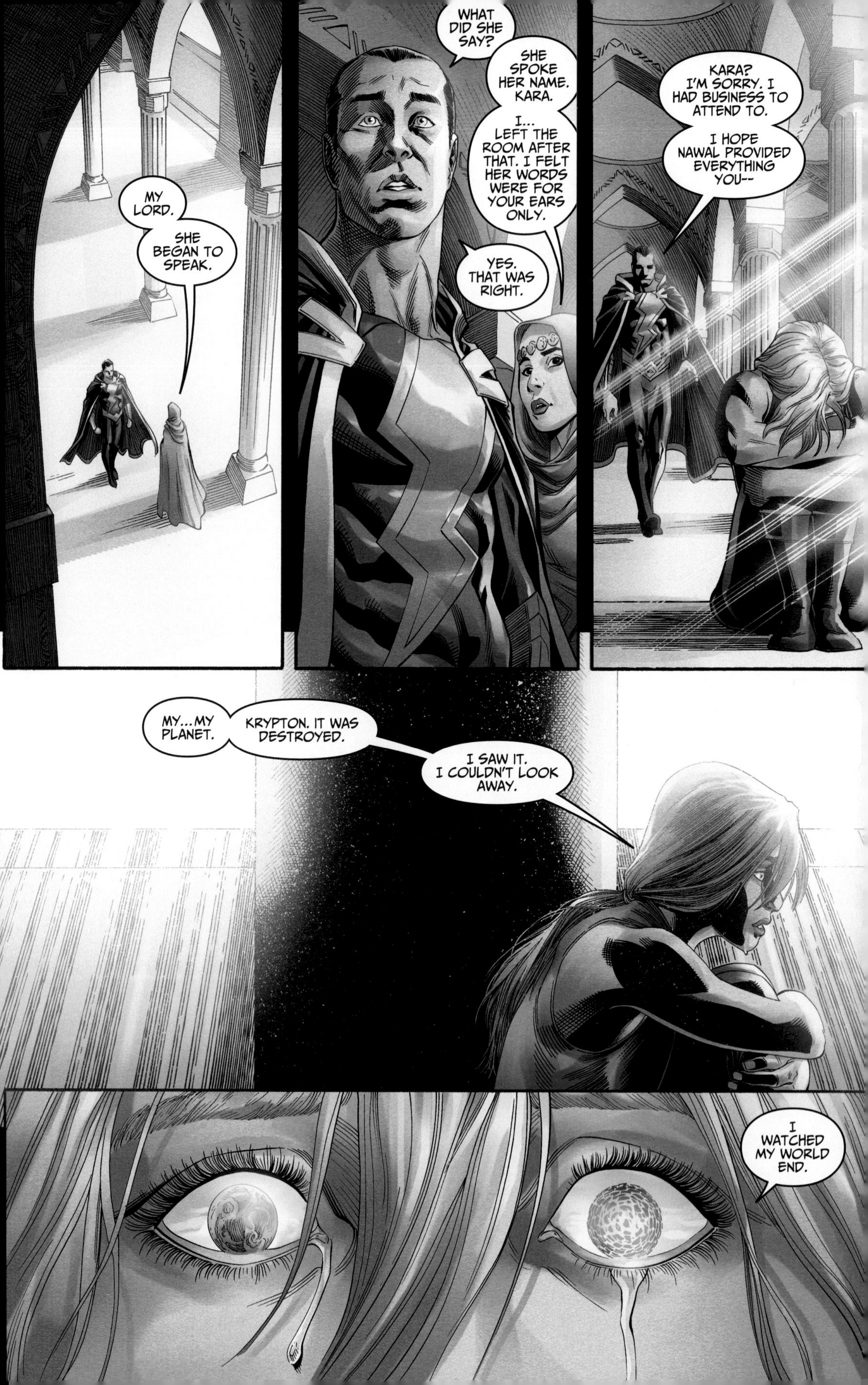
MY LORD.
SHE BEGAN TO SPEAK.
WHAT DID SHE SAY?
SHE SPOKE HER NAME. KARA.
I... LEFT THE ROOM AFTER THAT. I FELT HER WORDS WERE FOR YOUR EARS ONLY.
YES. THAT WAS RIGHT.
KARA? I'M SORRY. I HAD BUSINESS TO ATTEND TO.
I HOPE NAWAL PROVIDED EVERYTHING YOU--
MY...MY PLANET.
KRYPTON. IT WAS DESTROYED.
I SAW IT. I COULDN'T LOOK AWAY.
I WATCHED MY WORLD END.

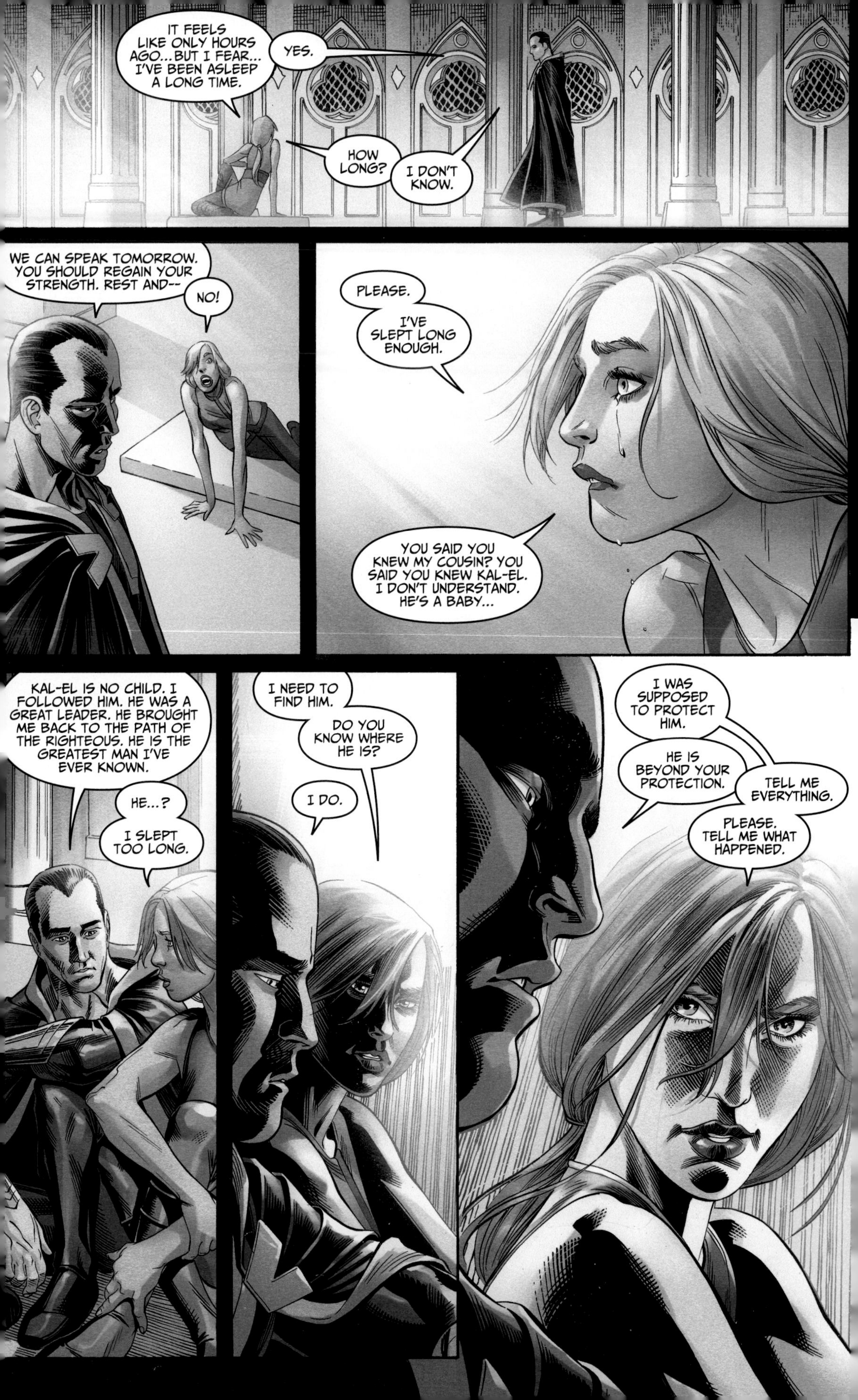
IT FEELS LIKE ONLY HOURS AGO...BUT I FEAR... I'VE BEEN ASLEEP A LONG TIME.
YES.
HOW LONG?
I DON'T KNOW.
WE CAN SPEAK TOMORROW. YOU SHOULD REGAIN YOUR STRENGTH. REST AND--
NO!
PLEASE.
I'VE SLEPT LONG ENOUGH.
YOU SAID YOU KNEW MY COUSIN? YOU SAID YOU KNEW KAL-EL. I DON'T UNDERSTAND. HE'S A BABY...
KAL-EL IS NO CHILD. I FOLLOWED HIM. HE WAS A GREAT LEADER. HE BROUGHT ME BACK TO THE PATH OF THE RIGHTEOUS. HE IS THE GREATEST MAN I'VE EVER KNOWN.
HE...?
I SLEPT TOO LONG.
I NEED TO FIND HIM.
DO YOU KNOW WHERE HE IS?
I DO.
I WAS SUPPOSED TO PROTECT HIM.
HE IS BEYOND YOUR PROTECTION.
TELL ME EVERYTHING.
PLEASE. TELL ME WHAT HAPPENED.

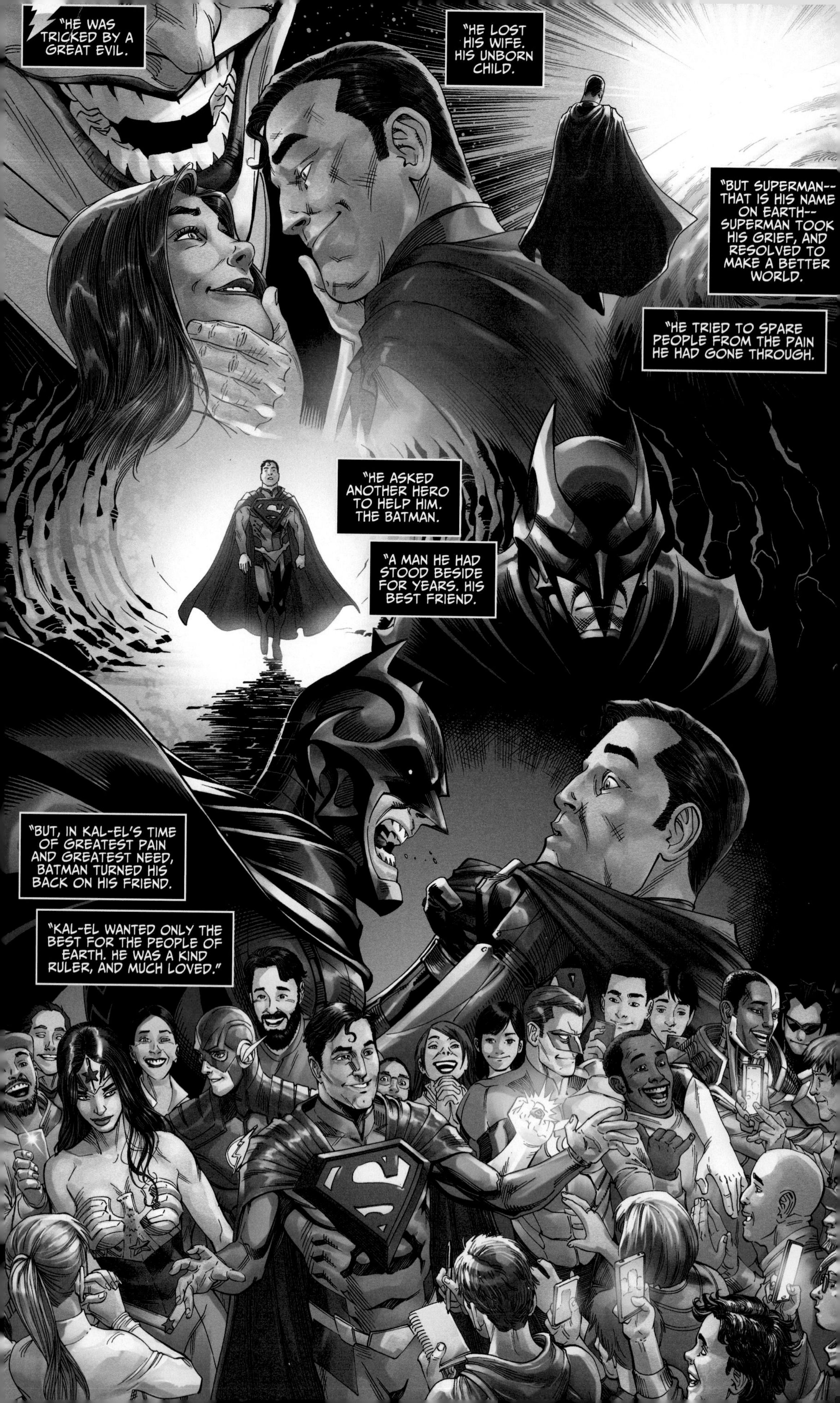
"HE WAS TRICKED BY A GREAT EVIL.
"HE LOST HIS WIFE. HIS UNBORN CHILD.
"BUT SUPERMAN--THAT IS HIS NAME ON EARTH--SUPERMAN TOOK HIS GRIEF, AND RESOLVED TO MAKE A BETTER WORLD.
"HE TRIED TO SPARE PEOPLE FROM THE PAIN HE HAD GONE THROUGH.
"HE ASKED ANOTHER HERO TO HELP HIM. THE BATMAN.
"A MAN HE HAD STOOD BESIDE FOR YEARS. HIS BEST FRIEND.
"BUT, IN KAL-EL'S TIME OF GREATEST PAIN AND GREATEST NEED, BATMAN TURNED HIS BACK ON HIS FRIEND.
"KAL-EL WANTED ONLY THE BEST FOR THE PEOPLE OF EARTH. HE WAS A KIND RULER, AND MUCH LOVED."

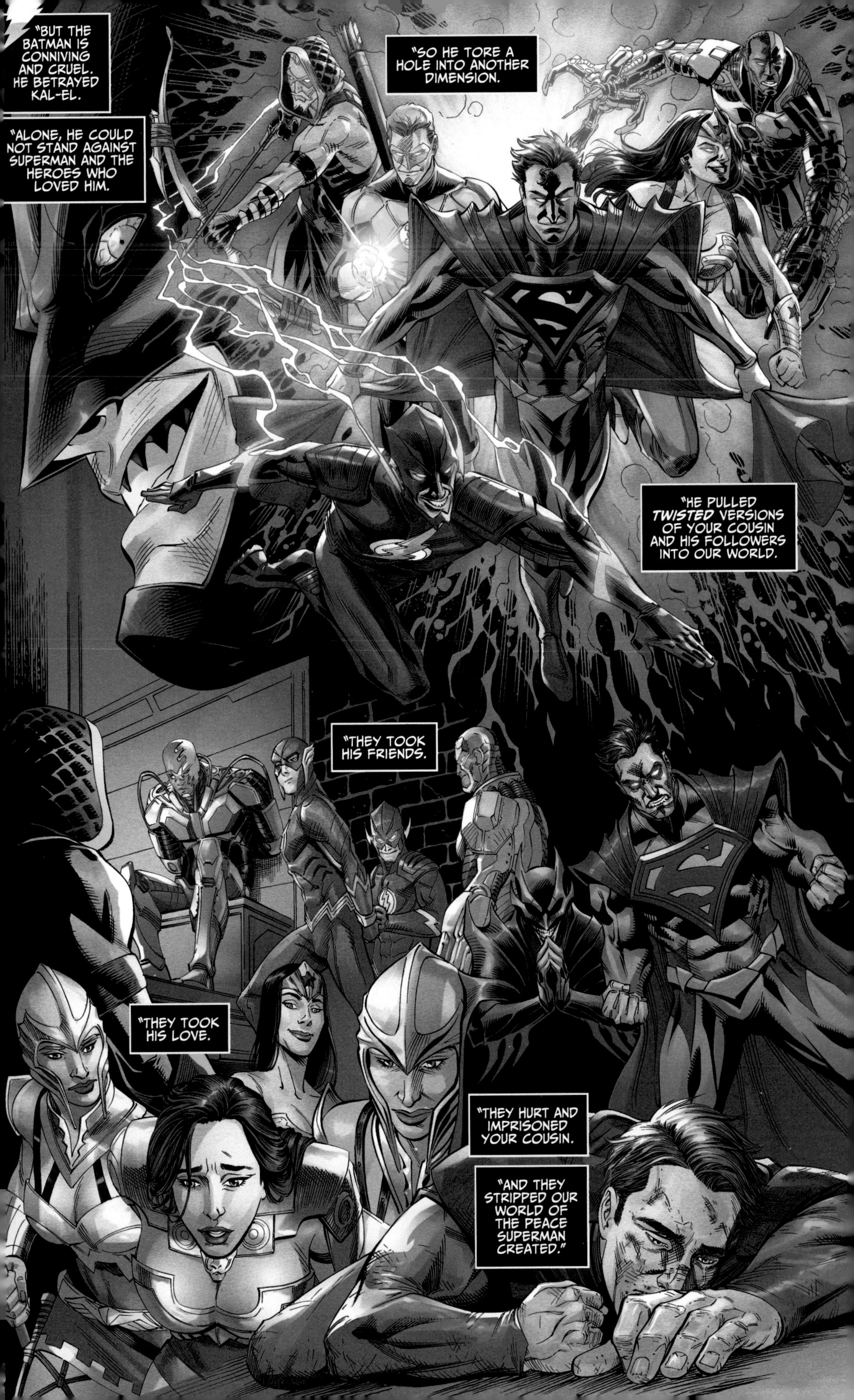
"BUT THE BATMAN IS CONNIVING AND CRUEL. HE BETRAYED KAL-EL.
"ALONE, HE COULD NOT STAND AGAINST SUPERMAN AND THE HEROES WHO LOVED HIM.
"SO HE TORE A HOLE INTO ANOTHER DIMENSION.
"HE PULLED *TWISTED* VERSIONS OF YOUR COUSIN AND HIS FOLLOWERS INTO OUR WORLD.
"THEY TOOK HIS FRIENDS.
"THEY TOOK HIS LOVE.
"THEY HURT AND IMPRISONED YOUR COUSIN.
"AND THEY STRIPPED OUR WORLD OF THE PEACE SUPERMAN CREATED."

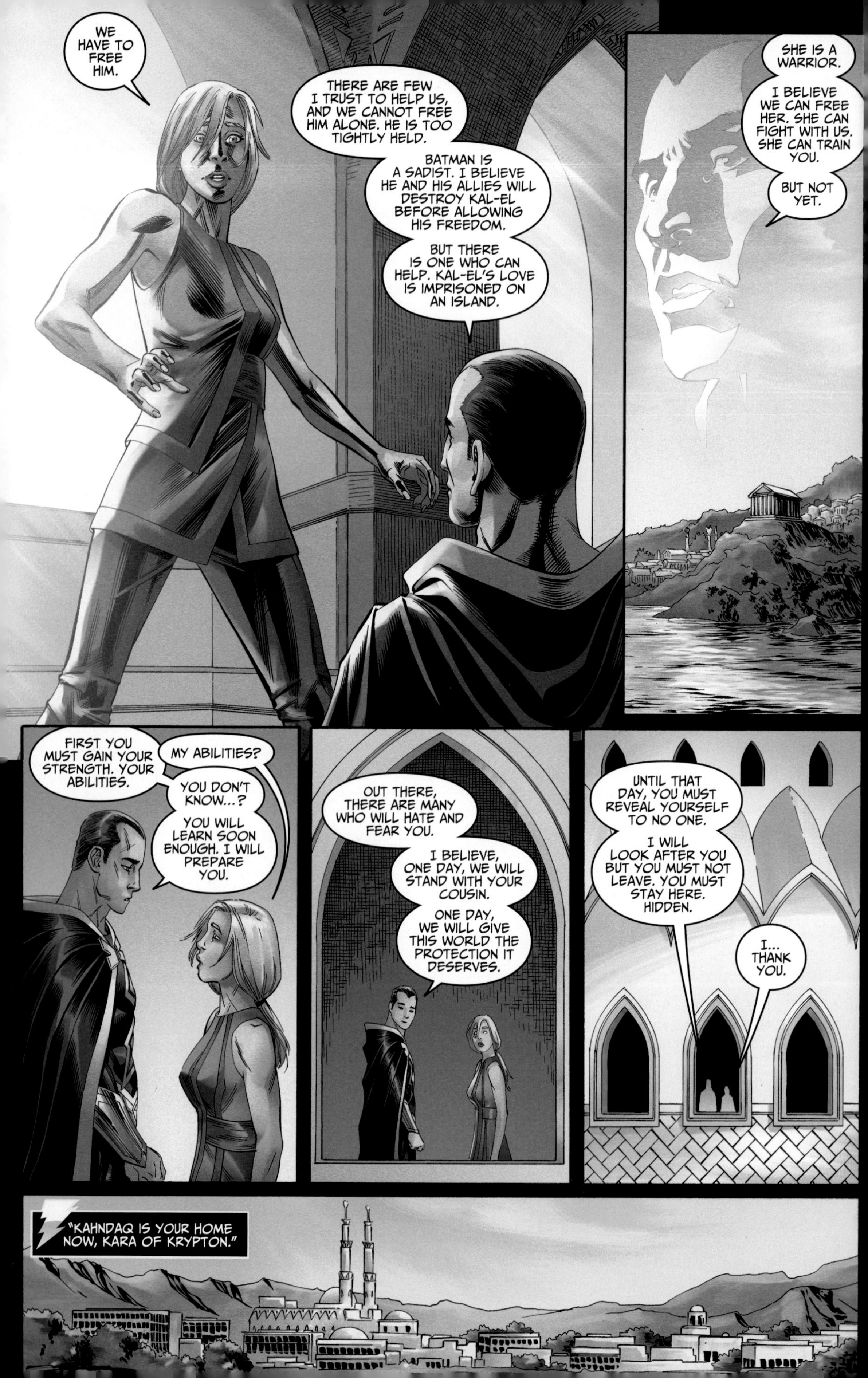
WE HAVE TO FREE HIM.
THERE ARE FEW I TRUST TO HELP US, AND WE CANNOT FREE HIM ALONE. HE IS TOO TIGHTLY HELD.
BATMAN IS A SADIST. I BELIEVE HE AND HIS ALLIES WILL DESTROY KAL-EL BEFORE ALLOWING HIS FREEDOM.
BUT THERE IS ONE WHO CAN HELP. KAL-EL'S LOVE IS IMPRISONED ON AN ISLAND.
SHE IS A WARRIOR.
I BELIEVE WE CAN FREE HER. SHE CAN FIGHT WITH US. SHE CAN TRAIN YOU.
BUT NOT YET.
FIRST YOU MUST GAIN YOUR STRENGTH. YOUR ABILITIES.
MY ABILITIES?
YOU DON'T KNOW...?
YOU WILL LEARN SOON ENOUGH. I WILL PREPARE YOU.
OUT THERE, THERE ARE MANY WHO WILL HATE AND FEAR YOU.
I BELIEVE, ONE DAY, WE WILL STAND WITH YOUR COUSIN.
ONE DAY, WE WILL GIVE THIS WORLD THE PROTECTION IT DESERVES.
UNTIL THAT DAY, YOU MUST REVEAL YOURSELF TO NO ONE.
I WILL LOOK AFTER YOU BUT YOU MUST NOT LEAVE. YOU MUST STAY HERE. HIDDEN.
I... THANK YOU.
"KAHNDAQ IS YOUR HOME NOW, KARA OF KRYPTON."

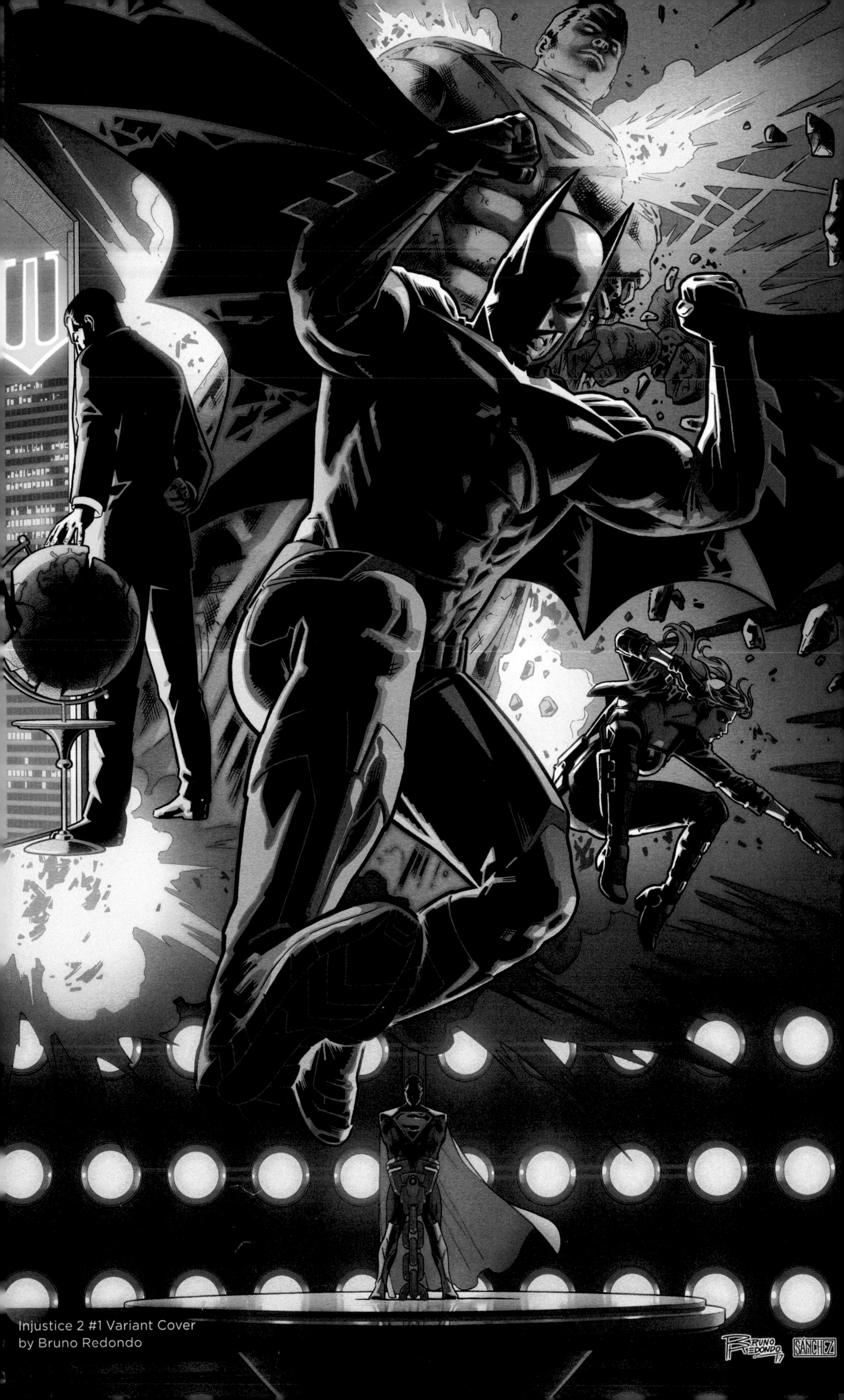

Injustice 2 #1 Variant Cover
by Bruno Redondo

Promotion Art for INJUSTICE 2

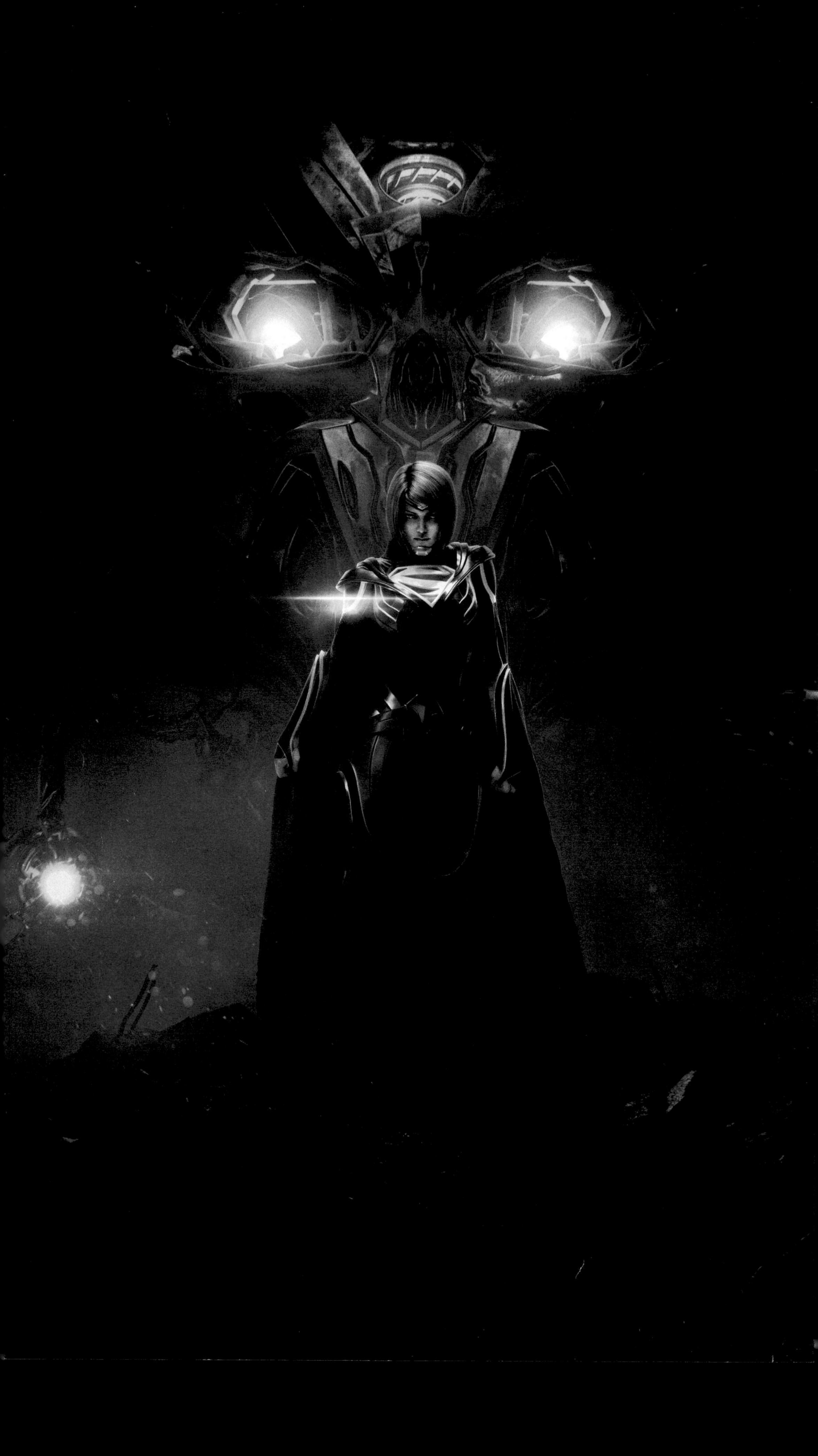

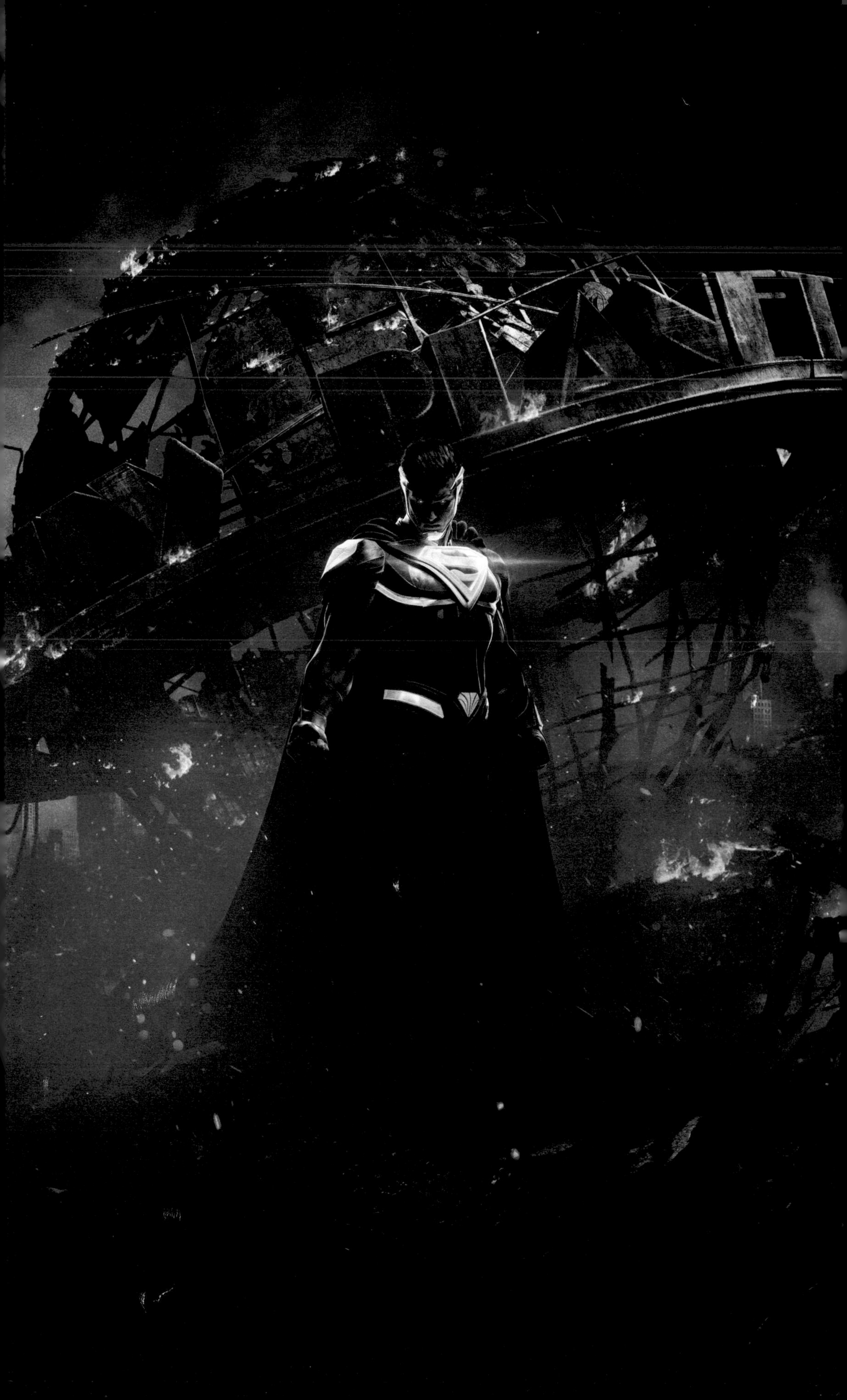

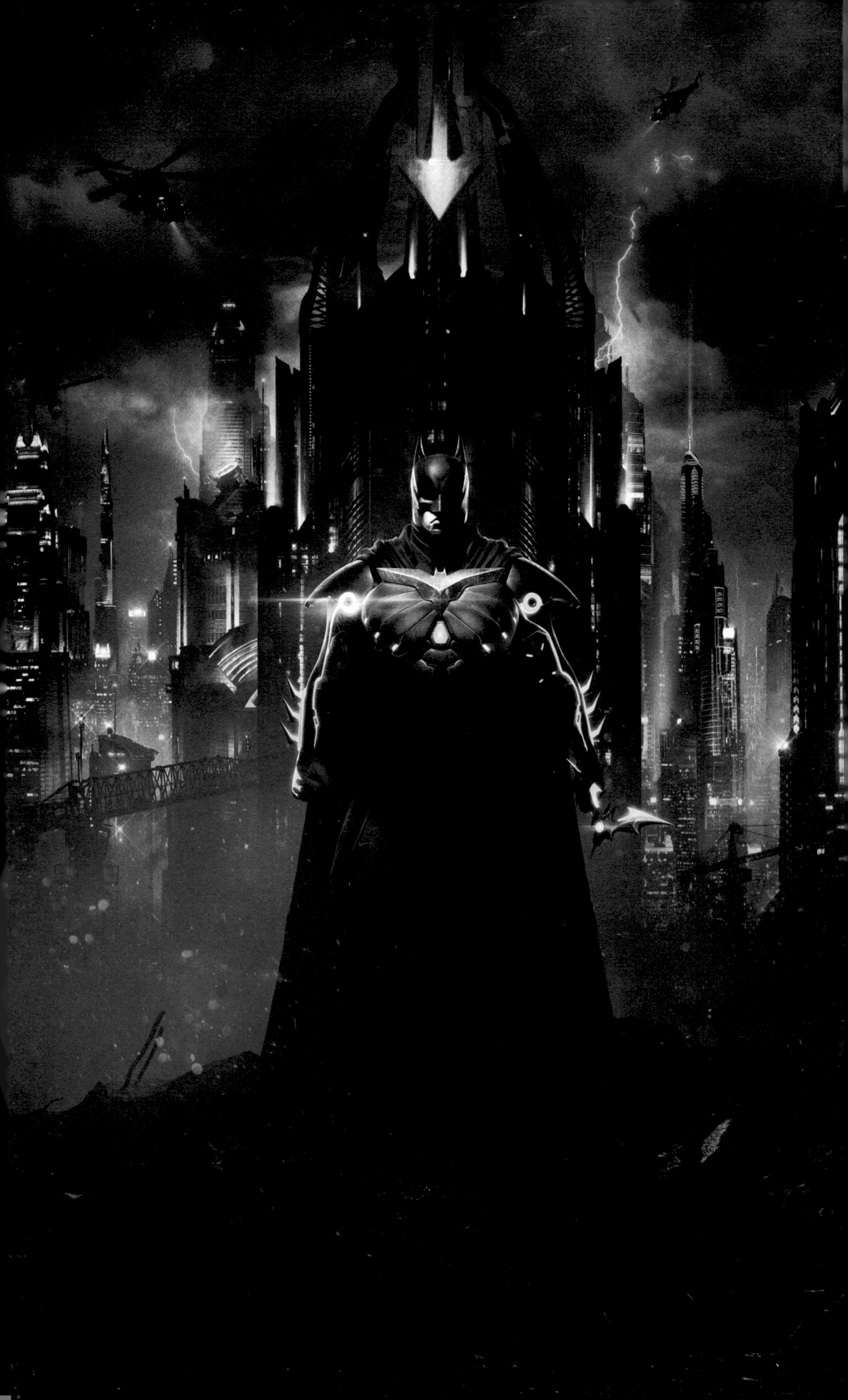

Character designs by Bruno Redondo

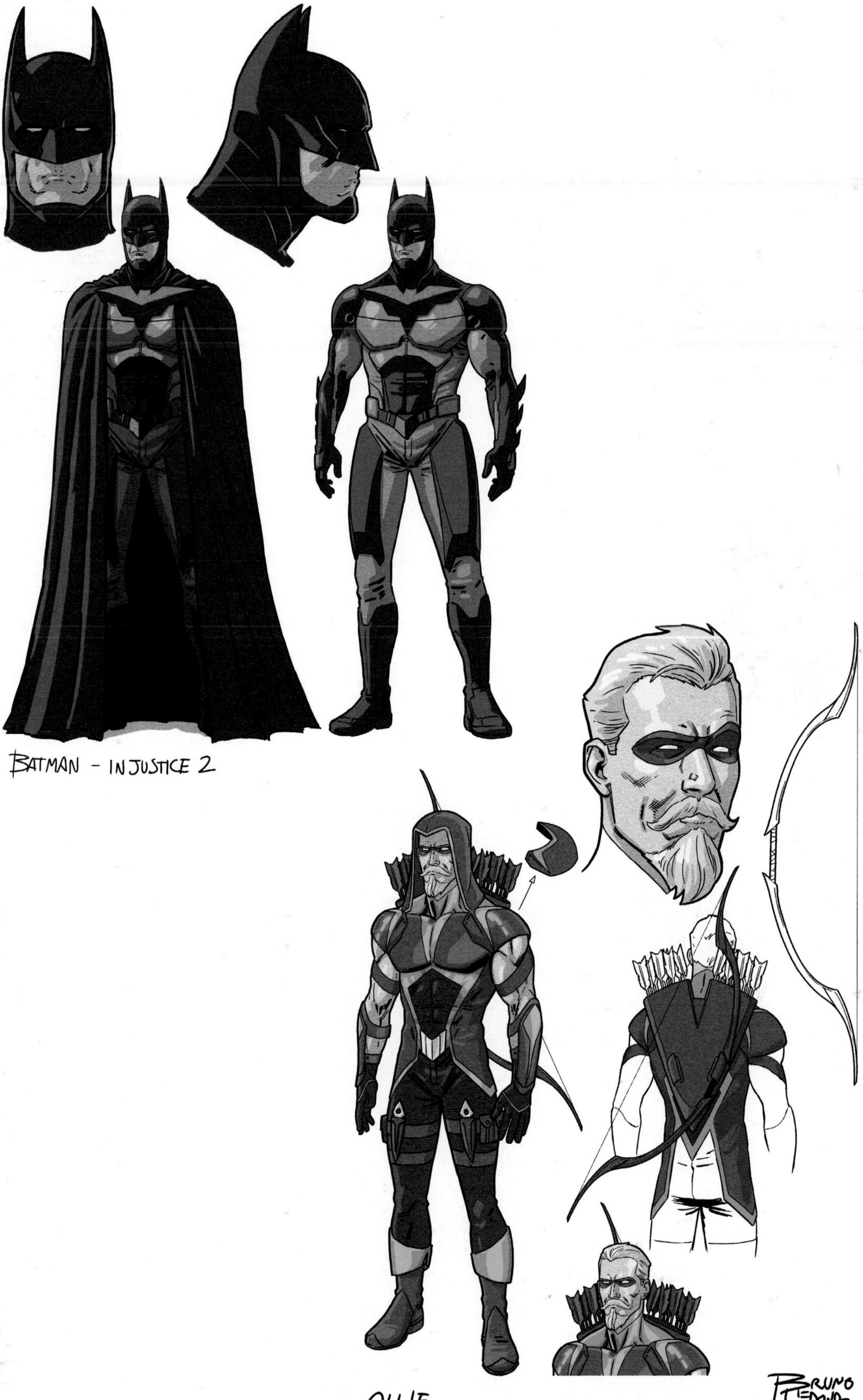
BATMAN - INJUSTICE 2
OLLIE
BRUNO REDONDO
16

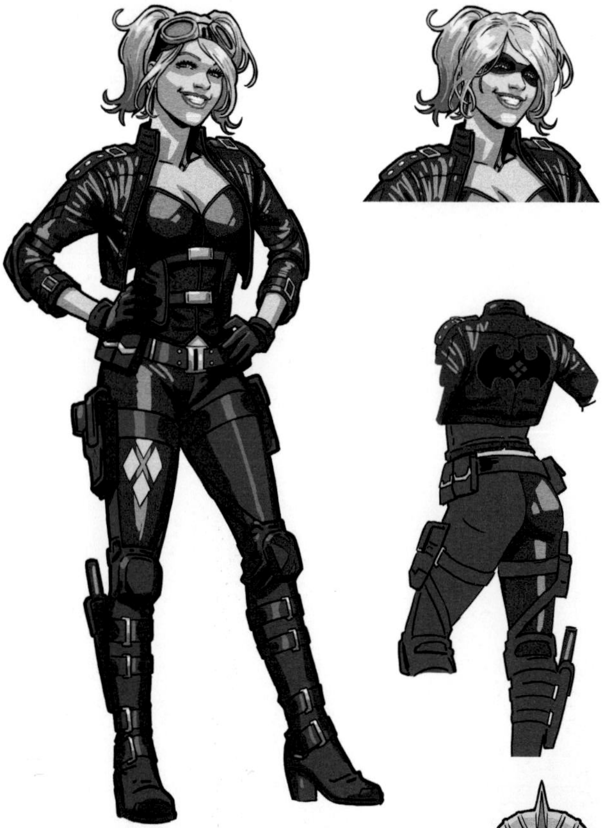

HARLEY QUINN

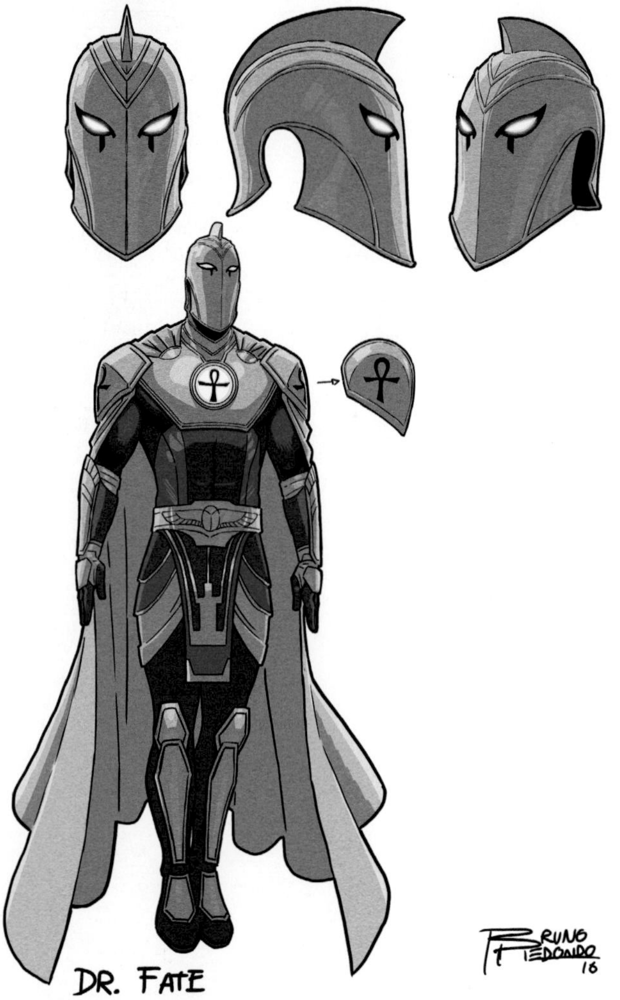

BRUNO REDONDO
16

DR. FATE